Lokopriya
GOPINATH BORDOLOI
An Architect of Modern India

LOKOPRIYA GOPINATH BORDOLOI

An Architect of Modern India

Edited by

LILY MAZINDER BARUAH

GYAN PUBLISHING HOUSE

NEW DELHI-110 002

GYAN PUBLISHING HOUSE
5 Ansari Road, Daryaganj
New Delhi 110 002

ISBN 81-212-0404-6

PRINTED IN INDIA

Published by Mrs. Gayatri Garg for Gyan Publishing House, New Delhi 110 002
Laser Typeseting by Rai Services (P) Ltd., Daryaganj, New Delhi 110 002
Printed at Goyal Offset Printers, Delhi

In the Sweet Hands of

Smt. SURABALA BORDOLOI

MY BELOVED MOTHER

and

WIFE OF LOKOPRIYA

FOREWORD

Lokopriya Gopinath Bordoloi whose birth centenary was celebrated by our nation last year, belongs to that remarkable generation which won freedom for India.

Bordoloiji personified the cultural ethos of Assam and deeply felt aspirations of the people of Assam. He was a dearly loved leader. The respect and affection with which he was held by the public had grown over long years of close and intense personal interaction between Gopinathji and the people of Assam. He had mingled with and become one with the common-folk in the towns, villages and hamlets and even in areas difficult to reach. He had first hand information of the requirements of the people and possessed the ability to organize social action alongwith party initiatives. The Naga Leader Phizo's admiration for Bordoloiji is well known (he had acknowledged Bordoloiji as a "Friend of Nagas"). The personality, perceptions and leadership of this outstanding patriot bear a continuing relevance today.

Gopinathji was acutely aware of the formidable complexity of social, economic and political problems which had kept the people of Assam trapped for centuries in poverty, ignorance and despair. He was aware that the people of Assam, though exceptionally gifted with the highest aptitudes, in a land richly endowed with natural resources, were poor and suffered greatly. Bordoloiji represented the urges and aspirations of the masses for peace, social justice and progress.

He appreciated, unerringly, that the problems and the challenges that confronted Assam, comprised only the Assamese facets of a sub-continental crisis that gripped the entire country. He saw that the causes of poverty, ignorance and frustration in Assam, as in the rest of India, were one and the same. He recognized that the very complexity and magnitude of these problems meant that effective solutions could be organized only on the basis of national unity and the power of concerted nation-wide effort. Such an approach was to him not only a matter of political ideology, but of indispensable, urgent and practical necessity.

It was therefore natural for Gopinathji to integrate the urge for freedom in Assam with nation-wide struggle under the leadership of Mahatma Gandhi. Gandhiji selected Lokopriya Gopinath Bordoloi as the first Satyagrahi in Assam, and, in turn, Bordoloiji's devotion to all aspects of Gandhian thoughts was total. His commitment to Gandhiji's call of rural reconstruction and promotion of Khadi and Village industries was reflected in the Gauhati Session of the Indian National Congress in 1926, where even the material for tents was made of Khadi. Gopinathji fully appreciated the value of rural industrialization of the context of the needs of economic growth in Assam and the tradition of cottage and village industry amongst the people.

Gopinath Bordoloi's leadership of the freedom struggle in Assam gave a larger dimension to the entire movement for Independence in India. A province in one corner of the sub-continent had come into the mainstream of national politics. His vision, dynamism and popular leadership contributed significantly to the totality of the nation's efforts to free itself from the foreign yoke and to emerge as a sovereign, independent nation wedded to the ideals of democracy, secularism and social justice. At the time of Partition, Gopinathji's understanding of the inner wishes of the people of Assam, his firm resolve, vision and leadership, account in great measure for Assam's position in the Union of India, and Assam's Statehood.

The experience of success during the struggle for freedom resulting from nation-wide action by people from different provinces, was clear proof of Gopinathji's perception that Assam's problems could be successfully tackled only by the people of Assam working in an atmosphere of national unity, and Centre-State and inter-State cooperation.

He was conscious of the fact that the requirements of the masses of India comprise a vast market encouraging sustainable socio-economic growth in Assam. The infrastructure in Assam that Gopinathji strove to develop was designed to draw upon the national economy for building Assam and contributing also to national wealth thus creating further potential for Assam's development. He realized that a closed economy confining Assam within itself would only constrict and retard Assam's potential for prosperity and security.

With far-sighted vision Gopinathji initiated the building of important institutions in all the key sectors of growth of Assam. He promoted primary, secondary and higher education, established agricultural and engineering colleges, Gauhati University, institutions for technical training and industrial development. It was Gopinathji of workers committed to the task of reviving and reconstructing Assam's socio-economic life.

In a crucial sector of public life–the identity of people of Assam, their culture, literature, dance, music and arts - Gopinath Bordoloi made a very important contribution. He was fully aware of and justly proud of the beauty, richness and ancient origins of Assam's cultural heritage and its intimate, living links with the ethos of Indian culture. (Gopinathji himself was an accomplished exponent of Assam's fine music and folk dance-forms.) He gave every assistance to the growth of Assam's language, literature and culture and encourged interaction with and the enrichment of the larger national cultural atmosphere.

It is this approach of cherishing, preserving and nourishing local cultural heritage and coordinating harmoniously with kindred cultures in the rest of the country that can strengthen the overall positive features of Indian society. Gopinathji's leadership in this respect was very significant and salutary.

Such a great individual–one who suffered personal hardship in the struggle for freedom, a leader who rendered historic service not only for the freedom of Assam but the creation of conditions of growth and well-being for the people of Assam, who contributed so richly to political and economic life and to cultural and literary processes and yet, who always remained modest, simple and true to the great mission of national reconstruction–such a person: Lokopriya Gopinath Bordoloi: belongs to that band of outstanding Indians whom the nation will always remember with respect and gratitude.

I congratulate Dr. (Mrs.) Lily Mazinder Baruah for her initiative in bringing out this biography. This biography of Bordoloiji, by his daughter, is a valuable contribution which deserves our appreciation and gratitude.

S. D. Sharma

(SHANKER DAYAL SHARMA)
Vice-President
India

17 July 1991
New Delhi

ACKNOWLEDGEMENT

I owe my deep sense of gratitude to all those who have rendered their valuable time and services to carry on the project, particularly to Dr. K.N. Baisya, Under Secretary, Assam Legislative Assembly who has constantly helped me to finalise the manuscript. Mrs. Puspalata Das, Ex-M.P. guided me to write the context of Bapuji's letters and advice report for which I remain thankful to her. Mrs. Rose, Mr. Rama Krishna and Mr. Banerjee need deep appreciation for their labour in getting the manuscript typed.

Heartfelt thanks go to Dr. Nirode Kumar Barooah and my respected Professor Naba Kanta Baruah and friend Dr. Indira (Mamoni) Raysom Goswami who gave me ideas to publish the book.

My thanks are due to my brothers late Brig. Dhiren Bordoloi (Rtd.), Professor Birendra Nath Bordoloi, Capt. Robin Bordoloi, Mr. Bolin Bordoloi and his staff of Tata Tea who inspired me to do the work. My late husband Dr. IKSM Baruah helped me tremendously to preserve the materials which have been added to this volume.

Mr. D.N. Choudhury who had been so kind to send me valuable information from the Indian Constitution deserves appreciation.

Mrs. Binita Mazinder Baruah, Mrs. Dipali Bhagabati, Miss Leena Bordoloi, Mrs. Pranita Phookan and Mr. Gautam Das have been constantly helping me in sorting out the work.

I thank the Editor, the Assam Tribune for allowing me to utilize his good office in order to compile the work and use the excerpts already published.

Last but not the least, I wish to thank the Gian Publishing House, New Delhi who came forward to publish this project work on Late Gopinath Bordoloi.

Guwahati

Lily Mazinder Baruah
Editor

PREFACE

The book was compiled by the editor while the birth centenary celebration of Lokopriya Gopinath Bordoloi–a true architect of modern India–was being observed throughout the length and breadth of the country. The work, thus, bears the prime significance of time.

Since 1857 turmoil was taking place into British India Lokopriya was born in 1890. He established his profile as a leader of backward State like Assam. He completed his academic career in 1917 obtaining M.A. and B.L. degrees although he began teaching as the Headmaster of a school. He later worked as an advocate at the Bar. But he was impressed by Gandhiji's clarion call to join the Non-Cooperation Movement, and having seen in him his political Guru in 1921 inspired to jump upon the freedom movement of India. A careerist and an outstanding legal practitioner Lokopriya became a changed man; he gave up regular earning professions and engaged himself in nation-building devotion till August 6, 1950 while he died in harness as the First Premier (Chief Minister) of Assam in free India.

Amongst the stalwarts of the freedom movement, statesmen, leaders and administrators of India in transition, Lokopriya was the man of words. And he was also a man of few words, but he remains alive : "Kirtiryasya sa Jivati" and his speeches too remind us of Bhavabhuti's saying: "The speeches of ordinary good men follow facts, while facts follow the utterances of primeval sages". His own writings and speeches as the editor embodied in this work are the ample proofs in highlighting Lokopriya's acumen on different contexts and occasions. The editor has done a marvellous task by collecting significant facts from its original writings which have been very carefully preserved either by herself or by her near and dear ones. Thereby she proves her eager and love to bring things in their originals in the true pursuit of knowledge to one who craves for it and is the real perspective. These original historical collections on personal endeavour are shined as pearls and added to the beauty of the book that needs in true perspective. Ten significant speeches, as many as twenty-eight personal letters corresponding with Gandhi, Nehru, Patel, Shri Prakash, Akbar Hydari, A. Clow, Mr. Debeswar Sarma and others would bring the readers of the book to understand the actual gravity of the political situations in the prevailing circumstances and how to handle them with a view to problem solving measures from the time point of view in the greater interest of the largest number of masses.

Similarly, four discussions and five articles of his own mind expressed on political philosophy, ethics, love for humanity are supplemented by as many as twenty-one articles written by Kalelkar, G.B.Pant, Dr. P.Sittaramaya, Jagjivan Ram, Dr. B.K. Bhattacharya, Prof. C.K. Mehta, Hem Barua, Satish Chandra Kakati and others. Ample references in this regard are the addition of obituaries.

His discussions with Mahatma Gandhi on a number of occasions would surely draw attention of everyone who would go through them.

Out of three Appendices of it, 'diary' reveals a part of the busy daily life which he led during pre-independence period of India. But prison life gave Lokopriya the tease he needed to make plan for future activities if India would win political freedom. Both leisure and a measure of detachment of his prison life shaped the future course of action firm in his mind. Whatsoever, it might not be unthinkable sometimes, the injustice, the unhappiness, the uncertainty, the brutality of the world oppress one and darken one's mind. With the British Government's inhuman actions and repressive Laws Lokopriya's mind and heart were occupied with patriotic and nationalistic ideas, cult of Swedeshi and Gandhian ideology but against colonial rules.

Out of six chapters of the book, Chapter III consists of the reports and memoranda which bear the report also drafted by Lokopriya as Chairman of the North-East Frontier (Assam) Tribal and Excluded Areas Committee and submitted to the Constituent Assembly that was chaired by Dr. Rajendra Prasad. The report strongly reflected the feelings of Gopinath Bordoloi about tribals of North-East as well as other areas of India. Ultimately, his observations and dream came into reality while Sixth Schedule took place in the Draft Constitution of India which was signed and approved by the Members of the Constituent Assembly on November 9, 1949.

Of many things, work, life, ethics, philosophy whatsoever may be, the present volume leads one who reads it as poet Rabindra Nath Tagore in his Gitanjali prays to behold :

> "Where the mind is without fear and the head is held high;
> Where knowledge is free;
> Where the world has not been broken up into fragments
> by narrow domestic walls;
> Where words come out from the depth of truth;
> Where tireless striving stretches its arms
> towards perfection;
> Where the clear stream of reason has not lost the
> way into the dreary desert stand of dead habit;
> Where the mind is led forward by thee
> into ever widening thought and action
> Into that heaven of freedom, my Father,
> Let my country awake."

The editor hopes to get a response from one and all and with full appreciation for her painstaking work.

Dr. K.N. BAISYA,
Under Secretary,
Assam Legislative Assembly

Dispur
The 19th March, 1991

SOME SIGNIFICANT SAYINGS OF LOKOPRIYA

"When an individual of a society respects the freedom of anotner and tries to work with goodwill, democracy becomes effective."

"By self-discipline and by such self control, every Constitution of the society such as Government employees, industrialists, merchants etc. should think in the same lines as to how he can work for the betterment of the society."

"Through a feeling of brotherhood, justice and morality it is our own duty to remove all these evils of the society."

"Congress does not want a constituent Assembly which will be subservient to the British Government. The British Government at least should give up the best for colonialism in India and until it recognise india to be an independent nation they should never hope to form any constituent Assembly."

"Hatred will lead to hatred; love will turn to love. Therefore if one is in quest of truth he will have to live a truthful life."

CONTENTS

CHAPTER I

Introduction

There may not be dearth of materials on Gopinath Bordoloi. Much has in the meantime been written on his meteoric career. His untiring efforts towards mapping Assam as well as framing the new Indian Constitution lined with Gandhian idealism had drawn sharp attention of each and every top ranking national leader then and have now been sense of esteem and love from every walk of life, people called Gopinath "Lokopriya". Over the years, Lokopriya has emerged as a veritable legend. As a true architect of modern India his birth centenary celebration is also nationwide observed in India. But even as we have discovered his versatility, there are reasons to claim of our own, we seem to have lost the 'man', Lokopriya Gopinath beneath a bevy of public roles. The reason behind urges us to bring to the public much more about Lokopriya which are not published till date. Hence, our endeavour in bringing out this book to public has been to present our readers not only the first Premier of Assam in Independent India, but Gopinath Bordoloi, the man, a leader, also a true architect of Free India. I hope, the study of present volume would benefit readers interested in the contemporary backdrop of geo-politico-sociology in general and researchers and students in particular who are keen to know the critical political scenario of India on the eve of Independence and immediately thereafter.

If we see it, the very theme reveals to most of us what he is a name in the political annals of Assam–a Gandhian, a freedom fighter, a statesman, a humanitarian, a born leader and saviour of Assam.

Gopinath Bordoloi was born in a small village called Raha in the district of Nagaon on the 6th of June, 1890. His father, late Dr. Budheswar Bordoloi was a Government servant. Among the five children, Gopinath was the third. Radical by nature, Gopinath was interested in studies from his childhood. It is worth mentioning that he completed reading the Mahabharata at the age of seven. Gopinath's elder sister Sashikala used to make fun of him, when she noticed him coming out of his room in the evening after his day long homework.

Gopinath also showed interest in games, drama, music, songs and art from his childhood. As his father was in a transferable job, his primary education was not confined to one place. It is noteworthy to mention that he had an innate sense of rhythm and had a natural ability to pick up tunes. Even in his later life, he would sing the folk songs of the various places he had been to with his father.

Gopinath lost his mother Praneswari, while he was only twelve years of age, at Barpeta. After this sad incident his father decided to settle in Guwahati. His only sister Sashikala was a widow. So with her four younger brothers she remained with her father.

Late Manik Chandra Baruah and Swami Sureshananda of Panchabati Ashram were the two personalities who stood by Gopinath when he was struggling to complete his education in Calcutta. His father, late Dr. Bordoloi had an earnest desire to see his son, Gopinath as a graduate in the family. But God snatched him away before Gopinath could attain the Bachelor of Arts degree. At that time, he fell seriously ill and narrowly escaped from collapse. A torrential outpour of misfortunes befell on Gopinath. He lost his elder brother, Indreswar who used to give him moral and financial support. Gopinath's days became cloudy for some time. Soon after, he overcame all those difficulties and came out successful in securing MA BL degrees in 1917.

His widowed sister, Sashikala had to burden herself with the responsibilities of all her younger brothers. Their income being meagre, she started weaving clothes to maintain the family. She was a poetess and a devoted social worker. Sashikala is remembered in Silpukhuri for the Naamghar she had built for the household ladies to offer their prayers in a common place.

She became busy with searching for a suitable match for her advocate brother, Gopinath. But the would be groom, who had already become a devotee of Deshbhakta Tarun Ram Phookan, started acquiring a passion for politics.

Being a Headmaster of Sona Ram School, Bordoloi almost regularly visited Phookan, his Guru. It was through him that he had heard about Gandhiji and turned with a fervour to the Independent Movement of India. Therefore, Gopinath was apprehensive that with his involvement in politics he may not be able to lead a happy conjugal life. But with his approval, the marriage took place. The bride was the only daughter of late Bhumi Kanta Mazinder Baruah of North Guwahati. Pretty Surabala, then a child of thirteen, got married to Gopinath on a moonlit night of April. She entered a house full of bachelors with the widowed sister, Sashikala as the only guardian. With the tender care of her sister-in-law and her husband's love the girl child learnt to manage the household chores. Under the loving guidance of her husband, she started learning sewing, reading, writing and also cooking non-vegetarian dishes. Hardly, after a year of their married life, there came Gandhiji's clarion call for the non-cooperation movement. Gopinath, a young man with a rebellious spirit, could not but respond to Gandhiji's call. He at once gave up legal practice and involved himself in the movement.

In 1921, when Gopinath Bordoloi saw Gandhiji for the first time in his life, he became a completely changed person. Bordoloi had a taste for fine clothes and preferred a comfortable life but after meeting Gandhiji he realized that one could go well without fashion. This is how Gandhiji influenced Bordoloi. He underwent a total transformation of mind and soul which lasted till the end of his life. The letters to his wife and children speak of the spiritual bent of mind that Gopinath possessed. He cherished a deep reverence towards all religions. I can't resist the temptation of quoting him from a letter written to his wife–"I have started writing on the lives of Prophets meant for boys of Bapa's age (teen aged Dhiren, his eldest son). As I did not get good books on Buddha and Mohammed, I have purchased some books.... At present I work 12 hours daily, 3.5 hours in spinning and winding, 1 hour in Geeta recitation, 1.5 hour in reading newspapers and journals and the rest 6 hours I read". Thus, late Bordoloi did not waste time, rather he had utilised it in a valuable way.

He sought Gandhiji's advice for every bit of work. He was his friend, philosopher and guide. It is found that the indomitable courage Bordoloi possessed was the source of all that he attained from Gandhiji. He followed Gandhiji in thought, word and deed.

Bordoloi was a man of few words. He believed in action. While in or outside the jail, we found him always busy with constructive work. Inside the jail, he alongwith his co-prisoners, always sat together and discussed about their future plan of work after attaining independence. He used to teach Kamla Miri how to read and write and spin.

The problems of the hill people of Assam occupied a special position in his mind. This is evident from his article entitled,"Our hill brethren of Assam," (included in Chapter V), which he wrote while in jail wherein he had very sensitively revealed his viewpoints. Discussion in the jail reveals his sentiments towards the hill people of Assam. He, thus, wrote, "What should be the boundary of the province under the new Regime of Independent India and what should be its composite parts? The principle of excluded area and partially excluded area should go. Representative Government should extend to these areas also. But arrangements for their protection and development should be specifically provided in the Constitution. A body of specialists with intellectuals of the locality should be set up to determine what protection and development should be given and how to give them. The frontier tracts such as the Balipara and the Sadiya frontier should also be included in the provincial administration".

Towards the border tribes of Assam, he said, "The policy to be followed should be one of complete non-aggression. The province should render all cooperation to develop themselves in their respective areas, and friendship with them should be cultivated. (A board of specialists, to study their mode of living etc., and to investigate the real needs and above all their psychology, should be set up)".

The above quotation is taken from his writings wherein he had expressed his concerns for the tribal people of Assam. An admirer of Gopinath Bordoloi, Sri Gurudatta Bhagavati while paying glorious tributes wrote about a discussion he had with Gopinath Bordoloi on the subject of the hill people. Bordoloi had expressed that independence would come to India only when not even a single tribe would be left uneducated. The feeling of hatred among hills and plains would vanish from the mind of the people.

Gopinath assumed power as the leader of the ruling party. He had also discharged the responsibility of framing the Constitution of India. He became the Chairman of the North East Frontier (Assam) Tribal and Excluded Areas Sub-Committee. Bordoloi, who was a cardiac patient, did not pay heed to his health. He single mindedly threw himself into his activities. His report to the Chairman, Advisory Committee of Fundamental Rights, Minorities Tribal Areas, etc. says,"The report has been drawn up by us after a tour of the province which included visits to the Lushai Hills District, the North Cachar Hills Sub-Division, the Mikir Hills, and the Naga Hills District. The Committee could not visit the Garo Hills District on account of bad weather and difficult communication and the Jowai Sub-Division of the Khasi Hills District could not also be visited for the same reason." The Naga Hills District and the Lushai Hills District hit a movement for secessionists. Bordoloi in his report mentioned, "In the Naga Hills the Committee had to face similar situation in the sense that certain officials were influencing extreme elements of the Naga National Council. Our proposals correspond fully to the spirit of the resolution of the Naga National Council passed at Wokha in June, 1946 and we feel confident that the majority of people in th Naga Hills District will find that our proposals go a long way towards meeting even their present point of view".

Bordoloi's untiring efforts to preserve and protect the interest of the Tribals of the Hills was duly felt by them. His sudden demise in 1950 was a bolt from the blue particularly to the Hills and plains tribal people of Assam. In a message to the Governor they said, "The whole of plains people of Assam convey to the Government of Assam their condolences on the sad demise of Sri Gopinath Bordoloi, the late Chief Minister, who through many diversities and difficulties successfully fought for the cause of Assam in general and of the plains and Hills Tribals in particular, before and after the transfer of power and at the time of framing the Constitution of free India."

Late A.Z. Phizo of Nagaland poignantly wrote in his condolence message, "With only a few others, Bordoloi saw, years ago amidst the gathering storm a patch of blue sky. In that great vision of his and his unremitting contribution towards its realization truly depicted the impress of his character which neither death nor time can rob away. In life Bordoloi was a friend of the Nagas whose friendship they held dear. Nagas have been made power today that he has gone".

While coming to the North Cachar Hills Sonaram Thaosen, Ex:MLA, a reputed leader, expresses with gratitude the efforts of the late Bordoloi, "The Bordoloi Sub-Committee has recommended for the district autonomy empowering the District Council to make laws and regulations on land, water, cattle markets, social customs, primary education, appointment of village headman and the chiefs etc. The recommendation was accepted in its entirety by the Constituent Assembly as a result of which the Sixth Schedule was incorporated in the Constitution of India and subsequently the District Councils were functioning in the hills since 1952". But analysing the present political situation in the state due to the tribal people, it seems that instead of trying to understand the spirit and objective of the Sixth Schedule and following the principles, the new leaders of the District Council are involved with ambitious schemes of the Government of India in which they have neither experience nor the public spirit and honesty to manage the schemes. This is the cause of the failure of the Sixth Schedule. Had Bordoloi lived for another five years, the relationship and political atmosphere may have remained healthier.

R. Thanlira, Ex.-M.P., Mizoram states, "Gopinath Bordoloi was definitely one of the major architects of the Sixth Schedule. The provisions of the Sixth Schedule have now become so popular that they are in use in every state." He further states, "During the three days he stayed in Aizwal, Gopinath Bordoloi could endear himself to the Mizo people so much so that the unexpected news of his death barely two weeks after his departure from Aizwal, struck the Mizo people like a bolt from the blue. In a heartfelt resolution adopted at a huge memorial service held on the 7th of August at Aizwal, the people of Mizoram expressed their due acknowledgement of Gopinath Bordoloi's love, sincerity, honesty and untiring effort to serve the country and, in particular, the backward and undeveloped tribal people."

Late Bordoloi's immense love towards the hill people made him write for them, work for them and represent their feelings in the AICC Session held in Dehradun. His writings found in his brief case four decades ago seem to have relevance today. We have not deleted any idea or expressions from the article in order to give an idea to the readers as to how late Bordoloi's heart cried for the well-being of the entire people of the region. We fervently hope that the present generation of the various ethnic groups mentioned and described in the article will appreciate the spirit and not act to the write up otherwise.

It is well known that Gopinath was one of the prime movers of the cause of education in the North East Region. To this end he wanted to see an ideal institute of higher learning, that is University, established in Guwahati, the seat of learning in the Assam of those days. And he could see it established two years before he expired in 1950. The article, "A case for a University in Assam," might be the write up he submitted as a memorandum to the then Government of Assam headed by Sir Saadullah against its proposed University Bill. We leave it to the readers to find out for themselves for this article why and how late Bordoloi fought for a University in Assam.

The article on Gandhiji's birthday, although it is a brief one is an eloquent tribute. Late Bordoloi wished to pay to the greatness and glory of the unique life of Mahatma Gandhi even while behind bars on the completion of his seventieth year. This shows his deep conviction in the ideology and philosophy of Gandhiji. It is worthwhile to note here how late Bordoloi could realize even in those far off days that the only answer to the question of extinction of all lives as faced by today's humanity lay in the Gandhian approach to life whether individual, social or political.

Late Bordoloi's personal letters as compiled in Chapter IV were available in our small collection. Apart from the political life of this personality, his letters from jail reveal his character as a responsible father in the proper sense of the term. Gandhiji has left an indelible imprint on his mind which made him follow a spiritual path. The tremendous task which he undertook after the death of Gandhiji to follow the path led by him to the political world was awe-inspiring.

Gopinath Bordoloi's contribution in the literary field was also immense. Being deeply involved in constructive works throughout his life, he made proper use of the short span of time, when he was in jail, to pursue his literary interests. He felt that one can serve humanity through writing also. To guide children and educate them into the values of life, he wrote the biographies of five prophets of the world. In his writings we find a tinge of romanticism. Vinoba Bhave on receiving Gopinath Bordoloi's "Gandhiji" wrote to Smt. Surabala Bordoloi, *"Bordoloi ki likhi huyi kitab ko hridayangam bi hogi."*

The book is in six chapters. All this is the history of Bordoloi who was a student of history. Now he himself created history–a legend. Although quite a few things said and discussed in, these writings have a great deal of relevance to the present state of affairs in the country. We hope the readers will be inspired to translate Bordoloi's dream into a living reality, which has in the present context become so great a necessity.

Late Bordoloi is rememberd by Gandhian stalwarts like Kaka Kalelkar 'as one of the noblest sons of India'. The Governor of West Bengal stated that Sri Bordoloi was "a selfless patriot and a pillar of strength to the national struggle in past years and now his statesmanship was an asset not only to Assam but also to whole of India." Rajendra Prasad, the then President of India poignantly remembered Bordoloi, "with his death a void is created in the public life of Assam and India which it will be very difficult to fill". Bordoloi had borne the burden of administering a most difficult province in very trying times. He was greatly loved and respected not only in Assam but outside the province also as a great fighter in the cause of freedom, and a good and considerate administrator. The Prime Minister Pandit Nehru remembered him thus, "For all of us and Assam particularly, this is a great loss of a brave fighter for freedom and one who in his high position as a Chief Minister of Assam faced courageously the many problems of that state". Sardar Vallabh Bhai Patel was shocked at the sudden demise of Bordoloi. He stated, "Assam's loss is too great to contemplate". Govind Vallabh Pant expressed shock saying, "The sudden death of Bordoloi caused an irreparable loss to the country particularly Assam. One of the foremost leaders in the struggle for independence he was the architect of new Assam, a universally esteemed and loved by his people, a thorough gentleman and a true friend. "The then Chief Minister of Sourashtra Dhebarje expressed Bordoloi's demise as, "a loss to India." Shukla, Chief Minister of Madhya Pradesh expressed shock over Bordoloi's death as "a national loss". Asaf Ali from Orissa stated that the "premature death is a serious loss not merely to Assam but to the whole country." Morarji Desai was grieved to hear of sudden death of Bordoloi. Balvant Rai Mehta expressed his grief at the sudden demise of Bordoloi saying, "India loses a tried and veteran patriot who has rendered yeoman services to the motherland in her hour of trial."

CHAPTER II

Speeches

GOPINATH BORDOLOI's first speech as the Leader of Opposition on the first day (BRITISH INDIA)

Election to the Speaker

Srijut GOPINATH BORDOLOI: Sir, I consider it a great privilege and a very happy coincidence also that my first speech in this House should synchronise with your elevation to the high dignity of the Chair. It is not indeed for me to dilate on the great honour and heavy responsibility of the great office that you are assuming today. No post, no office could be of greater honour than the one that could be given to you by the elected representatives of the people (hear, hear). Therefore, Sir, I consider that it is an elevation and I particularly feel honoured that the Congress Party has been able to furnish this House with the occupant of this Chair. Sir, your responsibilities are undoubtedly great. With a little perusal of the Government of India Act, we have felt that the position I mean to say, the position of the House is not as good as it should be. We think that a lot of improvement is necessary in order that the House as a whole may acquire those rights which are available in other legislatures in free countries. I feel, Sir, that the shadow of the Autocratic Governor does often extend even to the precincts of this House. I do not anticipate what will be done by you but I do feel that in your hands the collective freedom of the House as a whole will receive encouragement and with your wise guidance and

---

The Assembly met in the Assembly Chamber, Shillong, at 11 a.m. on Wednesday, the 7th April, 1937.

ruling you will create in this House precedents, which will create India's history. On behalf of the members of the Congress Party, I accord you our heartfelt congratulations on your elevation to this Chair.

GOPINATH BORDOLOI's first speech as the Premier of Assam in ASSAM LEGISLATIVE ASSEMBLY (BRITISH INDIA)

Proceedings of the Fifth Session of the First Assam Legislative Assembly, assembled under the provisions of the Government of India Act, 1935

Request for the adjournment of the session sine die

The Hon'ble SPEAKER : Hon. members are aware that the Leader of the Opposition Srijut Gopinath Bordoloi, was summoned by His Excellency to form a Ministry in the place of the Hon'ble Minister who resigned. May I enquire of the Hon. Leader of the Opposition what the present position is?

Srijut GOPINATH BORDOLOI: Mr. Speaker, Sir, on Tuesday evening at 7-30 p.m. I was called by His Excellency to meet him and to tell him whether I was prepared to accept the Government after the Hon'ble Chief Minister of the late Government has declared that he did not enjoy the confidence of the House. I told him that I would take the responsibility, but I would take some time to announce the names of the Cabinet and I took 3 or 4 days. Accordingly on Saturday last, I was again sent for and I met his Excellency at 3-30 p.m.

There I definitely told him that we were accepting office and that I would take time till 3-50 p.m., to announce the names of certain Cabinet members. Then at 5-30 p.m., I went again and submitted a list of members, and said that I would fill in the names of other members 3 or 4 days later. His Excellency was pleased to tell me that he would accept the names and that he would allow me to form the Government. This morning at 10-25 I again saw His Excellency with the list of Cabinet members which I have submitted and he has announced that the swearing-in will take place at

---

The Assembly met in the Assembly Chamber, Shillong, at 11 a.m. on Monday, the 19th September, 1938.

12-30 noon. With reference to our action, after we accept office, I desire to place before you our position in respect of the business of the House.

In the first place, the question were mostly from us. Not in all cases, or in many cases at any rate, the replies that would be given would be very much different from the replies now given by the present Government and, therefore, it is impossible for us to agree to answer the questions and to give replies to them. The same thing applies to resolutions also. Our attitude will be very different from the attitude that has been taken up by the present Government with regard to these resolutions. Thirdly, with reference to Bills in particular, in view of the fact that we accepted office, it will be necessary for us to withdraw some of those Bills and recast them in the right of the policy of the Government that we are going to pursure–I mean to say, by the Coalition Government.

Therefore, it is perfectly clear that in no circumstances could we transact the present business of the House unless we are given an opportunity of scrutinizing from our view point all these questions, resolutions and Bills. Unless we have a chance to look into them, it is impossible for us to take up any attitude and meet the House over this matter.

It may well be known to you that we have not been given any access to the files even now: And at 12-30 we take the oath of office. Within less than two hours, say at 2 P.M., for us to be able to do all the things that is expected of Government in this House, is impossible. Therefore, I would request you to adjourn the House sine die so that we may be in a position to scrutinize everything and get ready to face over the many questions that are now before the House.

GOPINATH BORDOLOI's first speech as the Premier of Assam in the ASSAM LEGISLATIVE ASSEMBLY (FREE INDIA)

Resolution offering Homage to the sacred memory of Martyrs of India's Freedom and recording sense of gratitude to Mahatma Gandhi

The Hon'ble Srijut GOPINATH BORDOLOI: Mr. Speaker, Sir, we most heartily and joyfully associate ourselves with the Resolution that you have placed before the House. In a moment like this–a moment which seldom

---

The Assembly met in the Assembly Chamber, Shillong, at 11 a.m., on Monday, the 1st September, 1947.

comes in the life of a people, we do indeed remember the sufferings and sacrifices of those who have gone before us and through whose ceaseless efforts we enjoy the benefit of freedom today. It is only proper that in moment like this we should be paying our humble tribute to the sacred memory of those heroes that figured in the history of this struggle; and however small and insignificant they might have appeared to an unappreciating world, they contributed their mite to the success of this unique and non-violent movement.

It would also be only in the fitness of things that we will be associating ourselves with that glory of tribute which you are offering to the Great Leader of India, Mahatma Gandhi. His has been a life very different from ours, and however lengthy an expression that we may have used, we cannot sufficiently describe him. Today he is in a sphere of activity very different from that of ours. He had his dream; but possibly his dream has only been partially fulfilled. Possibly certain reasons have compelled us to think of ourselves in terms of two different regions and acting in two different spheres of activities, but that Great Man has gone beyond and transcended beyond the limits of areas and denominations and is applying himself to the task which he feels has fallen on him. What we do feel at this moment most is the need of following his guidance which has always stood for truth and non-violence. Therefore, in this day of rejoicing we shall be failing in our duty if we do not remember that Great Man not merely as the creator of Free India but also for the great principles which he has put before mankind for the solution of all ills which beset them.

With these words, Sir, I associate myself with the Resolution that has been moved by you before the House.

Assam - A Gift of Nature

Mr. President, Ladies and Gentlemen,

I thank you for the honour you do me in asking me to come over here and to speak to you a few words about Assam. I appreciate your kindness, but I realize also my difficulty. To talk about a province in the course of 20 minutes or so would require such wit and brevity that, I am sure, I do not possess.

A part of the speech delivered by Lokopriya Gopinath Bordoloi in A.I.C.C. Session in May, 1949 at Dehradun.

I feel that I cannot congratulate you when some of you seem to say that you know so little about Assam. Assam is a part of this great country–beautiful and wealthy in all that nature has given, but poor and neglected in all that man has done. But I feel that if even today you begin to take an active interest in this part of India and her simple and unsophisticated people, much will grow and develop there for which you will have reasons to be proud and happy. In the busy world of today, we have hardly time enough to look around, and those who have it are engrossed with what is close at hand. Therefore, the beauty in looking at a thing as it is, the glory of helping one of your own, and of acting in collaboration with a weakly brother and a neighbour is lost sight of.

Yet not so were your forefathers, centuries and centuries ago, and I can tell you without encroaching on the field of the antiquarians, archaeologists and epigraphists, that Assam then known as Pragjyotish or Kamrupa and her people even from pre-historic times were better known to the rest of India than you seem to know their successors today. Recent researches into the pre-historic period show Pragjyotish flourished in about 1,000 B.C., when Lower Bengal was not there in existence. (Aryanization from the West continued from very early times, while its own *Adibasis* were respectively Austries, Mongolians, Tibeto-Burmans and Dravidians with their developed civilization. [Pragjyotisha has been mentioned both in the Ramayana and the Mahabharata, and from descriptions given, it would appear that the country stretched as far as the sea in the South and that it was also a hilly country. In the Ramayana it is stated that Pragjyotisha was built on a golden crested mountain which was 64 *jojanas* in extent and stood abutted on the bottomless Varunalaya (Sea). In the Mahabharata Bhagadutta, King of Pragjyotisha is also called Sailalaya (dwelling among the mountains) and it is stated that his troops consisted of Kiratas, Chinas and dwellers of the sea-coast. It is quite clear that the mountains mentioned were Assam ranges, and the sea was the Bay of Bengal which stretched up to this Hill range. In the West its boundary was Korotiya or Teesta, to the East as far as present Darrang District of Assam.] This geography is corroborated by the Buddhist records and Greek accounts of more historical period who refer to the land of Kamrupa as having the tributary of Laudhitya Sagara, (which is Brahmaputra) in the South with islands there, and to the West Kausika Kosi. Right from that time till 16th century when Thailand established their rule in the Eastern portion of the land Kamrupa stretched from Korotya River in the West which includes the modern districts of Jalpaiguri, North Rangpur and Dinajpur to the Eastern point of modern Assam with Bhutan Hills as the Northern boundary and the Southern Bengal in the South. Between 400 A.D. and 1000 A.D. there were many occasions when Western boundary was stretched up to River Kausika, now known as Kosi.

It may be seen that Kamrupa was always described by the writers who mentioned it as one of the great Kingdoms of Northern India and even at the cost of taking a bit of your valuable time, I want to mention to you some of the references to prove how much more the knowing people of India of ancient and medieval period knew of Assam than we do today. I have already mentioned the authors of the Ramayana and the Mahabharata. The Kalika Purana gives the description how Kamrupa came to get its name. In th 4the century A.D. the then "Prasasti"* of Samudra Gupta mentions Kamrupa as a frontier Kingdom of India in the East. The famous poet Kalidas who is said to be flourishing in the 5th century A.D. mentions Kamrupa and Pragjyotisha as the same Kingdom in his Raghuvangsam. In the Harshacharita of Banabhatta, Kamrupa Kings are mentioned chronologically for more than 100 years. In the Kashmere chronicle Raja Tarangini, mention is made of the King Meghabahana of Kashmere marrying Princess Amritaprabha, daughter of the Kamrupa King Samudra Varman. It is said that in the Swayambara held by her father, Meghabahana received from the princess Amritaprabha the bridegroom's garland, and what Amritaprabha did in Kashmere finds record in the same account.

Vincent Smith mentions the deputation of an embassy to China by the King of Devaka, a Kingdom east of Kamrupa in about 8th century A.D.

In the 10th century Rajasekhara, the court Poet of Mahipala, King of Kannauj mentions Pragjyotisha as one of the countries of Aryabara along with Magadha and Paundra (?) etc.

These foreign travellers of great renown also mention Kamrupa. Ptolemy, the Greek describes in his "Periplus of the Erithrian Sea" the country of Kamrupa at great length.

Huen Tsang went to Assam from Nalanda at the invitation of the King Bhaskar Varman and gave a full description of the land in the 7th century A.D.

In the 11th century A.D. the Arab traveller, Alberuni mentions Kamrupa among the Eastern countries of India.

*He (Samudra Gupta) performed Aswamedha Ceremony and the King of Kamarupa, Pushya Varman challenged his authority and submitted only after a severe battle.

It would, I believe, be of some interest to study the topography of the modern province today in particular reference to its flora and fauna and perhaps its forests and minerals. It will be seen that Assam today is mainly composed of the Valley of the Mighty Brahmaputra flowing between two mountain ranges the maximum height of the northern being as high as the Kanchanjhanga and the maximum height of the southern range being over 6,000 ft. Assam today has 56,000 sq. miles within its borders, leaving out 7,000 sq. miles of territory opting for Pakistan. Out of this nearly 36,000 are in Hills, and only 20,000 are divided between the Brahmaputra Valley and the Valley of Surma falling in Cachar Districts. Eleven to twelve lacs of hills people live in these Hill regions of 36,000 while 63 to 64 lacs of people live in the plains which include 25,000 sq. miles of the sandy land of the Brahmaputra and tracts of land in hollows, lands strewn with pebbles and sand. The figures that sometimes appear in papers about the availability of millions of acres of cultivable waste is a fable. If the forest and the cultivable and scientifically habitable land of the people could be distributed scientifically instead of 13 per cent of the land in reserved forests as now, we might have as much as 40 per cent to 50 per cent. The hill regions could have been organized for forest regeneration with hill people having recourse to settled cultivation instead of shifting ones as now. This might have saved the cataclysm to which the Province, nay, the whole region in the East is subject to the ravages of nature. One has only to describe a normal monsoon to show what it seems. Six to eight weeks before the monsoon begins, westerly and warm winds begin to blow continuously spreading the whole country with dust and seeds of various trees and plants. Then start the thunder, hails and showers, the sky gleams with brilliant light and the earth reverberates with heaven-rending sound, and almost every night from about the middle of April start heavy showers of rain. The rills and streams in the hills, which were so long dry, show themselves in sparkling white streaks in blue hills and begin to rush down; and as monsoon proceeds, join with hundred others to fill in the rivers both in the northern and southern ranges of the Valley. These rivers in their turn, again run down precipitously to the wide breast of the Brahmaputra which begins to froth and foam and boil striking terrors into the heart of men and beasts. The level of the mighty river rises to such heights that the whole of the Valley comes under water, and if it rains for any continuous period, flood and havoc are created both by the feeder rivers as also by the Brahmaputra. Before the monsoon starts, the lands in the hills are made ready for cultivation, earth there is loosened, and with the rush-down of this avalanche of water from the hills and mountains, not only are wild animals including sometimes elephants and big reptiles, flotilla of drift wood etc. are brought down but also very stupendously large quantities of soil, that spread themselves in the beds and the banks of the feeder rivers in the whole plains going as far as the Sea. No data about the quantity of this huge mass of soil is possible; but the fact that what were mere dots of earth in South Bengal Sea could form themselves into the big solid territory in course of 3,000 years only gives us some indication of what these rivers are doing for us.

This heavy rainfall which varies from 120" to 60" in plain regions and with as much as 500" in Cherrapunji has given Assam her richness in flora and fauna. The forests of Assam are rich both in hard and soft wood. Sal, Bansam, and Teak are some of the former, while Holong, Holok and Simmul are some of the latter. The former bring to the Government of Assam an annual revenue of Rs. 25,00000 to 30,00000, while the latter feed to the existing units of plywood factory with the possibility of 2 or 3 more besides supplying enough timber for a match factory or two. In the field of fauna, we yet retain in our three game sanctuaries rare type of rhinoceros, vast varieties of deer, wild buffaloes and almost in every forest big and small bears, tigers, leopards etc. and wild animals of all species and kinds are met even today. Elephants alone bring to the coffers of the Province not less than Rs.2,00,000 annually in the average. In the feathered kind also, apart from the common species that you find everywhere in India, birds of rarest varieties with beauteous plumage and with the sweetest of melodies greet you both in the forests and arbours of Assam. In winters descend from the heights of the Himalayas innumerable varieties of duck and goose, and come to feed in the jheels and low-lying fields of Assam which retain the flood water for almost the whole of the year.

In the hills and highlands are to be found the mineral wealth of the Province. The Northern Hills Range which falls within Bhutan and China......

India Attains Freedom

India has attained freedom and started a new life from today. Since 15th August 1947, the population of India has increased to a large extent and the diameter of the Indian territory has also widened much. In fact more than 2 lakh of people and 3700 sq. miles from the State of Khasi Hills

---

Lokopriya Bordoloi's address to the people on AIR on the occasion of Independence Day-1948.

have merged into this dominion. As a result, 13 lakh sq. miles of land and 14 crores of people today constitute India, this outstanding country in the globe. Whether it is for the better or worse, India will greatly influence the future of the world. Realising this, if we carry out the responsibilities that have come upon us as a consequence of the present situation, it will be to our credit and pride. From this day onwards our relationship with the British crown has come to an end. To me, the decision to be within the Commonwealth will not change our political standing. I believe that this decision is an inception for the promotion of Universal human welfare from a common platform. Twenty years ago exactly on this date under the leadership of Mahatma Gandhi and others pledged in spite of many sufferings and pain to bring freedom to India through the path of truth, non-violence and sacrifice. At the end of the 20th century, we have availed the opportunity to decide on our future independently as an independent nation. These happenings are astonishing as well as romantic. I hope we have been able to realize the miracle of truth and non-violence after the long struggle of 20 years. I think we do not cherish any sense of hatred against the foreign power which ruled us. It is really joyful that our leaders have expressed goodwill towards the Britishers without any reservation. The same thing may be expressed in our small state also. Although we were ruled by the British bureaucrats, merchants and planters and although we could not agree with them on the economic front, we can say without being hypocritical that our goodwill and wishes are always with them.

Today, on this memorable day, I also greet the people who are not citizens of this country. This democratic view has emerged as a result of the new ruling policy of India. At the time of framing the Constitution, there was a lot of criticism on the various articles of the Constitution by outsiders and within the Gana Parishad. There is no dearth of people who want to point out the defects of the Constitution. But if we all try to understand this immense endeavour of the main theme, then we will realize, it is an achievement for the whole of free India. It seems as though years of conservation in the form of meaningless rituals for instance, fortune in the name of religion and untouchability, have been put to an end by the mere stroke of a pen. Today it is a criminal law to think or to look down upon somebody as an untouchable. The troubles of the hills and plains and the other backward people will avail love and sympathy from the nation. It is the aim of the Constitution to remove poverty and illiteracy and place the common people on an equal status. If we can build our new democratic nation according to the main ideals, I am sure India will top the world politics.

Question is, will it be possible to create such a country? It is not possible for a nation to earn honours merely through assembly words or sentences or by composing linguistic essays. It is possible only wherein the people of that particular nation possesses the strength of justice, truthfulness and human values. Administration becomes effective within a good team of people. Probably, it is therefore said, that the administration of a society is determined by the character of the people. When an individual of a society respects the freedom of another and tries to work with goodwill, democracy becomes effective. If our own behaviour and the behaviour we expect from another one is in disharmony we are going against the lines of democracy. Democracy can never thrive here, let alone human welfare and progress.

But if we look back towards our past we find that the people of these eras lived a life of morality and truthfulness. It is not that the kings of these eras had no differences or that no wars were fought. These wars did not disturb the simple life of the peace loving people of the villages. This peaceful life was not lived under pressure of law or fear of punishment, but rather because the people of these eras were basically peaceloving and just and hence India attained her peak of civilizations in these eras. The emperors of the Buddhist Dharma, instead of trying to widen the boundaries of their empires, tried to arouse the dormant spiritual strength within each human being in order to remove the miseries of the people. To my mind, today it is not an impossible task to cultivate and attain the truthfulness and goodness which our people in the past possessed. It is a matter of grave concern that a nation which had arrived at such a degree of civilization and culture should at present fall into decadence. We should realize that it is because of the disintegration of the moral value that we lost our Independence. It is surely because of this we have suffered in the economic front as well. Therefore, we shall have to regain our moral strength to build a powerful India which will determine the future of the world. And keeping this ideal in mind Gandhiji has bid a stress on the fact that we should morally and spiritually build a strong society in this new era. But it seems that in attaining the power of Independence we have not paid heed to Gandhiji's instructions of building a moral society. It is inevitable that to live as an independent nation, one must follow the teachings of Gandhiji and there is absolutely no way out.

As individuals of an independent country people of different Constitutions must learn to work together in cooperation. Unity admits diversity is an eternal phenomenon of human life. Therefore, it is indispensable that the various people and constituencies must work for a common welfare, the welfare of the common people. When people of a constituency work for the fulfilment of their own vested interest, there arises chaos in the society and main goal is driven away far from the welfare of the common people. Truly, there are some parties in India who had falsely promised to solve the problems of society and resorted to the paths of violence. If this kind of treacherous attitude prevails amidst us, it is certain that democracy will not last long. The independence we have attained after a long saga of pain and suffering will have stripped us in no time.

We must realize that if the nation is to be based on our ideals as discussed above it will not be an easy task. It is only by leading a disciplined and restrained life can we make it possible. To be independent which we restraint and sacrifice we did not do during the period of the great movement. One who thinks for the future of the country has to shoulder more responsibilities. By self-discipline and by such selfcontrol, every constitution of the society such as Government employees, industrialists, merchants etc. should think on the same lines as to how he can work for the betterment of the society. Many a time we create our own problems and miseries. Famine, war, riots are all man-made. Whatever it be, when we are to face the problems, we should try to rectify the situation together with a common outlook, and share it equally amongst the various constituencies. Those people who work with anti social aims are detrimental to the society.

Through a feeling of brotherhood, justice and morality it is our own duty to remove all these evils of the society. Unsocial and wrong doings must be dealt against together. It is observed that anti-social elements by law and punishment cannot be removed. We should all co-operate and work to eliminate them. I believe that God revealed his will in the form of inspiration to the calm and dedicated people of today. Our administration has admitted this fact. Even the whole of the world is proceeding through this path of truthfulness. I have implicit faith that this mediation can never be attained through violence and bloodshed. This is possible only through non-violence and therefore we should follow the path of peace. Only then shall we be able to realise our ideal. To fulfil this great ideal, we should not give up our patience and goodwill. If the people of our democratic country are inspired by this aim, I hope we can develop an outstanding society in the world.

I believe that the world will be transformed into a peaceful place if people try wholeheartedly.

Long live Indian Democratic Nation.

THANK YOU

Courtesy of Awaham, a leading magazine of Assam published in Calcutta.

Addressing the Masses*

".....The British Government failed to fulfil the national demands of the Congress and in protest to it the Ministry submitted resignation and adopted a non-cooperation policy. The British expressed desire to seek cooperation from the Congress, although the speech of Lord Linlithgo delivered recently in Bombay seemed not to fulfil any demands of the Congress. But if the British changes their motive towards the Congress, Gandhiji hopes to come forward for some negotiation. The Congress Working Committee has given full power to Gandhiji to hold talks with the great Lord on the point. Gandhiji will try to convince the British Government to yield to the lawful and justified demands of the Congress. Peace and compassion depends solely on this talk."

Gopinath Bordoloi clarified Congress Party's stand to a group of youths of leftist party that Congress ideology would help to save democracy in India. He replied to their questions:

"Congress does not want a Constituent Assembly which will be subservient to the British Government. The British Government at least should give up the lust for colonialism in India and until it recognises India to be an independent nation they should keep in mind that they should never hope to form any Constituent Assembly. Congress is aware that if the British Government do not recognise this basic principle, Congress would never come to an agreement and it will definitely fight against the British Government."

Understanding Mahatma Gandhi**

Just a while ago today, the last day of the month, Bapuji left his mortal coils to join the abode of the immortals, never to return. His awe inspiring personality and philosophy had probably become a deep concern to all the great thinkers of India while he was alive for it promised an indis-

*Gopinath Bordoloi's speech in a mammoth gathering in Guwahati on the 24th January, 1940 regarding the political situation.

**Gopinath Bordoloi's AIR broadcast on 30th January'49 in Shillong - Gauhati Centre.

putable position among the most prominent men of the world. I would like to express a few thoughts on this occasion. To me personally, Gandhiji was my leader and my teacher.

Gandhiji was a preacher of all religions. Like all great men his vocation was clearly perceived by him and he chose to confine his field of activity to it. In Gandhiji's case it was service to mankind. His initiation began with the Indians in South Africa. He saw that his foremost duty was to bring justice to them. However, whatever Gandhiji undertook, even though confined to a particular country, the means he adopted to achieve his goals were not limited to either region or race for what he taught and practised were universal and eternal truths meant to bring solace to the people of the world regardless of time and place.

Gandhiji, being a sensitive child, sensed the evils of the foreign rule even in his childhood. However, it was only after he had completed his studies abroad and returned to India to start his spiritual practices that he realised the immensity of the evil he would have to battle against. But Gandhiji was born not only with extraordinary perception but also extraordinary strength of mind. His occupation led him to South Africa and there too he met with the same oppression of the White Administration that he saw in India–racism. On returning home he realized that the cankerous forces of Imperialism had spread all over Asia. It would not be appropriate on my part to elaborate on the historical aspect at this juncture. What I want to find out is that Gandhiji was against the British Administration because of its lack of humane sentiments. People were ruled not as human beings but automatons. This is what pained Gandhiji. Craze for power and greed for wealth had made the Britishers' callous attitude towards the people they ruled. Gandhiji had been a witness to the devastation of the first World War and therefore knew that as long as certain people remained power-hungry and exerted themselves upon others the world would never know peace or prosperity. In India, he had seen apparently supercivilised people change to human monsters when they came to power. Gandhiji was determined to fight all these forces till peace prevailed in India and the Universe.

Though Gandhiji was a religious preacher he was no moralist sermonizing on do's and dont's.

The very methodology he employed to fight the evils in society was a boon to it. Gandhiji could be called an interpreter of religion for he re-defined religion to us thus making it relevant to our daily existence.

Two thousand five hundred years ago another religious preacher had put forward the concept that every thought, word and deed had physical, mental and spiritual reactions. Although nobody can know a thought in our mind, the thought will manifest in a definite visible act. Therefore one should guard against evil thought. Not only did Gandhiji preach this principle, he himself strictly adhered to it. Hatred will lead to hatred; love will turn to love. Therefore, if one is in quest of truth he will have to live a truthful life. The quest may lead to a number of hindrances but one will have to be prepared to fight them with non-violence. Gandhiji lived this principle. His aim was to create a world wherein there was no hatred but only peace and joy. All the various activities he undertook in India were motivated by the will to establish peace. What was Gandhiji's chief concept behind all his principles? He believed that the ultimate truth was God and human being were God's creation, then what was the need to indulge in heinous atrocities in the name of religion? Whether one was a Hindu, Muslim, Christian, Jain or Sikh, the point of difference lay only in the procedure of prayer. Therefore, where is the ground for arguments about the superiority of any particular religion? All religions were equal for they were created by the same God. Our country is a diverse country with many people living together. It should be our duty to awaken a feeling of brotherhood amongst us. India would be a most wonderful country if we could make equality our religion. I should like to point out that the society Gandhiji envisaged was never against any religion nor did it worship a different God.

Gandhiji's approach towards the Harijans was born out of the same principle of equality. The Harijan too was a creation of the same God who had created us.

According to Gandhiji, to be mechanical in one's activities could be tolerated but a mechanical way of life would lead to disastrous results–it could make an individual an automation. Every human being is the reflection of God and carries in him the power to create.

No nation has the right to tyrannize over another nation or to deprive it of its independence. With the cooperation of the backward classes Gandhiji rebuilt the village organizations in line with the ancient Indian tradition, thus organizing a self-reliant society. Gandhiji aimed at building an organised society. But he did not begin with the Committees or bodies but with the very minds and hearts of the men who constituted these organizations. His aim was to make man worthy of being the highest creature of God's creation.

A year has rolled by and we are still making attempts at understanding Gandhiji. Unless our hearts are pure, our mind steady we shall never be able to understand this great man or his precepts. In spite of our meagre accomplishment our one achievement has been the practice of Gandhiji's principles.

We hope that the path of peace shown to us by this great and magnanimous thinker will enable us to reach our goal and thus transform his death into a source of inspiration for us.

Tribes of Assam

Mr. President, Sir, I did not want to participate in this debate. But it seems to me that many Members are not fully cognisant of the tribal situation in Assam, and what is more, many have not been able to appreciate the background of the recommendations of the Advisory Sub-Committee set up by the Constituent Assembly for the purpose of inquiring into the tribal situation in Assam.

I wish to state, Sir, that there are three categories of tribals in Assam. There are the plains tribals–men who were the original inhabitants and who have a culture and civilization of their own. They were gradually absorbed into the folds and the culture of other plains people to put more appropriately the Aryan culture. These people have now been classed with the minorities, just as the Scheduled Classes and they have been granted the same right as the other minority community.

Then there are the hill tribes proper. These again can be divided into two clear categories. One such class of hill tribes is administered by the Governor as the Agent of the Governor-General of India and the other class, coming under the Sixth Schedule, is proposed to be administered as autonomous groups. We are not concerned with the first category in the Sixth Schedule except to the extent of the provision contained in paragraph 17 which says that any area now administered by the Governor as the Agent of the Governor-General, can be brought under the category of autonomous districts in his discretion only under certain circumstances. For that purpose the Governor has been given power as mentioned by me under paragraph 17.

Speech delivered by Gopinath Bordoloi in the Parliament regarding Sixth Schedule.

Now I would like to give this information to the House that in the Agency areas these tribes have no self-governing institutions of their own at the present moment. The Draft Constitution provided that these areas should be administered directly by the Governor without any restriction whatsoever. But the time may come when they may become fit to govern themselves. The proposal is that at that time they may be brought under the category of autonomous districts. These areas lie on the northern banks of the Brahmaputra on the foothills of the Himalayas. The others who come under the category of autonomous districts are those who inhabit the southern bank of the river bordering Burma and Pakistan. There are some six different types of tribes among them and the autonomous districts are envisaged for them.

Now I want to place before you the background in which this draft had to be formulated. It is not unknown to you that the rule of the British Government and the activities of the foreign missions always went together. These areas were formerly entirely excluded areas in the sense that none from the plains could go there and contact them. That was the position till 15th August 1947, when India became independent. The foreign rulers till then had in these areas power to send out of the place anyone they desired within 24 hours. Again, Sir, some of these areas were war zones. During the war, the then rulers and officers developed in the minds of these tribal people a sense of separation and isolation and gave them assurance that at the end of the war they will be independent states managing their affairs in their own way. They were led to believe that the entire hill areas would be constituted into a province and put under some irresponsible Governor. You might possibly have read in the papers that plans were hatched in England in which the ex-Governor of Assam evidently took part, to create a sort of a kingdom over there.

Now, with this background, Sir, our investigation began early in 1946. People of this area were already fully suffused with these ideas of isolation and separation. The most important fact that presented itself before this Committee was whether for the purpose of integration the methods of force, the methods of the use of the Assam Rifles and the military forces, should be used, or a method should be used in which the willing co-operation of these people could be obtained for the purpose of governing these areas.

Sir, it is necessary to mention here that there are certain institutions among these hill tribals which, in my opinion, are so good that, if we wanted to destroy them, I considered it to be very wrong. One of the things which I felt was very creditable to these tribals was the manner in which they settle their disputes. Cases which would go in the name of murder according to our Penal Code were settled by these people by the barest method of Panchayat's decision and by payment only of compensation. Then, the democracy which prevails there–though limited in the sense it is confined only to the tribals of a clan or region–will rouse the admiration of any disinterested student. And again take the instance of their village administration. The district authorities have indeed very little to concern themselves with the way things go on there. Take again the case of the Nagas who distributed the entire functions of the society to certain age groups of people in their society. The boys would perform certain simple functions, leaving the sturdier functions of the State to the adults, while the elders would give their judgments in case of disputes and order distribution of lands for jhumming and things of that kind. In other words, they are exercising a certain amount of autonomy which, I thought and the members of the Tribal Sub-Committee thought should be preserved rather than destroyed. What is necessary for good government is already there.

It is true that some of these tribal people sometimes indulge in head-hunting, but it should be clearly understood that this is only when there is enmity of one clan against another. These people nurtured a spirit of collective hatred in them for generations. The point therefore that presented itself to us was whether we should raise in them a spirit of enmity and hatred by application of force or whether we should bring them up under the broad principle of government by goodwill and love. The Advisory Committee thought that the latter course was the course that should be adopted. I myself am a firm believer in Gandhian principles. If therefore Gandhian methods are to be followed, there is no alternative but to adopt the course which we have thought was the best method. Now, with background the draft was prepared and was placed before you. In the meantime, great changes have come in the structure of the Government of India. More powers are being vested in the Centre today than it was contemplated then. Therefore, those powers at present have to be put in the appropriate place. The trend of criticism on the amendments that have been submitted seems to indicate that we gave more powers to these autonomous Councils, perhaps very much beyond what the State Legislature of Assam could. I do not agree with this view. As a matter of fact, most of these provisions are nothing more than translating something which already prevails in the tribal societies, and therefore we are not giving too much as has been pointed out by some of my friends.

Then coming to the amendments which have been moved by Mr.

Chaliha, excepting for–what he was objecting to that a particular place Dimapur has been included in the Naga Hills, the rest have all been accepted by the Drafting Committee. It is true that the area was included in the Naga Hills only for administrative convenience. The Drafting Committee have however provided for two things. First that any area as a whole could be excluded from the autonomous district. Secondly, it has also been provided that the men who are living there or in similar area shall have the right of exercising their vote in a neighbouring general constituency.

I submit, therefore, that nothing has been proposed there which is not in line with the pattern and the structure of the Constitution which we are framing for the whole of India, and that wherever there was any anomally, that anomaly has been removed. That is all that I have to say. I therefore request that the movers of these amendments take into consideration the background of the draft and also the peculiar conditions which prevailed in the hills before.

Presidential Address

President, of the Reception Committee Mondal Kanang Sanmilan, my dear friends, Kanangu and Mondals and respected members present.

I would like to express my deep sense of gratitude for the honour you have given electing me as the President for the second time within a span of four years. Whatever reasons may it be, in 1937, I had offended you by not being present in the last conference, but probably having attended this meeting I am sure I have been able to satisfy you.

In response to your love and honour, except speaking a few words to you I have nothing else to give you. But that too has been already told and now I don't know what should I explain to you.

Actually, whatever, I spoke in 1937, there cannot be any addition to it. I have come to learn that you had read out my speech in the last conference. Therefore, except a few points which I would add to my lecture now, I would feel it enough. On my experience as an administrator

---

Speech delivered by Gopinath Bordoloi on Mondal Kanangu Conference on October 7, 1940.

for the last fourteen months I can only say that the same thought is in my mind as I had three years back. I had told at that time that according to the Act, where an officer of high rank enjoys a salary ranging from Rs. 400-500 to Rs. 2,500 Rs. 3,000 per month and the lower cadres are to remain satisfied with a meagre Rs. 15 Rs. 20 per month, I should say that I have no confidence over such an Act. Such type of an administration should be immediately brought to an end.

Our only intention of resigning from the ministry and coming back to the people is because there should be a reform in this Act and another Act should be introduced in accordance to the condition of our State. It is sure if the present Congress ideology does not change and thereby the power comes to common people, Congress would not go under such Act to rule. This great Act may immediately be formed or it may become successful after a great hardship and after a long time. But whenever it may be, I doubt whether we shall be able to help you duly until the work is being done.

The two grave defects of the Government of India in reference to services:

(I) Cost of administration in services including 62 per cent equivalent of 10-6 in the rupee. Of this most of the money for whatever reason it might be must be paid unless a radical change in the administration involving the substitution of present Constitution Act by a mere equitable Act. No civilized country spends that percentage.

(II) But in spite of this expenditure, the poorer classes of public servants have hardly a living wage. This is due to the fact that we are compelled to pay the higher services in thousands, where we might have paid in hundreds, were of provincial services. We are not privileged to reduce the pay of these external services at certain times. In no civilized country this is true. The London Constables get 120 to 100 p.m. while the Inspectors get 300-350 p.m. The result is to create an aristocracy of services. They naturally come to look down upon village life as completely unsuitable to the status they enjoy and are inclined to look down upon the village officials as equivalent to menials. The village lifes is the heart of the country linguistics, and a new and artificial town the exploitation of the village.

My sympathies are entirely with you because you live in the village and work in the village. I do sincerely believe that the present scale of pay of Mandals and Kanangoes is inadequate. But I feel the inequity is bound to continue till we can bring in a new order and new state in the society.

I feel, even being a Government servant, you can be helpful in bringing into existence that condition, a Mondal or a Moral as I said.

A Meeting with Mahatma

A Historic Talk of Gopinath Bardoloi with Gandhiji

It may be some time in 1947 that I met Gandhiji again. The division of India was effected and referenda in Sylhet and NWFP were also over in favour of the Muslim League. Murder, arson, loot and rape–each community trying to out-do the other in the two Punjabs–had begun on a scale never dreamt of. Referendum had decided the cessation of certain areas from India to Pakistan but the boundaries were yet to be determined by a Commission. Judges appointed by India and Pakistan both for the Punjab and Bengal including Sylhet could not agree and a British arbitrator had to do the final work.

On the Assam side the Eastern Pakistan claimed the inclusion of Cachar, Goalpara and what not. The Judges were hearing the cases and the air was thick with all sorts of rumours. While at Delhi I found that some Khasi gentlemen and ladies having leaning for the Muslim League went there to meet Lord Mountbatten and Jinnah. Serious misgivings arose in my mind as to what the off-shoot of this Commission would be. I spoke to Panditji about it and he wanted me to meet Lord Mountbatten and tell him the facts I mentioned to him. So, I went and told him that by any interpretation of the terms of reference of the Boundary Commission, Cachar and Goalpara did not come under the purview of the Boundary Commission. He agreed with me regarding the interpretation of the reference, but he said that since the whole matter was left to arbitration and the whole inquiry was in the nature of a judicial proceeding, it would not be proper for him to give a clear direction; but again, he repeated to me that the terms were so obvious that they could not include the two districts.

Misgiving on Shillong

Then he asked me whether I knew of any place of higher altitude in Sylhet. I said, a large part of Sylhet is below sea level and I knew of a place which

---

This recorded note of the late Gopinath Bardoloi about a historic interview which he had with Gandhiji immediately after the partition of the country was published on the occasion of his fifteenth death anniversary.

was higher than two to four hundred feet. Then he brought me near a map and pointed out Shillong and the lower slopes of Khasi Hills. He said these areas were in Pakistan. I said that Shillong was the capital of Assam. I came back without any more thought on the subject of this query then. In the meantime, the Khasi friends had an interview with Liaquat Ali and were arranging similar interviews with leaders of Pakistan. On the second day, it suddenly flashed on me if Lord Mounbatten's query was not in any way connected with these moves and interviews. In my suspicion I argued within myself if Lord Mountbatten might not also think in the way as the Khasi representatives. To whom shall I go in this hour of doubt, misgiving and confusion but to one who has always removed them with his loving sympathy?

It was some time towards the end of July or beginning of August, 1947, and Gandhiji was sitting in his usual seat with only Srimati Amrit Kaur in the room. I narrated to him my fears and troubles mentioned above. But before I quite finished, he said: "I have heard all about your attitude regarding separation of Sylhet. Why did you agree to the referendum?" I told him that I was no party to it. But immediately came the retort, "Can anything happen in a province without its Prime Minister becoming a party to it?" I then told him all I knew: how Lord Mountbatten at a lunch to which I was invited, said that he presumed I was indifferent about Sylhet going to Pakistan. I told him, however, that, while it was true that a large number of the people in Assam Valley wanted Sylhet to be separated and, at one time, even the Hindus of Sylhet wanted the same, the Congressmen of both the places wanted to live together as they fought a common fight together for ten long years under my leadership for weal or for woe. I told him also how Lord Mountbatten met the leader of Sylhet, the then Home Minister of our Cabinet (Basanta Kumar Das), the same evening at a garden party and how the latter agreed to the referendum and how the Working Committee of the Congress endorsed it. I then put to him, "How can I fight the Working Committee?" Then he said rather firmly, "Did I not tell you that you should be prepared to fight any wrong? Why did you not do so? Seven years ago you did a mistake in adopting satyagraha in trying to follow the Working Committee."

Then referring to the subject under discussion he said, "I can do little for you. You had better go to the Sardar." I said, "I shall surely go to him, but Bapu, you must do something." He was then as if thinking aloud–

"Once you agree to an evil, you do not know where it will lead you." I was sitting there full 8 to 10 minutes mute, while he was talking to himself and partially to Srimati. I read on his face a bitterness and a despair which, during the course of 25 years experience, I had never seen before. He spoke in a very low tone: "I am never a man given to suspicion, much less act on suspicions. But looking at things around me, I feel suspicious of even the best actions of the Britisher." Then he became silent. I again repeated, "Bapu, will you not do anything for me?" He did not reply but told me again, "Go to the Sardar." I obeyed him and went to the Sardar the next morning. I narrated my doubts and fears in the same way as I did to Bapuji; but Sardarji said that I was wrong in my suspicions, and that if I felt so strongly, why did I not speak to him earlier. I came back with the impression that he considered I was childish in my fears.

Misunderstanding

And verily I was. The next evening Sardarji gave a party at the Imperial Hotel to the Rulers of the States and their representatives in the Constituent Assembly, to which he invited Lord Mountbatten and all his colleagues in the Cabinet, the Premiers of the provinces and many personages. I had only been 3 or 4 minutes in the room when Sardarji stated without any introduction of the subject, "You see, Bardoloi, there was clear misunderstanding...." But by the time being I began to understand him, an Aide-de Camp of His Excellency would talk to me. I went with him immediately and was about to take a seat nearby; but he made me sit by his side on the same seat he was occupying. He said, "On the day I met you, I could not explain to you certain things, which were yet confidential, but I can speak to you now. You see, Sir was offered the Governorship of East Bengal. He had three small children and his wife (he mentioned their age). He could not keep them in Dacca in this heat. He was, therefore, wanting to know from me if there was any cooler place of higher altitude in East Bengal where he could keep his wife and children. He had just left my room when you came in; and who could give better information about East Bengal and Sylhet than you? I, therefore, wanted to know from you all about these places. And you possibly thought that I was thinking of ceding these areas to East Bengal, and then you spoke to Gandhiji"–with that he gave a big pinch to my arm. "As you know now, nothing could be further from my thoughts. I shall write to Gandhiji, but go and tell him all that I have told you" (words are mine). All that I could say was that I was extremely sorry and ashamed. I told him that I am never a man given to suspicions; but in the extraordinary times and circumstances in which we were living, I had subjected to unfounded doubts and fears. I told him how grateful I was for the frank manner in which he explained the matter to me. I could not meet Gandhiji; but I wrote to him to say how great was Lord Mountbatten and how small I was, and what a fool I had been to trouble him with my doubts and fears.

Who Wants Me?

I was in the course of some of my visits during this time, that I perceived the inner agony from which he was suffering on account of the division of India, and the crimes that followed thereon. In one of those moments Bapuji uttered: "Who wants me now?" I felt a sort of dart in my heart and came out with tears in my eyes.

People like us thought that since Independence has come, we would all settle down to the construction of a new India, and of a new province. But it appeared, to my great sorrow, that forces of disruption took possession of the minds of some people more than they had possibly at any time. Selfishness of the worst type seemed to take possession of men, from which even some Congressmen did not seem to escape. In this province the aftermath of Sylhet transfer and the attendant evils of transfer of the poor clerks rendered the political situation bitter, and not a few letters were received by me threatening my murder by unknown hand. I was feeling perplexed as to what would be the best way to fight these evils–whether by remaining in Government or going out of it; and I wrote a lengthy letter to Bapuji. But a long time after, he wrote back to say that while the conclusion arrived at by me was quite correct (my desire to resign), he would not hazard any advice as it would amount to a blind man leading the blind, and asked me to approach Kaka Saheb for advice. But what he wrote to me in the end of the letter was of importance. He wrote, "set apart some time every morning and pray."

The last time that I saw him was when he was undergoing fast in the Birla House for the pacification of the communal feelings that were creating a wave of crimes in Delhi itself. The facts and the circumstances of this episode are so well-known that I do not propose to bring my imperfect knowledge of things to describe the causes and effects of the same. It was 2 o'clock when I arrived at Birla House and directly went to the yard where Gandhiji was lying on the cot in the December sun of New Delhi. Maulana Abul Kalam Azad Saheb was discussing with him the conditions under which Gandhiji would be prepared to break his fast. I went and caught hold of his feet for a few seconds and kept standing near his legs for about 10 minutes, while the conversation was going on. He only smiled at me. I had full opportunity of studying his face and the pose in which he lay on the cot. He was speaking in low but distinct tones with usual emphasis. He had the Burma hat given to him by Thakin Nu on his head, and his whole face was aglow with a radiance that I had not seen in him for several months. He was protected from the western sun by Dr. Sushila Nair and some other ladies. But nobody could miss the beaming happiness that was radiating from his face, apparently arising out of divine duty done. Every moment of the talk, however, made me anxious about his condition-It was passing the seventh day of his fast; and I decided not to speak anything, although I came with determination to ask him to break the fast.

Immediately after the Maulana had finished, he beckoned me to his side, with a smile which will linger in my memory all the rest of my life. I took one step towards him, and told him that I had nothing to say and, with a namaskar, left his side to the place where the Maulana was talking with Dr. Nair and others. I did not listen to the conversation; but all the time I was contemplating on Bapu's fast and the duty that the same imposed on us.

The Last Interview

Little could I imagine then that this was the last time that I would have the chance of meeting him. Today I feel an agony in my heart when I feel that I did not go near him even when he beckoned me, although I did so from the tenderest of feelings in me.

It was 6-15 p.m. on the 30th of January, when a newspaper correspondent of Shillong asked me on the phone whether I had heard that Gandhiji was shot dead while going to the prayer. I simply did not believe him, but the next minute and the minute next and so on, did my phone began to ring, sounding the same ominous query. I now felt it must be real and felt so stunned that I became mute for the time being. I did not really know what to do, where to go. And again came the conviction that it cannot be at all true. I then sought a call with Dr. Bidhan Chandra Roy, and, in 5 minutes, I got him to be only told the light of India and the world had gone out from us forever.

Is it possible to describe, in words, the void that we are all feeling at this separation? To me, he had always been a force influencing or trying to influence every thought and action of my life. I know that I could not even expect to live up to what he wished of us; but the very fact that he was looking at us even from a distance, used to inspire us. During the last six years I felt that he infused in me a strength which only a spiritual leader could bless his follower with. His advice was seldom in the nature of "do this, and do that"; but always to inspire me with courage to fight out anything that I consider evil or wrong.

Bapu's Advice

There is a reference in the report before us. There are three things in which you seek my advice. It is this. Do as you think best in each case. Really I am useless as any body else should be without being in the scene. You are the best judge. Act fearlessly. Do not mind even if you may find you make a mistake. Freedom is not embarrassing but if you think it to be so you will always be a slave even if the chains are of gold.

Restriction Orders: My opinion in each case like this is that every order of the kind should be disobeyed. But if a particular person feels otherwise he or she should act accordingly. My advice may be disregarded as one of perfection. If I were you, I should allow Pushpalata to obey her own conscience.

Parliamentary Duties : I have read your thing carefully. I am myself in doubt. But on the whole my personal opinion is that if I am a member, I should go and attend the Assembly. Assam is a most peculiar case. What may apply to Bombay ought not be made applicable in Assam. Hence I say quite seriously, act as the dictate of your heart tells you. If by coming you discover your heart the visit will have been worthwhile. Not even you take readymade opinion from me. It may flatter my vanity but not serve you.

Enrolment of Members: Strictly speaking an illegal organisation cannot enrol members. But we are doing many illegal things. You may add this one.

Relationship with Communists : I am of your opinion.

Assembly Politics regarding Change of Ministry etc.: Both sides are right and both sides are wrong. You will be more wrong if you take away my opinion and act on it. I tell you if you are a leader, act as a leader and not my follower. You are right in consulting me as would be in consulting any body else. But ultimately you should do what appeals to you as right even if the whole world is against you. This is Satyagraha, this is Leadership.

Gandhiji's advice on the report submitted to him.

"The programme of constructive work is more than law and parliamentary works. Its completion means complete swaraj won by truth and non-violence. What is true of you is true of every Congressman be he or she great or not. This is my message. Try to learn from men here how it works and how ennobling it is".

N.B.: While Gandhiji was observing silence as one of the 'bratas', he wrote the following words with a copying pencil on a scrap of paper. The original scrap paper is unfortunately lost. Smt. Pushpalata Das ex-MP and a veteran Gandhian has explained the contents that Gandhiji advised Gopinath Bordoloi regarding constructive work in Assam.

An Account of the Interview with Mahatmaji

Kasturba Memorial Fund : "On the 10th February '45 we interviewed Gandhiji and spoke to him about the necessity of training female workers, who had volunteered to work for the Kasturba Memorial Fund Scheme and accordingly, had applied to us. Mahatmaji said that not a training school has been opened yet anywhere not even at Sevagram. But to quote his words he remarked that there is no institution here does not mean that nothing is being done here. Much is being done but not of an institutional character yet. He, however, requested us to see round people connected with these works. On the other hand, he remarked that 'Forty is a good number. Why should they wait if they had any action in mind? Let them give the lead.' It seemed to us that some kind of model institution at Sevagram was in contemplation.

In order to explain things to the organising Secretary we fixed up a special appointment by wire and saw Mridula Ben on 12th February. She told us that she had already accepted the model scheme put up to us by Bhandary in so far as it related to the Provincial and District organisation concerned and that she had written to our Secretary accordingly on the 25th or 26th January last. As regards the scheme for Provincial Training she told us that some schemes have already come and that if any scheme was given it might be put up before the Executive Committee. We accordingly formally addressed a letter to (copy of which is enclosed wherewith) submitting alongwith it the scheme of training in maternity and child welfare (in midwifery and nursing etc.) outlay of Rs.1,10,000 only for equipment and for general expenses of Rs. 6,000 a month. We pointed out that proportion of both the initial as well as the recurring expenditures should be borne by the Central Trust Fund in view of the training which would be given to the women workers under the Memorial Funds. A copy of this letter was presented to Gandhiji with a copy of the scheme; and on the 13th interviewed him again. After perusing the scheme he remarked as follow: 'I have read the scheme carefully. It lacks details. But the Board would not consider it. It will go to the Advisory Medical Committee. Dr. Baruah may appear before it. It will meet here on Saturday and Sunday. After it advises, the Board will study it and vote'. After this talk we met Mridula Ben again and after the matter was explained to her she said that she would put up the scheme before the Advisory Medical Committee and then the Board. On Thakkar Bapa's asking us to stay till he arrived at Wardha we decided to wait for another day and actually met him at the Wardha Station and went with him up to Sevagram discussing this scheme. He also said that the scheme would be put up before the

Medical Committee. He was, however, insistent that the institution itself must be established atleast some twenty miles from a town.

We think it will be worthwhile to immediately enquire whether the scheme was actually put up before the Medical Committee and if so with what result. As may be known Dr. Baruah could not appear before the Medical Committee. If the matter has not been disposed off yet, Dr. Baruah may well go and attend the next meeting of the Committee.

As regards the training in the educational portion of the scheme is concerned, we Shrimati Ashadevi and also other persons interested in the affair under the instruction of Gandhiji. It appeared to us that syllabus for the scheme was only under preparation and it may take a month more before it is ready. We are afraid we shall have to wait till then. It appears to be the wish of Gandhiji and all other friends of Wardha and Sevagram that one or two ladies with initiative and insight should be sent to Sevagram to stay there for a month or so in order to not merely get adequate idea about the subjects of training but also to imbibe the spirit in which the provincial training centre is to be run.

We discussed various other details with the Organising Secretary and other workers but do not propose to discuss them in this note.

Constructive Work : As regards the constructive work there seem to be general approval of our scheme among all the experts in Khadi, Village Industries, Go-seva and agriculture, basic education etc. whom we met, including Gandhiji. As regards individual workers wanting to carry on the work he said, 'you should let him do on his own responsibility. An individual becoming his own organisation naturally is above any other organisation. He must act as he chooses and take the consequence.' For works in the Ashram and the training of the workers in a provincial institution Gandhiji advised us to see Krishna Das Jaju, Secretary, All India Spinners' Association, Parnekar of Go-seva and Agriculture, J.C.Kumarappa and Jhaverbhai P.Patel of Village Industries and Ashadevi of Basic Education, each of whom we saw more than once. We purchased all the available literatures and made mental note of what they said. On the question of opening a provincial centre they said that a syllabus covering a period of training from six months to four years was in preparation, possibly only a shade difference with that of the Kasturba's. Ashadevi is the Secretary of this committee. Here also the main point that was stressed by every one of them was not so much to mechanical training for workers in crafts but imbibing the spirits and the philosophy of the whole endeavour of establishing self-dependent units of villages under Gandhiji's leadership. Here also all of them requested us that person or persons who will be in charge of the provincial training centre must stay for two or three months in Sevagram and Wardha...

Representation before the Cabinet Mission

(Extracts from the Minutes of the Meeting between the Cabinet Delegation, Field Marshal Viscount Wavell and Gopinath Bordoloi on Monday April 1, 1946 at 4.50 p.m.)[1]

Secret

Bordoloi said, in reply to a question from the Viceroy Field Marshal Wavell that he was prepared to make a statement of what he regarded as the best method of bringing about a political settlement, but he desired to make it plain at the outset, that the Congress President alone was competent to speak on the general question, and he could give only personal opinion. He felt that under a Constitution of United States type, a real adjustment between the Muslim League and Congress would be possible. The Centre would have to retain responsibility for communications, defence, foreign relations, special powers for emergency measures together with the right to take for these purposes. But to secure this, the complete separation desired by Mr. Jinnah was not necessary and it would be sufficient if more powers were given to the units. He felt that Jinnah should accept this point of view. He considered the two-nation theory to be necessary to proceed without accommodating him. The process of giving the Muslim a share in the administration must, he felt, be a democratic one.

In his view, Jinnah's stand would, if acceded to, result in civil war, but if he refused to come to an agreement, independence must nevertheless be granted and given, if necessary, without him. No one should be allowed to arrest the process.

If Jinnah agreed to formation of Provinces based on linguistic divisions (and this was what the Congress had desired for many years),

---

[1]The Transfer of Power, Vol. VII, (1942-47) p.76, edited by Nicholas Mansergh.

the Province (Assam) should have greater autonomy than under the 1935 Act. The Centre's powers should be limited, and the residual powers should rest with the Provinces. A United States of India was the ideal, the main executive functions remaining with the Provinces.

As regards what was immediately possible, he pointed out that if Jinnah reached some agreement with the Congress, it would be easy to effect a settlement. He stressed that a near failure of agreement (Sic) on account of unreasonableness must not stand in the way of transfer of power. A government should immediately be set up at the Centre, by asking the Provinces to nominate persons to a panel from which the Victor would choose his interim government. Even if Sindh and Bengal stood out, 27 out of India's 32 crores would be represented. In his view Punjab would come in. The provisional government, summoned in this way would have the function of setting up a Constituent Assembly, negotiating with Jinnah if nessesary, drawing up a Constitution for new India and conducting negotiations with the states. The British Government would have to make it clear that power had really been transferred to this provisional government and any delay in the transfer would be highly dangerous.

Condition in Assam

He then described the situation in Assam. The Province (with Sylhet included) has been a unit for about 3,000 years. The Assam kingdom had been maintained until the British arrived. At that time, the district of Sylhet was a part of Bengal, and though there had been several attempts by the Muslims to conquer the Province, in 1901 there were only 7 per cent of Muslims in the population excluding Sylhet. The juncture of Assam with Bengal in 1905 led to a large infiltration of Muslims with the result that the Muslim population had grown from 3 lakhs to 13 lakhs in the Assam Valley proper. Only Muslim immigrants had entered. And in Assam with Sylhet district combined there were now 33 per cent of Muslims. It was preposterous for Jinnah to say that the whole of Assam should be included in Pakistan.

In reply to Sir Stafford Cripps, Bordoloi said that Congress would not object to the transfer of Sylhet to Bengal, as its people and culture were predominantly Bengali. Before 1874, the district was administered by a commissioner. In 1874, it was decided to include the district as part of Assam. In 1924 and again in 1926, the Assam Legislative Council passed a resolution that the district should be transferred to Bengal and a similar resolution was passed by the Bengal Legislative Council in 1926.

Now, however, the Muslims of Sylhet opposed the separation of the district from Assam, as they gained advantages in the way of representation in government services etc. and Sylhet being permanently settled deficit district, which has to be maintained by the people of Assam Valley, the relations between the two regions were liable to be strained. This was the main argument for cutting off Sylhet from the Province.

It was a Province with considerable resources, but the Government of India by absorbing the royalty on oil, had taken a great deal of money out of it. About 260 million lbs of tea were produced every year, 90 per cent of which was exported but the export was realised by the Government of India in Calcutta, and the revenue lost to the Province. In return, the Province, though one of the poorest, got only 30 lakhs subvention from the Central Government. To enable Assam to utilise its resources in its own interest, he felt that the fullest possible autonomy should be given to it.

In reply to a question from the Viceroy, Bordoloi said that he could not agree that there was a large area of uncultivated land in Assam; this was Muslim League's propaganda. The Muslim League has been sending in Muslims to occupy grazing areas, and these Muslims from Bengal were maiming and killing cattle and oppressing the inhabitants. On account of this, Muhammad Saadullah has agreed that they should be evicted, but until now nothing has been done, and the present government intended to carry out his policy in accordance with the agreement. It was incorrect to say that there was vacant land available. Much of the land was under water for a large part of the year. It was true that in the hills there were undeveloped areas, but one had to avoid denudation, and most of the land would be required to make up economic holdings. In the valleys too, once land had been provided for those with uneconomic holdings (e.g. with less than one acre) there would not be enough land to go round. It was untrue that Congress was preventing export of grain from the Province.

The Hill Tribes

As regards the position of the hill tribes, he wished to produce a memorandum by Rev.J.J.M.Nichols Roy, a Khasi Christian and a Minister in the present Assam Government. The hill people were also anxious for some degree of autonomy, and although the tribes in north of Assam were generally still somewhat savage, the relation between the hill people in the south and those in Assam valley were friendly. The Khasis have an advanced form of self-government. The Jayantias were also in an advanced state of civilisation. He had no doubt that these tribes would be willing to be associated with the Assam Government, though they would desire a high degree of autonomy. He would like Manipur state to be in a similar position and he hoped that the ruler would agree.

The tribes in the country north of Brahmaputra would be administered by the Provincial Government. Part of the cost was now being met out of provincial revenues, and the expenses of the Assam rifles were shared between the Central and Provincial Governments. Some provision for the external defences would be necessary, but he felt sure the provincial resources were adequate to pay for administering this area. Sir Stafford Cripps pointed out that the matter would be one for arrangement between the Centre and the Provinces, and Bordoloi concurred.

The Secretary of State said that the delegation at this stage was to explore the situation. If there were to be a Pakistan region, including Eastern Bengal, Sylhet might go with East Bengal. Did Bordoloi agree that on this hypothesis, the remainder of Assam could unite with the main part of India? Bordoloi replied that loss of Sylhet would not make much difference to communication between Assam and the rest of India.

Bordoloi said that he was definitely against Pakistan, but the land tenure etc. in Sylhet were similar to those in Bengal and if there was a hypothetical United States of India, the district should form part of Bengal area. He had no doubt that the Congress would be willing to meet the expenses of the tribal areas, though external defence would have to be paid by the Centre.

The Constitution-making Body

The Secretary of State informed Bordoloi that one purpose of their visit was to accelerate the setting up of a Constitution-making body. What were Bordoloi's views on the best method of selecting such a body? Bordoloi replied that he thought it was unnecessary to delay for adult franchise, and the representatives should be sent to sit with people from other Provinces. The selection need not, however, be limited to people with seats in the Legislature. The best people would be wanted, and there should be powers to send names from any part of India, and for the Constitution-making body to coopt in case of need. All communities should as far as possible be represented.

Even if Jinnah did not agree to the Interim Government, the Provinces should have the right to send in a panel of names, not necessarily from the Province itself. Panel of names could be submitted by each Government as responsible to the Legislature i.e. they would be selected rather than elected.

In conclusion, Bordoloi asked whether he could take any message from the delegation. Sir Stafford Cripps said that he felt that it was for Indians to help at this stage and the Secretary of State added that their cards had been placed to make the independence of India an accomplished fact and were whole-hearted and sincere in this attempt.

(Courtesy : Director Public Information, Govt. of Assam.)

Appeal

On the very day of announcement by the British Cabinet Mission of May 16, 1946, the Assam P.C.C., which was in session at Gauhati, sent a telegraphic message to the Congress Working Commitee in session in New Delhi, intimating the universal feeling of apprehension of the people of Assam, and lodging emphatic protest against the Grouping clauses in the State Paper and G.N.Bordoloi, who was then in New Delhi, was also instructed telegraphically to meet Congress Working Committee and represent Assam's case and acquaint the Committee with Assam's strong opposition and her refusal to accept the Grouping Plan.

Accordingly, G.N.Bordoloi met Congress Working Committee and submitted a Memorandum on 19th May, 1946.

On June 10, 1946, the Assam Congress Delegation headed by M.Tayyebulla, President A.P.C.C, met the Congress Working Committee at New Delhi where Mahatma Gandhi was also present, and submitted a Memorandum and urged upon Congress Working Committee to lend full support to Assam in her decision not to accept under any circumstances whatsoever, the provision of decision by simple majority of votes in Section "C" in the matter of settling her Constitution.

Maulana Abul Kalam Azad, the then Congress President, gave on behalf of the Congress Working Committee, full assurance of support and also conveyed through the Assam Delegation a message of sympathy and support to the people of Assam. This allayed, for the time being, to a great extent the anxiety of the people of the Province.

In July, the Assam Legislative Assembly elected Assam's ten representatives to the Constituent Assembly including the three Muslim League members and gave a clear Mandate in a Resolution which was passed without division not to go into Section and accept the Group Plan of H.M.G. State paper (Vide Annexure IV).

On September 25, 1946, the Assam P.C.C. President M. Tayyebulla and the A.I.C.C. Members of Assam met Mahatmaji and other Congress leaders at New Delhi during the A.I.C.C session and obtained further assurances of strong support to Assam. Mahatmaji advised on the very line of his recently published Srirampur Note on December 17, 1946, wherein he advised Assam not to go into the Section if full assurance is not given by the Congress (vide Annexure III).

But H.M.G. Statement of December 6, 1946, which now seeks to alter and add to the May 16 State Paper fundamentally, has given a rude shock to the people of Assam in particular, by its interpretation of the Grouping Clause and thereby raised a deep universal feeling of alarm and resentment in the Province. Assam finds herself in grave peril, facing a crisis indeed !

On December 9, 1946, G.N.Bordoloi on behalf of the Assam Members of the Constituent Assembly, submitted a Memorandum to the Congress Working Committee in regard to the stand of Assam vis-a-vis H.M.G. Statement of December 6, and represented Assam's case fully (Vide Annexure I).

On December 10, 1946, President A.P.C.C. sent a telegraphic message to Congress President and the Members of the Working Committee and Mahatma Gandhi (at Srirampur) conveying Assam's decision not to accept under any circumstances whatsoever to submit to simple majority vote in Section C for the settlement of Assam's Constitution as contemplated in the recent H.M.G Statement and ask for assurances of support (Vide Annexure II).

On December 1, Bejoychandra Bhagavati, Secretary Assam P.C.C. and Mahendra Mohan Choudhury, Secretary Assam Congress Parliamentary Party, were deputed to meet Mahatma Gandhi at Srirampur and seek his advice. Mahatmaji handed over to them a note giving his advice, which was published in the Press on December 23, 1946 (Vide Annexure III).

G.N. Bordoloi and prominent Assam Constituent Assembly Members thereupon met the Congress Working Committee at New Delhi and acquainted them of the new position of Assam and Gandhiji's advice in the matter of Grouping and Section.

On return from New Delhi, G.N. Bordoloi made a full statement before the Provincial Congress Working Committee on December 26, 1946, regarding the position of Assam obtaining in the counsels of the Congress Working Committee and Constituent Assembly. The Working Committee thereupon having reviewed the whole matter adopted a Statement which will speak for itself (Vide Annexure V).

To place the decision and point of view of the Assam P.C.Working Committee, contained in the Statement, Deputation was appointed to meet the Congress Working Committee at New Delhi during the A.I.C.C session as well as to meet A.I.C.C. Members and others and make all possible efforts to obtaining the fullest support and a final decision of the A.I.C.C in the full satisfaction of the people of Assam.

The question of Assam, and of N.W.F.P. and the Sikhs, vis-a-vis Grouping and Section is today a vital issue of All India importance before the Indian National Congress and the whole country. The A.P.C.C., therefore, appeal to the Congress Working Committee, Members of the A.I.C.C. and the Members of the Constituent Assembly to lend their fullest support to the just and righteous cause of Assam in their hour of grave crisis in her national life when her very existence is in peril.

To

The President, Indian National Congress, New Delhi
December 9, 1946

Dear Friend,

On account of the recent statement of the British Cabinet with reference to Sections and Groupings, and the method of work therein, we the members of the Constituent Assembly from Assam elected according to Congress directions deem it our duty to make the following observations in order to emphasise the attitude which we have been all taking on these very important questions :

1. It may be recalled that soon after the Cabinet Mission's proposals of May16, 1946 was published, Srijut Gopinath Bordoloi submitted a memorandum to the Working Committee on the May 19, criticising the proposals not only on account of their falling far short of the Congress claim that the Constituent Assembly was the sovereign authority, but also how they would perniciously affect the Province of Assam. What interpretation HMG give today was visualised in that Memorandum and the fact that Assam shall be forced to enter into Group 'C', that her Constitution would be framed by the majority of members sitting in the Section and that there would be no room for revision of the Constitution as framed by the Section, was clearly pointed out. On June10, a deputation from the Assam Provincial Congress Committee which was led by the President himself waited upon the Members of the Working Committee with another Memorandum which stressed on the evils of the Cabinet Mission's proposals, in almost identical terms. On both these occasions President Maulana Azad and the members of the Working Committee were pleased to assure both Sjt. Bordoloi, the leader of the Congress Assembly Party as well as the deputationists of the Assam Province Congress Committee that the case of Assam would receive proper consideration at the hands of the W.C. and that necessary direction would be given for action to be taken by the Legislative Assembly in this behalf.

2. While Sjt. Bordoloi was here he requested the W.C. to give him a draft of a resolution to be moved in the Assam Legislative Assembly determining what attitude the elected Members of the Constituent Assembly should adopt regarding the whole question. Such a resolution could not be handed over to Sjt. Bordoloi at that time but a resolution drafted by a Member of the W.C. was sent to President Maulana Azad for approval with a letter through a special messenger. After going through the draft Maulana Sahib replied to the above letter on the following lines:

"The present problem is only concerned with Grouping and you already know the decision of the W.C. about it. You should, therefore, bring a motion in the light of the above decision, the wording of which may be formulated by the Board mentioned above (Selection Board of Constituent Assembly Members)."

Accordingly, the Board adopted the draft resolution with slight modification and that resolution was adopted in the House without any division. It will be seen that the main points stressed therein are :

(i) That the representatives elected by the Assam Assembly alone shall frame and settle the Constitution of Assam in a meeting or meetings in which only they i.e., the representatives elected by the Assam Legislative Assembly to the Constituent Assembly shall take part.

(ii) That the said representatives shall not take part in any meeting or meetings of any Section or Group of Provinces for the purpose of settling the Constitution for the Province of Assam.

(iii) That the said representatives shall resist all or any attempt made to set up a Group Constitution for the settlement of questions relating to any subject or subject in which the Province of Assam is interested or concerned being dealt with by any such group of Provinces on the basis of majority of votes.

On July 22,1946 Pandit Jawaharlal Nehru who became the President of the Congress in the meanwhile wrote to Sjt. Bordoloi that you should not boycott the section which he said from a cursory reading of the resolution passed by the Assam Legislative Assembly regarding Grouping, that there was some confusion in the resolution regarding Section and Grouping. He added "That a Section may definitely decide not to form any Group and yet may continue as a Section to consider Provincial Constitution. Thus, making the Provincial Constitution representative of the Province need not be outvoted by others". In reply to this it was pointed out to him by Sjt. Bordoloi that all that was meant in the resolution was that the Provinces should be allowed to function as a unit in the Section and that the Section should not be made to consist of so many Members from the Provinces. He pointed out that the Provincial Constitution must be framed by the Province in the question alone. On the Broadcast speech given by Pandit Jawaharlal Nehru after his assumption of the office as the Head of the Interim Government defining his Government's attitude towards Section and Groupings, it was further pointed to him by Sjt. Bordoloi that his declaration for going into Sections without at the same time making any reference to the method of discussion in the Section created great confusion in the minds of the people of Assam. To that letter he was pleased to reply on September 27, 1946 as follows:

"I fully appreciate the feeling in Assam in regard to Sections or Grouping. I think that our position safeguards your sentiments completely. Having accepted the document of May 16 we have inevitably to accept going into Sections, but the question arises as to how we shall function in these Sections. You are right in saying that I did not go into this matter in my broadcast because I did not wish to raise controversial issues there.

But our position is clear that Provincial autonomy must be maintained and a Province must decide both about Grouping and about its own Constitution. It is true that we have accepted the Federal Court's decision in regard to interpretation and we must abide by that decision of ours. But in no event are we going to agree to Province like Assam being forced against its will to do anything".

It is possibly not necessary for us to mention here that the Working Committee in their sitting both in July and August had made it unequivocally clear that Provinces would frame their own Constitution and shall be free to go to Group Constitution or not as they liked.

H.M.G. have now given a completely different interpretation from what the Congress Working Committee gave and on the basis of which they held out assurances to the people of Assam. If H.M.G.'s proposals are to be accepted both our Constitution as well as Grouping will be determined by the majority of the Constituent Assembly Members sitting in Group 'C',with the inevitable result that we shall be thrown entirely at the mercy of the Muslim League both for our Provincial Constitution as well as our Grouping. With this perspective of Section before us, we, the Members of the Constituent Assembly from Assam, can have but only one decision; and, that is that we refuse to go to that Section. We feel that our position is being rendered still worse by the attitude of the Working Committee in agreeing to accept the decision of the Federal Court in all matters of controversy between the Congress and the Muslim League. H.M.G. have already announced that their latest interpretation of the Statement of May 16, was based on the best legal advice and that it was the essential part of their Scheme. We cannot in these circumstances think that there is any scope for the decision of the Federal Court.

Moreover, the mandate of the Assam Assembly leaves us no room for acting in any other way than to refuse to go to Section.

It seems quite clear to us:

(1) That under no circumstances could the Working Committee agree to the interpretation which has been put to section 19(5) & (6).

(2) That their previous decision to abide by the arbitration of the Federal Court cannot hold good under the existing altered circumstances.

(3) That in view of the British Government's attitude of trying to impose condition upon the Constituent Assembly should declare itself as a Sovereign Body and should proceed to frame the Constitution according to their old viewpoint not only in Reference to Sections and Grouping but on all other matters.

We shall be grateful to be informed about the decision of the Working Committee.

Yours Sincerely,
Sd/- Gopinath Bordoloi
and others.

Annexure II

1. Congress President, Kriplani.
2. Vice-President, Nehru interim Govt.
3. Sardar Patel.
4. Dr. Rajendra Prasad.
5. Chairman, Constituent Assembly.
6. Gopinath Bordoloi, Member Assembly.
7. Bejoychandra Bhgavati, Secretary Assam Congress Care Gopinath Bordoloi
8. Mahatma Gandhi, New Delhi.

Assam can under no circumstances accept British Government's interpretation of Section deciding matter by simple majority votes or federal court decision as binding on Assam Grouping with Bengal.

Assam shall resist any forcible, compulsory imposition of Constitution notwithstanding approval by Muslim League as against all canons of democracy, self-determination stop, Assam case special and peculiar, stop Assembly July resolution, Assam Congress directive mandate must stand, Assam must be left free to settle own Constitution in sovereign Constituent Assembly, pray help Assam in gravest peril by advising and permitting members never to accept section C majority decision or any federal court decision of compulsory groupingwise assurance allaying universal deep feelings.

President Tayyebulla
Secretary Siddhisarmah
Assam Congress.

Annexure III

Gandhi's Advice to Assam

Two Assam friends Bijoy Chandra Bhagabati and Mohendra Mohen Chaudhuri saw Gandhiji on the morning of December 15,1946 on behalf of Bordoloi. They asked him what Assam was to do with regard to the question of Grouping. It was the question of life and death for Assam. They did not wish to be grouped with Bengal. Some people told them that they would be helping the League if they stay out. Assam could not be allowed to stand in the way of the progress of the rest of India and so on. They had asked the Working Committee. There did not seem to be any clear guidance from them. So they had come to him for advice. In reply GANDHIJI SAID : "I DO NOT NEED A SINGLE MINUTE TO COME TO A DECISION FOR ON THIS I HAVE A MIND. I AM A CONGRESSMAN TO THE VERY MARROW, AS I AM MAINLY THE FRAMER OF CONSTITUTION OF THE CONGRESS AS IT STANDS TO-DAY. I TOLD BORDOLOI THAT IF THERE IS NO CLEAR GUIDANCE FROM THE CONGRESS WORKING COMMITTEE, ASSAM SHOULD NOT GO INTO THE SECTIONS. IT SHOULD LODGE ITS PROTEST AND RETIRE FROM THE CONSTITUENT ASSEMBLY. IT WILL BE A KIND OF SATYAGRAHA AGAINST THE CONGRESS FOR THE GOOD OF THE CONGRESS".

Rightly or wrongly the Congress has come to the decision that it will stand by the judgment of the Federal Court. The dice are heavily loaded. The decision of the Federal Court will go against the Congress interpretation of Grouping as far as I can make out for the simple reason that the Cabinet has got legal advice which upholds their decision. The Federal Court is the creation of the British. It is a packed court. To be consistent the Congress must abide by it whatever it may be.

If Assam keeps quiet it is finished. No one can force Assam to do what it does not want to do. It must stand independently as an autonomous unit. It is autonomous to a large extent today. It must become fully independent and automomous. Whether you have that courage, grit and the gumption, I do not know. You alone can say that. But if you can make that declaration it will be a fine thing. As soon as the time comes for the Constituent Assembly to go into sections you will say Gentlemen Assam retires. For the independence of India it is the only condition. Each unit must be able to decide and act for itself. I am hoping that in this, Assam will lead the way. I have the same advice for the Sikhs. But your position is much happier than that of the Sikhs. You are a whole Province. They are community inside a Province. But I feel every individual has the right to act for himself, just as I have.

Q But we are told that the framing of the Constitution for the whole of India cannot be held up for the sake of Assam. Assam cannot be allowed to block the way.

A. There is no need to do that. That is why I say I am in utter darkness. Why are not these simple truths evident to all after so many years? If Assam retires it does not block but lead the way to India's independence.

Q. The League has said that the Constitution framed by the Constituent Assembly cannot be imposed on unwilling Units. So, if some parts do not accept it, the British Parliament won't accept it.

Gandhiji flared up at this question. "Who is the British Government? If we think independence is going to descend on our heads from England or somewhere,we are greatly mistaken. It won't be independence and we will be crushed to atoms. We are fluctuating between independence and helpless dependence. The Cabinet Mission's plan lies in between. If we act rightly transfer will be the full blown flower of independence. If we react wrongly the blossom wither away. Mind you, the League standpoint is quite correct. If they stand out, the Constituent Assembly cannot impose its Constitution on an unwilling party. The British Government has no say in the matter one way or other.

The British cannot interfere with the working of the Constituent Assembly. Supposing the vast majority including the Muslims and others form a Constitution, you can defy the British Parliament if it seeks to interfere. Power is in your hands. Some such thing happened in Ireland only recently. And De-Valera is no non-violent fighter. The position of

India is far better than that of Ireland. If we have not the penetration we will lose the advantage we have as it is apparently being lost today.

If Assam takes care of itself the rest of India will be able to look after itself. What have you got to do with the Constitution of the Union Government. You should form your own Constitution. That is enough. You have the basis of a Constitution all right even now.

I have never despised the 1935 Constitution. It is based on provincial autonomy. It has the capacity for fullest growth, provided the people are worth it. The hill people are with you. Many Muslims are also with you. The remainder can be too, if you act on the square.

You will have to forget petty jealousies and rivalries and overcome your weakness. Assam has many weaknesses as it has strength for I know my Assam.

"With your blessings we can even go outside the Congress and fight". The friends put in.

Gandhiji replied that in 1939 when there was question of giving up the Ministry, "Subhas Babu opposed it as he thought Assam's was special case. I told Bordoloi that there was much in what Subhas Babu has said and although I was the author of that scheme of boycott I said Assam should not come out if it did not feel like it. But Assam did come out. It was wrong".

The friends said, "Maulana Sahib had then said that exception could not be made in the case of Assam".

Gandhiji said, "Here there is no question of exception, Assam rebelled and that civilly. But we have that slavish mentality. We look to the Congress and then feel that if we do not follow it slavishly something will go wrong with it. I have said that not only a Province but even an individual can rebel against the Congress and by doing so save it assuming that he is on the right. I have done so myself. Congress has not attained the present stature without much travail. I remember 1918. I think there was the Provincial Conference of the Congress workers of Gujarat at Ahmedabad. The late Abbas Tyabjee Saheb was in the chair. All the old guards were there. Ali Brothers had not yet joined hands with me fully as they did later on. The late Patel was there, and I moved the non cooperation resolutions. I was non-entity then. A Constitutional question arose. Could a Provincial Conference anticipate the decision of the Congress? I said "Yes": A Provincial Conference and even a single individual could anticipate the Congress for its own benefit. In spite of opposition of old hands, the resolution was carried. That paved the way for the Congress to pass a similar resolution at Calcutta. India was dumb founded at the audacity of a Provincial Conference passing the resolution.

We had formed Satyagraha Sabha outside the Congress. It was joined by Horiman, Sarojini Devi, Sankarlal, Umar Sobhani, Vallabhbhai the mischief making Sardar. I was ill. The Rowlatt Act was passed. I shook with rage. I said to the Sardar I could do nothing unless he helped me. Sardar was willing. And the rest you know. It was rebellion but a healthy one. We celebrate the April 6 to the 13th. You have all these historical instances before you.

"I have given you all this time to steal your hearts, to give you courage. If you do not act correctly and now, Assam will be finished. Tell Bordoloi not to lose its soul. It must uphold it against the whole world. Else, I will say that Assam had only mankinds and no men. It is an impertine suggestion that Bengal should dominate Assam in any way."

The friends asked if they could tell the people that they have rebelled against the Congress with Gandhiji's blessings.

"Talk of God's blessing", said Gandhi, "try to dissuade us, we won't listen".

ANNEXURE IV

Resolution of the Assam Legislative Assembly, July 16, 1946

The Resolution

Premier Bordoloi then moved the following motion :-

Whereas this Assembly after a very careful consideration of the statement made by the British Cabinet delegation and the Viceroy on May16 last, is of opinion that the Province of Assam has an undoubted claim to have the Constitution of the Province framed and settled by its own representatives, elected to the Constituent Assembly, and that it will be detrimental to the interests of the Province of Assam to form any section or sections or group or groups with any other Province of British

India for the purpose of settling the Constitution for the Province of Assam, and

"Whereas this Assembly is of opinion that no Group Constitution should be set up for any Group of Provinces including therein the Province of Assam and that no Provincial subjects in which the Province of Assam is interested or concerned should be dealt with by any such Section or group of Provinces, this Assembly directs its ten representatives elected by it as laid down in the said statement of May 16 last to act in the manner as set forth below:

That the said representatives shall frame and settle a Constitution for the Province of Assam at a meeting or meetings at which only they, that is, the representatives elected for the Constituent Assembly, by the Assam Legislative Assembly shall take part.

"That the said representatives shall not take part in any meeting or meetings of any Section or Group of Provinces for the purpose of settling the Constitution for the Province of Assam:

"That the said representatives shall resist all or any attempt made to set up Group Constitution for the settlement of questions relating to any subject or subjects in which the Province of Assam is interested or concerned or for any such questions being dealt with by any such group of Provinces on the basis of majority of votes; and

That the said representatives shall take part in the meeting of the Constituent Assembly for the purpose of framing and settling the Union Constitution and in all matters relating to the Union Constitution".

ANNEXURE V

Statement of Assam Provincial Working Committee

26 December, 1946

Read Memorandum submitted to the Congress Working Committee at New Delhi by G.N. Bordoloi on December 10, 1946 and Assam P.C.C. President's telegrams to Congress President and certain Members of the Congress Working Committee and Mahatma Gandhi, dated December 10, 1946 also G.N. Bordoloi's letter, dated New Delhi, December 10, 1946 to Mahatmaji and Mahatmaji's directions given in his letter sent through Bijoy Chandra Bhagabati, M.L.A., Secretary, Assam P.C.C. and Mohendra Mohan Chaudhari, M.L.A., Secretary, Assam Congress Parliamentary Party, who met Gandhiji at Srirampur (Bengal) on December 17, 1946.

Heard G.N. Bordoloi, who, upon his return from New Delhi today, made a statement before the Assam P.C. Working Committee about Constituent Assembly and Congress Working Committee, with special reference to the matter of Section and Grouping.

The Working Committee of Assam P.C.C. hereby endorses the aforesaid telegrams of President Assam P.C.C. and Bordoloi's Memorandum to the Congress Working Committee.

The Working Committee, Assam P.C.C. appreciate the stand taken by the Congress Working Committee in maintaining that "the interpretation of British Government in regard to the method of voting in the Section is not in conformity with Provincial autonomy, which is one of the fundamental base of the Scheme proposed in the Statement of May 16". The Committee, however, feel that the Statement of Congress Working Committee of December 23, 1946 is not enough to assure the Province of Assam of sufficient safeguards against the repugnant declaration of H.M.G. Statement of December 23, 1946 seeking to determine Provincial Constitution, as well as Group Constitution, by simple majority of votes of the Provinces sitting together in a Section. The Committee are of opinion that the recent interpretation of the British Government on this subject, has not only gone beyond the Statement of May 16, to the detriment of the Provinces like N.W. F.P. and Assam, but it is also against the assurance of safeguard given to the Sikhs for their protection. Assam can, under no circumstances, accept the interpretation of H.M.G. Statement of December 6. Assam must be left free to settle her own Constitution in sovereign Constituent Assembly.

The W.C. of the Assam P.C.C. is of the considered opinion that, so far as the Province of Assam is concerned, Assam's entry into the Section in the existing circumstances will be suicidal. In terms of the Statement of H.M.G. Assam decides to go into the Section, she cannot by the dissociation of her Constituent Assembly members except the Muslim League group, from Section C, claim to be unrepresented and thereby avoid a Constitution imposed on her.

The Committee is further of opinion that if the Working Committee cannot give assurance of protection to these Provinces and to the Sikh minority, they should carry on the work of the Constituent Assembly regarded as a sovereign body, in accordance with its own interpretations and in complete disregard of the H.M.G. Statement of 6 December.

The Assam P.C. Working Committee's decision to stay out of the Section is determined by the general principle of self-determination, autonomy for the provinces and fundamental principles of democracy, for which the Congress stand, while conceding to the Muslim League demand for framing a Provincial Constitution, or a group Constitution, by the strength of simple majority of votes of other Provinces in the Section, is nothing but concession to coercion and force.

The Committee, therefore, strongly urge the Congress Working Committee and the A.I.C.C. to give clear and unequivocal direction to the Provinces aforesaid and give full assurance of protection to the minorities. The Committee accordingly requests the Congress President and the A.I.C.C. to issue special directions to Assam in this behalf.

This W.C. hereby deputes the President, Assam P.C.C., the Assam A.I.C.C., member and Sjts. D. Sarmah, B. Bhagawati, Secretary, A.P.C.C. and O.K. Das to meet the Working Committee in this behalf; and Sjts. G.N. Bordoloi and S.N. Sarma, General Secretary, A.P.C.C. to acquaint Mahatma Gandhi at Srirampur with the present position of this province in reference to the recent British Government's Statement.

CHAPTER III

Report and Memoranda

(II) Report of the North-East Frontier (Assam) Tribal and Excluded Areas Sub-Committee

July 28, 1947

From

The Chairman,
North-East Frontier (Assam) Tribal
and Excluded Areas Sub-Committee.

To

The Chairman
Advisory Committee on Fundamental Rights
Minorities Tribal Areas, etc.,
Constitutent Assembly of India
Council House, New Delhi.

Sir,

I have the honour to forward herewith my Sub-Committee's report on the Tribal and Excluded Areas of Assam. The report has been drawn up by us after a tour of the Province which included visits to the Lushai Hills District, the North Cachar Hills Sub-Division, the Mikir Hills and the Naga Hills District. The Committee could not visit the Garo Hills District on account of bad weather and difficult communication and the Jowai Sub-Divsion of the Khasi Hills District could not also be visited for the same reason. We, however, examined witnesses and representatives of the Garo Hills District at Gauhati and also paid a visit to certain Garo villages on and near the Goalpara road. At most of the places we visited, we had to be satisfied with a visit to the headquarters of the district of tract and with a visit to one or two villages in the neighbourhood. To visit places in the interior would have taken us a great deal more of time and delayed our report considerably. Representatives of the tribes, however, visited the headquarters, even from long distances, and on the whole we feel that we have been able to get into contact with all the important representatives of the hill people and to take their views of the future administration of the areas. We have also taken the views of the different political organizations in the Province and recorded the evidence of officials.

2. Except for the Frontier Tracts and Tribal Areas, we coopted two members from the tribes of each of the districts visited. The coopted members, with the exception of Kezehol (representative of the Kohima section of the Naga National Council and himself an Angami) who submitted his resignation during the final meeting at Shillong discussed the proposals and signed (subject to dissent in the case of Khetloushe and Aliba Imti) the minutes of the meeting.*

3. In connection with the cooption of members we would like to mention the "District Conference" convened by the Superintendent of the Lushai Hills as an elected body purporting to be representative of the whole of the Lushai Hills. The election to this body which consisted of twenty chiefs and twenty commoners with the Superintendent himself, a President was boycotted by the Mizo Union which was the only representative body of the Lushais at that time and clearly could not be regarded by us as representing more than a section of opinion, largely that of certain officials and chiefs controlled by them. Consequently, the criticism that we coopted members without consulting the Superintendent or his conference carries, in our opinion, no weight.

4. In the Naga Hills, the Committee had to face a similar situation in the sense that certain officials were influencing the extreme elements of Naga National Council. Discussion on number of points could not be carried on to the full extent on account of lack of agreement within the Naga National Council but we understand that on the occasion of the Governor's visit to Kohima, the more reasonable elements put forward their views. We find that our proposals not only contain the substance of these but go further in some respects. The resignation of Kezehol was due to the fact that his section of the Naga National Council was dissident. Our proposals correspond fully to the spirit of the resolution of the Naga National

Council passed at Wokha in June 1946, and we feel confident that the majority of people in the Naga Hills District will find that our proposals go a long way towards meeting even their present point of view.

5. Our report (Volume I) is divided into two parts and the evidence forms a separate volume (Volume II).* In the first part of our report we have given a bird's eye view of the areas as a whole, noting in particular their common features and giving the framework of the scheme of administration recommended by us. In part II a largely descriptive account of the different areas is given separately and we have mentioned their special features or needs.

6. We regret that our colleague Aliba Imti has not been able to attend the meeting to sign the report and hope that he will be able to attend the meeting of Advisory Committee.

I have the honour to be,
Sir,
Your most obedient servant
G. N. Bordoloi
Chairman.

Part I

Introductory : The Excluded and partially Excluded Areas of Assam as scheduled by the Order-in-Council under the Government of India Act, 1935 are as follows:

Excluded Areas: The North-East Frontier (Sadiys, Balipara and Lakhimpur) Tracts.

The Naga Hills District.

The Lushai Hills District.

The North Cachar Hills Sub-Division of the Cachar District.

Partially Excluded Areas : The Garo Hills District.

The Mikir Hills (in the Nowgong and Sibsagar District). The British portion of the Khasi and Jaintia Hills District, other than Shillong Municipality and Cantonment.

There is also an area to the east of the Naga Hills District known as the Naga Tribal Area, the position of which is covered by the provisions of Section 311 (I) of the Government of India Act. The Tirap Frontier Tract which adjoins the Lakhimpur Frontier Tract has no defined boundary with Burma.

The Assam Tribal and Excluded Areas Sub-Committee is required to report on a scheme of administration for all these areas.

2. General Description–(a) The Frontier Tracts: The Schedule quoted above shows the North East Frontier Tracts as excluded areas. In considering the list of areas to be excluded or partially excluded and making recommendations to H.M.G. in 1935 the Government of India wrote as follows:

"Balipara, Sadiya and Lakhimpur are essentially frontier areas inhabited by tribes in an early stage of development. Balipara has no defined outer boundaries and extends to the confines of Bhutan and Tibet". It will be seen that it was mentioned that Balipara has no definite outer boundaries but the position of Sadiya and Lakhimpur or the Tirap Frontier Tract was apparently the same. On the Frontier Tract in fact, the boundary with Burma has yet to be settled and all three regions include considerable areas of as yet virtually unadministered and only partially explored territory. The position of Balipara and Sadiya however differs from that of the Tirap Frontier in that there exists a boundary between Tibet and India. The facts are that in 1914 there was a tripartite convention with Tibet and China regarding the relation of the three Governments and in particular regarding the frontier between India and Tibet. The convention which contained an agreement about the frontier line between India and Tibet was ratified by the Tibetan authorities at Lhasa, and the line known as the MacMahon Line was indicated on a map of which a copy was given to the Lhasa Government which acknowledged it. The existence of this line was for a long time not known to the Assam Government, and on the other hand, it was found that there was no notification under Section 60 of the Government of India Act, 1919 specifying the northern frontier of Assam, with the result that the MacMahon Line which is the frontier between Tibet and India is the legal boundary of Assam as well. In practice the position is peculiar. Though the Governor of Assam is vested with authority over the Frontier Tracts, it is taken to be exercised, not by virtue of the provisions applicable to excluded areas of the Government of India Act, 1935, but as the agent of the Governor-General under Section 123 of the Act, vide notification No. I-X dated the 1st April 1937 of the Government of India in the External Affairs Department (Appendix B). All the costs of administration of the tracts are also borne by the Central Government and the Central Government are inclined to treat them as tribal areas within the meaning of Section 311 of the Government of India Act. On the other hand, the local officials treat the area as consisting of two parts, one, which they call the Excluded Area and stretches up to the "Inner Line" boundary, and the Tribal Area which by them is understood to mean the area beyond the "Inner Line" boundary. The "Inner Line" boundary is roughly along the foot of the hills and the area bounded by it is occupied by a somewhat mixed population, while the hill portions beyond it are purely inhabited by the tribes. This treatment again does not appear to be strictly justifiable in law though it may be convenient to think of the administered plains portion of the area separately from the not fully administered hills. Since the frontier tracts are administered in practice by the Central Government as tribal areas the absence of a notification under Section 60 of the Government of India Act, 1919 was regarded as an oversight. The position of these areas will be discussed further at a later stage, but it is clear from the foregoing that the Naga Tribal Area on the Eastern Frontier and the Balipara, Sadiya and Lakhimpur or Tirap Frontier Tracts on the North-Eastern Frontier fall under one category. The Balipara Frontier Tract which includes the Subansiri area is the Tract over which there is as yet the smallest measure of control and administration. This tract and the Sadiya Frontier Tract are inhabited by tribes such as the Senjithonji, Dafla Apa Tani, Momba (Balipara), the Abor, Mishmi, Hkampti (Sadiya). The Tirap Frontier contains Singphaws (who were originally Kachins) and a number of tribes classed as Nagas, while the Naga Tribal area is largely inhabited by Nagas of the Konyak group. The policy on these frontiers is to establish administration and control over the whole area right up to the frontier, and a five year plan mostly covers the Sadiya and Balipara Tracts but a few schemes of the Naga Tribal Area are also included in it. A separate plan for the development of the latter is under consideration.

(b) **The Excluded Areas :** The Excluded Areas of the Naga Hills District, the Lushai Hills District and the North Cachar Hills Sub-Division fall within the second category of areas over which the Provincial Ministry has no jurisdiction whatever and the revenues expended in this area are not subject to the vote of the Provincial Legislature. The Naga Hills District is the home of a good number of tribes classed as Naga, such as Angami, Ao, Sema, Lhota. Adjoining it is the Naga Tribal Area in the eastern portion of which a good deal of head hunting still goes on. Though the tribes are all called Naga, they speak different languages and have differing customs and practices also. The Lushai on the other hand, though consisting of number of clans, are practically one people and speak a common language. The Kuki in the North Cacher Hills and elsewhere are people of the same stock as Lushai or Mizo and speak the same language or dialect. The Lushai Hills District except for an inappreciable number of Lakhers in the extreme south contains a uniform population. The North Cachar Hills, on the other hand provide sanctuary for the Kachari, Naga, Mikir and Khasi. The largest of the tribes here are the Kachari and the villages of the different tribes are more or less interspersed...

(c) **Partially Excluded Areas :** The third category is the Partially Excluded Areas consisting of the Khasi Hills District (British portion), the Garo Hills District and the Mikir Hills which fall in two districts viz., Nowgong and Sibsagar. These areas are administered by Provincial Government subject to the powers of the Governor to withhold or apply the laws of the Provincial Legislature with or without modification, or to make special rules. The Khasis, incidentally, are the only one of the tribes in this area who speak a Monkhmer language; all the other tribes speak Tibeto-Burmese languages. Generally speaking, they inhabit the areas which bear their names but there are villages outside these districts which also contain some of the tribes. Thus, the Garo inhabit a number of villages in the Mymensing district of Bengal in addition to many villages in the districts of Kamrup and Goalpara in Assam. The Khasi population is not only to be found in the British portion of the Khasi and Jaintia Hills, but the States (which comprise a fairly large area) round about Shillong are inhabited by the Khasis. These States, twenty-five in number, have the special feature that their chiefs are actually elected in a few cases by free election, though in the majority of cases the election is confined to a particular clan, the electorate consisting of Myntries of the clan only in some States, by a joint electorate of Myntries and electors elected by the people in general in others. The States have comparatively little revenue of authority and seem to depend for a good deal of support on the Political Officer in their relations with their people. There is a strong desire among the people of the States to "federate" with their brothers in the British portion, a feeling which the people on the British side reciprocate. Some of the Siems also appear to favour amalgamation but their idea of the Federation differs from that of the people in that the chiefs seek a greater power for themselves than the people are prepared to concede to them.

Of the people in the Partially Excluded Areas, the Khasi are the most advanced and the Mikir the least. Unlike the Naga and the Lushai Hills these areas have had much more contact with people in the plains, situated as they are between the valleys of the Brahmaputra and the Surma. They have representatives in the Provincial Legislature who, in the case of the Garo and the Mikir Hills, are elected by franchise of the Nokmas and the village headmen respectively.

3. **Development :** As regards the degree of development and education in the Excluded and Partially Excluded Areas, the most backward areas,

comparatively, appear to be the Mikir and the Garo Hills, both of which are Partially Excluded Areas. The Frontier Tracts, parts of which must be inhabited by people with no contact with civilization or education, are of course on a different footing. The Khasi Hills have probably benefited by the fact that the capital of the Province is situated in them. In the Garo Hills, Christian Missions have spread some education along with Christianity but the Mikir Hills have suffered from the fact that they are divided between two districts Nowgaon and Sibsagar, and thus nobody's child. Partial exclusion has in a way been responsible for their backwardness also, since both the Governor of the Province and the Ministry can disclaim the sole responsibility for the area. The Sub-Divisional Officer and Deputy Commissioners of these hills moreover, seem to have taken little interest in them and hardly any touring has been performed by officers in the Mikir areas. On the whole, however, the Hill Districts show considerable progress. The Khasi Hills have provided Ministers in the Provincial Government. The people of the Lushai Hills who have benefited by the activities of the missionaries among them cannot be said to be behind the people of the plains in culture, education and literacy. In literacy particularly, they are in a better position than a good number of the plains areas and the general percentage of literacy among them is about 13 per cent, while the literacy among men only is about 30 per cent. Among the Naga also it may be found a number of persons of college education, though the district as a whole appears to be less advanced than the Lushai Hills. In the Naga Hills, the demand for education is keener in the Mokokchung Sub-Division than in the Kohima Sub-Division. In the North Cachar Hills, the development of the people has not been impressive and the Sub-Division as a whole should be classed as more backward than other areas and comparable with the Mikir rather than the Lushai Hills. While education has made some progress in all these areas, the conditions of life and pursuit of non-agricultural occupations cannot be said to have reached the level attained in the plains, although the degree of intelligence necessary is undoubtedly available in most of the areas, even in the tribal areas. We were in fact impressed by the intelligence of the Abor and Mishmi, the Sherdukpen, the Hkampti and even the Konyak of the tribal area. The skill of many of the tribes in weaving and tapestry contains the elements of a very attractive cottage industry ... at present articles are made largely for personal use ... but agriculture is practically the only occupation of the Angami in the Naga Hills under terraced and irrigated cultivation and the advanced cultivation in the Khasi Hills, the mode of agriculture is still the primitive one of jhuming. Portions of the forest are burnt down and in the ashes of the burnt patch the seeds are sown; the following year a new patch of forest is felled and cultivated and so on the first patch perhaps being ready again for cultivation after three or four years. The jhuming patches develop a thick growth of bamboo or weeds and trees do not grow on them. Thus the method is destructive of good jungle. In certain parts, of course, conditions may be said to be unfavourable to the terracing of the hillsides and there is no source of water supply other than rainfall. In the Lushai Hills for instance comparatively few areas have the gradual slope which renders terracing easy; in the North Cachar Hills Sub-Division, irrigation is difficult to arrange and the small hamlets occupied by the tribes cannot provide enough labour for terracing work. Attempts have, however, been made to introduce terracing and improved methods of cultivation as well as the growing of fruits, and there is little doubt that good progress will soon be feasible in these directions. A certain amount of political consciousness has also developed among the tribes, and we were much impressed by the demand of the Abor in the Sadiya Frontier Tract for representation in the Provincial Legislature. The idea of Government by the people through their chosen representatives is not a totally new conception to most of the hill people whose ways of life centre around the tribal and village councils, and what is required now is really an understanding of the mechanism and implications as well as the responsibilities of the higher stage of administration and the impracticability as well as the undesirable results of small groups of rural population being entrusted with too much responsibility. Generally speaking, it can be stated that all the excluded areas of the Province, not taking into account at this stage the frontier and tribal areas, have reached the stage of development when they can exercise their votes as intelligently as the people of the plains. On the ground of inability to understand or exercise the franchise, therefore, there is absolutely no justification for keeping the excluded areas in that condition any longer.

As regards the Frontier Tracts, not only has there been little education except in the fringes or plains portions, but administration has yet to be fully established over large tracts and the tribes freed from feuds or raids among themselves and from the encroachment and oppression of Tibetan tax collectors. The removal of the trade block set up by these Tibetans on the Indian side of the MacMahon Line sometimes creates delicate situations. Thus, the country is in many ways unripe for regular administration. Only when the new five year programme has made good headway will there be an adequate improvement in the position. Even the village councils in these tracts appear to be ill-organized and there seems to be little material as yet for local self-governing institutions though it may be possible to find a new people who can speak for their tribe. The plains portions are, however, on a different footing and the question of including them in the Provincial Administration needs careful examination. For example, we are of the view that prima facie there is little justification to keep the Saikhoaghat, the Sadiya plains portion and possibly portions of the Balipara Frontier Tract under special administration.

4. The Hill People's Views : Though the Constituent Assembly Secretariat and we ourselves, issued a leaflet to provide information and create interest in the political future of India, the Constituent Assembly's functions and the objects of our tour, the Hills people, even of the Excluded Areas, were not found lacking in political consciousness. Perhaps not without instigation by certain elements, this consciousness has even instilled ideas of an independent status the external relations under which would be governed by treaty or agreement only. In the Lushai Hills District the idea of the Superintendent who constituted himself the President of the "District Conference" which he himself had convened (see para 5 part II) was that the District should manage all affairs with the exception of defence in regarding to which it should enter into an agreement with the Government of India. A "Constitution" based on this principle was later drafted by the Conference. (The great majority of the Lushai however cannot be regarded as holding these views and it is certain officials and chiefs.) In the Naga Hills, although the original resolution as passed by the Naga National Council at Wokha contemplated the administration of the area more or less like other parts of Assam, a demand was subsequently put forward for "an interim Government of the Naga people" under the protection of benevolent "guardian power" who would provide funds for development and defence for a period of ten years after which the Naga people would decide what they would do with themselves. Here again it seems to us clear that the views of a small group of people, following the vogue in the Naga Hills of decisions being taken by general agreement and not by majority ... gained the acceptance of the National Council, for little more purpose than that of presenting a common front. In other areas more moderate views prevail. In the Garo Hills the Draft Constitution asked for all powers of Government including taxation, administration of justice etc. to be vested in the legal council and the only link proposed with the Provincial Government was in respect of a few subjects like higher education, medical aid etc. other than the subjects of defence, external affairs and communications which were not provincial subjects. In the Mikir Hills and in the North Cachar Hills, which are the least vocal and advanced of the areas under consideration, there would probably be satisfaction if control over land and local customs and administration of justice are left to the local people. The Khasi Hills proposals were for a federation of the States and British portions; otherwise the proposals were similar to those made for the Garo Hills. A feeling common to all of the Hill Districts is that people of the same tribe should be brought together under a common administration. This has led to a demand for rectification of boundaries. The Lushai want the Kuki of Manipur and other areas in their boundaries, the Naga want the Zemi areas of the North Cacher Hills included in their district and so on.

5. Political Experience : Except for the Municipality of Shillong, there are no statutory local self-governing bodies in any of the Hill Districts. The Partially Excluded Areas have elected representatives in the Provincial Legislature but in the Garo Hills the franchise is limited to the Nokmas and in the Mikir Hills to the headmen. Generally, however, the tribes are all highly democratic in the sense that their village councils are created by general assent or election. Chiefship among certain tribes like the Lushai is hereditary (although certain chiefs have been appointed by the Superintendent) but among other tribes appointment of headmen is by common consent or by election or, in some cases, selection from particular families. Disputes are usually settled by the Chief or headman or council of elders. In the Naga Hills what is aimed at is general agreement in settling disputes. Allotment of land for jhum is generally the function of the chiefs or headmen (except in the Khasi and Jaintia Hills) and there are doubtless many other matters pertaining to the life of the village which are dealt with by the chiefs or elders, but while this may form a suitable background for local self-government the tribes altogether lack experience of modern self-governing institutions. The "District Conference" of the Lushai Hills, the Tribal Council of the North Cachar Hills and the Naga National Council are very recent essays in organizing representative bodies for the District as a whole and have no statutory sanction. While there is no doubt that the Naga, Lushai, Khasi and Garo will be able to manage a large measure of local autonomy, the North Cachar tribes and the Mikir may yet want a period of supervision and guidance.

6. The Special Features : Whatever the capacity of the different councils or conferences to manage the affairs of the areas may be, the general proposals for the administration of these areas must be based upon the following considerations:

(a) The distinct social customs and tribal organizations of the different people as well as their religious beliefs: for instance, the Khasi and the Garo have a matriarchal system, the Lushai have hereditary chiefs, the Ao Naga have got the council of elders called 'tatar' which is periodically renewed by election. The laws of succession of the Lushai permit the youngest son of the family to succeed to the property of his father. Similarly, in the case of the Garo, the youngest daughter gets her mother's property and so on. Christianity has made considerable headway among the Lushai, Khasi and the Garo, but large number of the hill people still continue their own tribal forms of worship which some people describe as 'animism'.

(b) The fear of exploitation by the people of the plains on account of their superior organization and experience of business: the hill people fear that if suitable provisions are not made to prevent the people of the plains from acquiring land in the hill areas, large number of them will settle down and not only occupy land belonging to the hill people but will also exploit them in the non-agricultural professions. Thus, the hill people seem to attach special value to the present system of an 'Inner Line' to cross which non-tribals entering the area require a pass, and the provisions prohibiting non-tribals from settling down or carrying on business without the approval of the district officer. It is felt that even industries should not be started in the hill areas by non-tribals because that might mean exploitation of the people and the land by the non-tribals. In addition to these main points there is the question of preserving their ways of life and language, and method of cultivation etc. Opinions are expressed that there could be adequate protection in these matters only by transferring the Government of the area entirely into the hands of the hill people themselves.

(c) In making suitable financial provisions it is feared that unless suitable provisions are made or powers are conferred upon the local councils themselves the Provincial Government may not, due to the pressure of the plains people, set apart adequate funds for the development of the tribal areas. In this connection we invite a reference to views expressed in the Assam Government's Factual Memorandum on p.67 of Constituent Assembly Pamphlet" Excluded and Partially Excluded Areas" -I.*

7. **Provisions of 1935 Act :** The provisions of the Government of India Act are based on the principle that legislation which is passed by the Provincial Legislature is often likely to be unsuitable for application to the Hill Districts. The mechanism provided for "filtering" the legislation is therefore to empower the Governor of the Province to apply or not to apply such legislation. The full implications of the provisions of the Government of India Act are discussed in the Constituent Assembly pamphlets on "Excluded and Partially Excluded Areas" Part I & II* and it is perhaps not necessary to discuss them exhaustively here. The main features of the provisions are that certain areas have been scheduled as Excluded or Partially Excluded; it is possible for areas to be transferred

from the category of Excluded to the category of Partially Excluded to the category of non-excluded; legislation will not apply automatically to any such scheduled area even if it is a Partially Excluded Area, but will have to be notified by the Governor who, if he applies them at all, can make alterations. The revenues for Excluded Areas are charged to the revenues of the Province, and special regulations, which do not apply to the rest of the Province, may be made by the Governor in his discretion for excluded and partially excluded areas.

8. **Future Policy:** The continuance or otherwise of exclusion cannot be considered solely from the point of view of the general advancement of an area. If that were so, all that would be necessary in the case of areas like the Lushai Hills which are considered sufficiently advanced would be to remove the feature of exclusion or partial exclusion. Such action may be suitable in the case of certain Partially Excluded Areas in other parts of India. But in the Hills of Assam the fact that the hill people have not yet been assimilated with the people of the plains of Assam has to be taken into account though a great proportion of hill people now classed as plains tribals have gone a long way towards such assimilation. Assimilation has probably advanced least in the Naga Hills and in the Lushai Hills, and the policy of exclusion has of course tended to create a feeling of separateness.

On the other hand, it is the advice of anthropologists (see Dr. Gupta's evidence*) that assimilation cannot take place by the sudden breaking up of tribal institutions and what is required is evolution or growth on the old foundations. This means that the evolution should come as far as possible from the tribe itself but it is equally clear that contract with outside influences is necessary though not in a compelling way. The distinct features of their way of life have at any rate to be taken into account. Some of the tribal systems such as the system of the tribal council for the decision of disputes afford by far the simplest and the best way of dispensation of justice for the rural areas without the costly system of courts and codified laws. Until there is a change in the way of life brought about by the hill people themselves, it would not be desirable to permit any different system to be imposed from outside. The future of these hills now does not seem to lie in absorption in that the hill people will become indistinguishable from non-hill people but in political and social amalgamation.

9. **The Hill People's Land:** The anxiety of the hill people about their land and their fear of exploitation are undoubtedly matters for making special provisions: it has been the experience in other parts of India and in other countries, that unless protection is given, land is taken up by

people from the more advanced and crowded areas. The question has already acquired serious proportions in the plains portions of Assam and the pressure of population from outside has brought it up as a serious problem which in the next few years may be expected to become very much more acute. There seems to be no doubt whatever therefore that the hill people should have the largest possible measure of protection for their land and provisions for the control of immigration into their areas for agricultural or non-agricultural purposes. It seems also clear that the hill people will not have sufficient confidence if the control on such matters is kept in the hand of the Provincial Government which may only be too amenable to the pressure of its supporters. Even the Head of the State under the new Constitution will probably be an elected head, and even though he may be elected also by the votes of the hill people, they may still have the fear that he will give way to the pressure of the plains people on whose votes he may be largely dependent. The atmosphere of fear and suspicion which now prevails, even if it is argued that it is unjustified, is nevertheless one which must be recognized and in order to allay these suspicions and fears, it would appear necessary to provide as far as possible such Constitutional Provisions and safeguards as would give no room for them. Moreover, in the areas where no right of private property or proprietary right of the chiefs is recognised the land is regarded as the property of the clan, including the forests. Boundaries between the area of one hill or tribe are recognised and violation may result in fighting. Large areas of land are required for jhum and this explains in part the fear of the tribesmen that its availability will be reduced if incursions by outsiders is permitted. In all the hill areas visited by us, there was an emphatic unanimity of opinion among the hill people that there should be control of immigration and allocation of land to outsiders, and that such controls should be vested in the hands of the hill people themselves. Accepting this then as a fundamental feature of the administration of the hills, we recommend that the Hill District should have powers of legislation over occupation or use of land other than land comprising reserved forest under the Assam Forest Regulation of 1891 or other law applicable. The only limitation we would place upon this is to provide that the local councils should not require payment for the occupation of vacant land by the Provincial Government for public purposes or prevent the acquisition of private land, also required for public purposes, on payment of compensation.

10. Forest : As part of the question of occupation of land, the transfer of the management of land now classed as reserved forest has also been raised. We have recommended that the legislative powers of the local Councils should not cover reserved forests. While accepting the need for centralized management of the forests, we would strongly emphasise that in questions of actual management, including the appointment of forest staff and the granting of contracts and leases, the susceptibilities and the legitimate desires and needs of the hill people should be taken into account, and we recommend that the Provincial Government should accept this principle as a part of its policy.

11. **Jhuming :** We recommend further that the tribes should have the right of deciding for themselves whether to permit jhum cultivation, or not. We are fully aware of the evils of jhum cultivation that it leads to erosion, alteration of the rainfall, floods, change of climate etc. The tribes may not always be aware of these dangers but they have definitely begun to realize that settled or terraced cultivation is the better way. The Angam terrace now on a large scale and in most of the hills definite attempts at introducing settled cultivation are being made. The main difficulty however is the fact that all hill areas do not lend themselves to terracing equally well and in some parts, there may be a portion which could be terraced without prohibitive cost, or economically cultivated, by this method. Terracing means labour, a suitable hillside and the possibility of irrigation. When these are not all available it is obvious that the tribes cannot be persuaded to take up terracing and continue jhum. While, therefore, we feel strongly that jhuming should be discouraged and stopped whenever possible, no general legislative bar can be imposed without taking local circumstances into account. Besides there is a feeling among the tribes that jhuming is part of their way of life, and that interference with it is wanton, and done with ulterior motives. The wearing out of that feeling must come from within rather than as imposition from outside which may cause undue excitement among the tribes. We propose therefore that the control of jhuming should be left to local councils who, we expect, will be guided by expert advice.

12. **Civil and Criminal Courts :** On the principle that the local customary laws should be interfered with as little as possible and that the tribal councils and courts should be maintained, we recommend that the hill people should have full powers of administering their own social laws, codifying or modifying them. At present the Code of Criminal Procedure and the Civil Procedure Code are not applicable to the hill districts though officials are expected to be guided by the spirit of these laws. In practice, criminal cases, which are not of a serious nature like murder and offences against the State, are left to the tribal Councils or Chiefs to be dealt with in accordance with custom. Usually offences are treated as matters for the payment of compensation and fines are inflicted. There appears no harm and a good deal of advantage in maintaining current practice in this respect

and we recommend accordingly that all criminal offences except those punishable with death, transportation or imprisonment for five years and upwards should be left to be dealt with in accordance with local practice and that so far as such offences are concerned the Code of Criminal Procedure should not apply. As regards the more serious offences punishable with imprisonment of five years or more we are of the view that they should be tried henceforth regularly under the Criminal Procedure Code. This does not mean that Tribal Councils or courts set up by the local councils should not try such cases and we contemplate that whenever they are capable of being empowered with powers under the Criminal Procedure Code this should be done. As regards civil cases (among the tribes there is little distinction between criminal and civil cases) we recommend that except suits arising out of special laws, all ordinary suits should be disposed of by the Tribal Councils or courts and we see no objection to the local councils being invested with full power to deal with them, including appeal and revision. In respect of civil and criminal cases where non-tribals are involved, they should be tried under the regular law and the Provincial Government should make suitable arrangements for the expeditious disposal of such cases by employing Circuit Magistrates or Judges.

13. Other Local Self-Government : As regards such matters as primary schools, dispensaries and the like which normally come under the scope of local self-governing institutions in the plains it is needless for us to say that the Hill District should get all such powers and except in the North Cachar Hills and the Mikir Hills, we are opinion that the Hill people will be able to take over control of such matters without much difficulty. With a view to providing some training and thereby smoothening the transition, the Chairman of our Sub-Committee has already taken up the question of establishment of councils with powers of local boards. The difference between the councils we contemplate for the Hill Districts and Local Boards will already have been clear from the foregoing paragraphs. It is proposed to entrust these councils with powers of legislations and administration over land, village forest, agriculture and village and town management in general, in addition to the administration of tribal or local law. Over and above these matters and tribes are highly interested in education and feel that they should have full control over primary education at least. We have considered this question in all its aspects and feel that the safe policy to follow in this matter is to leave it to the local councils to come to a decision on the policy to be followed. We recommend that primary education should be administered by the Local Councils without interference by the Government of Assam. The Assam Government will however always be available to provide such advice and assistance as

Local Councils may require through its Education department particularly with reference to the linking up of primary with secondary education. As regards secondary school education we do not consider that the Hill People in general are able to look after this subject themselves nor do we consider that this stage should be left without some integration at least with the general system of the Province. There is of course no objection to Local councils being made responsible for the management of secondary schools where they are found to have the necessary material. But we consider that no statutory provision for this is necessary and that it should be open to the Council and the Government of Assam by executive instructions to make the necessary arrangement in all other matters usually administered by local boards and we consider that on account of the special circumstances in the hills the councils should have powers to make their own administrative regulations and rules. We expect however that in all matters particularly those involving technical matters like the management of dispensaries or construction of roads the Local Councils and their staffs will work under the executive guidance of the corresponding Provincial Department.

For the Mikir and the North Cachar Hills, we recommend that the necessary supervision and guidance should be provided for a period of six years which we expect will be the term of two councils by the appointment of the District or Sub-Divisional Officer, as the case may be, as ex-officio President of the Council with powers, subject to the control of the Government of Assam, to modify or annul resolutions of the Council and to issue instructions as he may find necessary.

14. Finance–(a) Powers of the Council : The next question we propose to consider is finance. A demand common to the Naga Hills, the Khasi and Jaintia Hills, the Garo Hills and the Lushai Hills is that all powers of taxation should vest in the National Councils. The Conference of the Garo and of the Khasi and Jaintia Hills suggested a contribution to the provincial revenues or a sharing of certain items. If this were accepted even the Centre would have no powers to levy finances in these areas. Suggestions regarding contribution to provincial revenues are obviously based on the assumption that the district, in addition to what it needs for its own expenditure, will have a surplus to make over to the Provincial Government. In the case of the Garo Hills, it was suggested that the abolition of Zamindari rights in that area would result in a considerable augmentation of the revenues of the district which would then be able to spare certain sum to the Provincial Government, and generally the idea seems to be that given sufficient powers the districts will be able to increase their revenues by exploitation of forests, mineral and hydro-electrical potentialities. Not only do some of the districts feel that they will have plenty of money in due course but the demand for all powers of taxation is based to a large extent on the fear that if the Provincial Government has those powers they may not get a fair deal and there may be diversion of money to other districts. Districts which, on the other hand, feel that they do not command potential sources of revenue or atleast realize that the development of the resources will take time during which they remain deficit can only make a vague demand for allocation of funds from a benevolent province or Centre to supplement local resources.

The question of finance and powers of taxation in an atmosphere of suspicion and fear is not an easy one. Any surplus district is likely to examine the provincial expenditure with a jealous eye to find out whether it gets a good share of expenditure for its own benefit or not. The extreme case is the expectation or demand that all the revenue derived from a particular district must be spent within that district itself. It is obvious however that where different districts are functioning under a common Provincial Government, revenues of the whole area becomes diverted to a common pool from which they are distributed to the best possible advantage of the Province as a whole. Should all powers of taxation and appropriation of revenues be placed in the hands of the hill districts, the plains districts will not fail to make a similar demand, and if they do there would be little justification to refuse it to them. The concession of such a demand to the various districts virtually amounts to breaking up the Provincial Administration. Besides, giving unregulated powers of taxation in general to small units is undesirable as it would result in different principles, perhaps unsound principles, being adopted in different places for purposes of taxation and in the absence of coordination and provincial control, chaos is more likely than sound administration. Further, it is obvious that a local council and a local executive would be much more susceptible and amenable to local pressure and influence than either the Provincial Government or its executive and will, therefore, not find it possible to undertake measures of taxation which the Province as a whole can. Even if taxes can be adequately resorted to by the local council, the proposal that an appropriation could be made for the provincial revenues does not sound practicable, for what the quantum of that will be is to be determined only by the National Council and it is quite obvious that the Council will decide the quantum from the point of view of its own need rather than the needs of the Province as a whole. The areas which feel that they have large potential sources of revenue must not forget that their demands for educational and other development are also very large and expanding. Various other factors such as the efficiency of tax collection and the cost of collecting staff have to be taken into consideration and we are of the view that the only practicable way is to allocate certain taxes and financial powers to the Councils and not all powers of taxation. Accepting this conclusion then we can consider what powers they should have. It goes without saying that they should have all powers which local bodies in a plains district enjoy and we recommend that in respect of taxes like taxes on houses, professions or trades, vehicles, animals, octroi, market dues, ferry dues and powers to impose house tax or poll tax, land revenue (as land administration is made over to the Councils), levies arising out of the powers of management of village forest, such as grazing dues and licences for removal of forest produce.

(b) Provincial Finance: There is no doubt that for some time to come the development of the hills must depend on the rest of the Province and they will be regarded as "deficit areas". As their development must be regarded as a matter of urgency considerable sums of money will be required but it is equally certain that measures of development are needed in other districts also and the claims of the hills will not find a free field. The expenditure on the Excluded Areas has so far been a non-voted charge on the provincial revenues but unless it is provided in the Constitution that sum considered necessary by the Governor for the hills will be outside the vote of the Legislature. We have to consider how the provision of adequate revenues can be secured. In this connection, we would point out the admission in the Factual Memorandum* received from the Government of Assam that while the Excluded Areas have benefited by the provision in the Government of India Act regarding them, the Partially Excluded Areas in respect of which the funds are subject to the vote of the Legislature have suffered greatly. In particular, the position of the Mikir Hills seems to be a bad example. Here, only a small proportion of the revenue derived for the area which contains rich forests is utilised in the district and the position in respect of provision of schools, medical facilities etc. is unsatisfactory. We have noted the views of witnesses from the various political organizations that there is a lot of goodwill among the plains people towards the tribes but we feel that a more concrete provision is necessary as practical administration must be taken into account. It is admitted all round that the development of the hills is a matter of urgency for the Province as a whole and there should therefore be a good measure of support for a specific provision.

Coming to the actual provision to be made, it has been suggested in some quarters, that the revenue to be spent within a hill district should be earmarked by provision in the Constitution and should form a definite proportion of the revenues of the Province. This, in our opinion, is an impracticable proposition since any statutory ration is invariable for a number of years and there are no simple considerations on which it can be based. If it is based on the population, it is obvious that the expenditure would be totally inadequate, for the hill areas are generally sparsely populated. On the other hand, if a certain stage of development has been reached the provision of funds on the basis of area may amount pampering the tracts, while revenue is needed elsewhere. We have no doubt that the fixation of a rigid ratio by statute would not be suitable for the Provincial Government to work on and may not be in the interests of the hills themselves. We feel that placing the sums outside the vote of the Legislature is likely to be distasteful to the Legislature and contrary to the democratic spirit and proceed therefore to consider an alternative.

It appears to us that the main reason why the needs of the hills are apt to be overlooked is due to the clamour of more vocal district and the facts that there is little attention to or criticism of the provisions made for the hills, which in the case of voted items are merged in general figures. If, therefore, a separate financial statement for each such area showing the revenue from it and the expenditure proposed is placed before the Legislature, it would have, apart from the psychological effect, the advantage that it would draw attention specifically to any inadequacy and make scrutiny and criticism easy. It can of course be objected that criticism may be ignored and that the separate statement may therefore not serve any really useful purpose, but we nevertheless recommend the provision of a separate financial statement as likely to fulfil its purpose. We also recommend that the framing of a suitable programme of development should be on the Government of Assam, either by statute or by an Instrument of Instructions, as an additional safeguard.

(c) **Central Subventions :** While the Province may be expected to do its best to provide finances to the limit of its capacity, it seems to us quite clear that the requirements of the hill districts, particularly for development schemes, are completely beyond the present resources of Assam. Though the districts are more developed than the frontier tracts in respect of which the Central Government has recognized the need for special grants for development, the position of the hill districts in comparison with the plains districts is not radically different. The development of the hill districts should for obvious reasons be as much the concern of the Central Government as of the Provincial Government. Bearing in mind the special position of this Province in respect of sources of Central revenue, we consider that financial assistance should be provided by the Centre to meet the deficit in the ordinary administration of the districts on the basis of the average deficit during the past three years and that the cost of development schemes should also be borne by the Central Exchequer.

We recommend statutory provisions accordingly.

(d) Provincial Grants for the Local Councils : Some of our coopted members have expressed the apprehension that the sources of revenue open to them may not provide adequate revenue for the administration of the District Council, particularly where there are Regional Councils. We have not made a survey of the financial position of the new councils and their requirements in the light of the responsibilities imposed on them but we recognize their claim for assistance from general, provincial revenues to the extent that they are unable to raise the necessary revenue from the sources allotted to them for the due discharge of their statutory liabilities.

15. Control of Immigration : The hill people, as remarked earlier, are extremely nervous of outsiders, particularly non-tribals, and feel that they are greatly in need of protection against their encroachment and exploitation. It is on account of this fear that they attach considerable value to regulations like the Chin Hills Regulations under which an outsider could be required to possess a pass to enter the hill territory beyond the Inner Line and an undesirable person could be expelled. They feel that with the disappearance of exclusion they should have powers similar to those conferred by the Chin Hills Regulations. The Provincial Government, in their view, is not the proper custodian of such powers since they would be susceptible to the influence of plains people. Experience in areas inhabited by other tribes shows that even where provincial laws conferred protection on the land they have still been subjected to expropriation at the hands of money lenders and others. We consider therefore that the fears of the hill people regarding unrestrained liberty to outsiders to carry on money lending or other non-agricultural professions is not without justification and we recognize also the depth of their feeling. We recommend accordingly that if the local councils so decide by a majority of three- fourths of their members, they introduce a system of licensing for money lenders and traders. They should not of course refuse licence to existing money lenders and dealers and any regulations framed by them should be restricted to regulating interest, prices or profit and the maintenance of accounts and inspection.

16. Mines and Minerals : The present position is that except in relation to the Khasi States all powers are vested in the Provincial Government. The hill people strongly desire that revenues accruing from the exploitation of minerals should not go entirely to the Provincial Government and that their Council should be entitled to the benefits also. In order to ensure this they demand that control should be vested in them in one way or another. We have considered this carefully keeping particularly in mind that the Khasi Hill States are now entitled to half the royalties from minerals and feel that the demand of the hills should be met, not by placing the management in their hands, but by recognizing their right to a fair share of the revenue. The mineral resources of the country are limited and it is recognized by us that the issue of licences and leases to unsuitable persons is likely to result in unbusinesslike working and devastation. We consider that the best policy is to centralize the management of mineral resources in the hands of the Provincial Government subject to the sharing of the revenue as aforesaid and also to the condition that no licences or leases shall be given out by the Provincial Government except in consultation with local council.

17. Legislation : The position under the Government of India Act, 1935 has already been described. It has been argued in some quarters that no Provincial Legislation should be applicable to the hills except with the approval of the hill council. This, we consider, is a proposition which cannot be acceded to without reservation. It is true that no legislation is now applicable without a notification by the Governor but the Governor in practice would apply the legislation unless there is a reason why it should not be applied, while the Council would probably be guided by other consideration. There are many matters in which the legislature has jurisdiction which have nothing to do with special customs in the hills and to provide that such legislation should not apply directly would only amount to obstruction or delaying the course of legislation which ought to be applied. It may also frustrate the application of a uniform policy through the whole Province and subject everything to the limited vision of a local council. The hill districts will of course have their representatives in the Provincial Legislature and we feel that a bar should be placed only in the way of Provincial Legislation which deals with subjects in which the hill councils have legislative powers or which are likely to affect social customs and laws. We consider therefore that there is no need for a general restriction in clause L of Appendix A to this part. We have also included in this draft a clause concerning the drinking of rice-beer which is very much a part of the hill people's life. We feel that the Council should have liberty to permit or prohibit this according to the wishes of the people. We would draw attention to the fact that the rice-beer (Zu or Laopani) is not a distilled liquor consumed by tribes in other areas.

18. Regional Councils : The conditions obtaining in the Naga Hills and the North Cachar Hills in particular, need special provision. The Naga Hills are the home of many different tribes known by the general name of Naga; in the North Cachar Hills, there are Naga, Kachari, Kuki, Mikir and some Khasi or Syntang. Other hills also contain pockets of tribes other than the main tribe. The local organizations referred to earlier have themselves found the need for separate sub-councils for the different tribes and the conditions are such that unless such separate councils are provided for the different tribes they may not only feel that their local autonomy is encroached upon but there is the possibility of friction also. We have, therefore, provided for the creation of Regional Councils, if the tribes so desire. These Regional Councils will have powers limited to their customary law and management of their land and villages. We also propose that the Regional Councils shall be able to delegate their powers to the District Councils.

19. **Emergency Provisions :** The picture drawn thus far is therefore that of an Autonomous Council for the district with powers of legislation over the land, village, forests, social customs, administration of local law, powers over village and town committees, etc., with corresponding financial powers. These are far in excess of the power of local boards. What if the Council or the executive controlled by it should misuse the powers or prove incapable of reasonably efficient management? Some of the hill districts are on the borders of India. What if their acts prove prejudicial to the safety of the country? Experience all over the country indicates that local bodies sometimes mismanage their affairs grossly. We consider that the Governor should have the power to act in an emergency and to declare an act or resolution of the Council illegal or void, if the safety of the country is prejudiced and to take such other action as may be necessary. We also consider that if gross mismanagement is reported by a commission, the Governor should have powers to dissolve the Council subject to the approval of the Legislature before which the Council, if it so desires, can put its case (see Clause Q of Appendix A).

20. The Frontier Tracts–(a) Central Administration Recommended: We have indicated the difference between the Frontier Tracts and other Hill Areas already. It is clear that the legal position on the Balipara and Sadiya Frontier Tracts is that they are part of the Province right up to the MacMahon Line. Regular Provincial administration is however not yet possible (except perhaps in the plains portions before the Inner Line) on account of the circumstances prevailing there. The policy followed in these tracts as well as on the Tirap Frontier (where there is no delineated frontier with Burma yet) and the Naga Tribal Area is that of gradually extending administration. We recommend that when the Central Government which now administers these areas (and which we consider it should continue to do with the Government of Assam as its agent) is of the view that administration has been satisfactorily established over a sufficiently wide area, the Government of Assam should take over the administration of that area by the issue of a notification. We also recommend that the pace of extending administration should be greatly accelerated and that in order to facilitate this, steps should be taken to appoint separate officer for the Lohit Valley, the Siang Valley and the Naga Tribal Area which at present is in the jurisdiction of two different officers (the Political Officer, Tirap Frontier Tract and the Deputy Commissioner, Naga Hills District). We have provided that the administration of the areas to be brought under the Provincial Administration in future should also be similar to that of existing hill districts.

(b) **Lakhimpur Frontier and Plains Portions :** Regarding the Lakhimpur Frontier Tract, it appears to be the view of the External Affairs Department that this tract does not differ from the plains "and need not be considered in relation to the problems of the hill tribes." Our information goes to show that a portion of the Lakhimpur Frontier Tract was recently (during the war) included in the Tirap Frontier Tract. The view of the Political Officer regarding this portion differed from that of other witnesses and the circumstances here seem to need closer examination, as the Political Officer has stated that the area is inhabited by Fakisls who should be brought into the regularly administered area if possible. About the Lakhimpur Frontier Tract which is under the Deputy Commissioner, Lakhimpur we have no hesitation in recommending that it should be attached to the regular administration of the district. The report of the Deputy Commissioner produced before us in evidence is clear on the point. We also conclude from the evidence collected at Sadiya that the Saikhoaghat portion of the excluded area, south of the Lohit river and possibly the whole of the Sadiya plains portions up to the Inner Line could be included in regular administration, but feel that the question needs more detailed investigation and recommend that it should be undertaken by the Provincial Government. The portion of the Balipara Frontier Tract round Charduar should be subjected to a similar examination, and the headquarters of the Political Officer of this tract should be shifted into the hills as early as possible.

(c) **Posa Payments :** Certain payments are being made at present to the tribes on the North East Frontier. In the Balipara Frontier Tract payments called posa which total in all to about Rs. 10,000 per year, and certain customary presents, are paid. These are vestigial payments of sums which the tribes used to claim in the days of the Ahom kings whether by way of quid pro quo for keeping the peace on the border and not raiding the plains or in recognition of a customary claim on the local inhabitants or territory. On the Tirap Frontier a payment of Rs.450 per year is made to the Chief of Namsang as lease money for a tea garden. We have considered the question whether these payments should be continued in view of the costly development schemes being undertaken, and have come to the conclusion that it would be a mistake to stop them. The effect upon the tribes of such a step would be the feeling that the first act of the new Government was adverse to them and the result of any disaffection in this area might seriously jeopardise our aims of establishing administration and bringing the tribes, who are well disposed at present, into the fold of civilization within our boundaries. The payments are negligibly small in comparison with the large sums of money required for these areas and we recommend that they should continue unchanged at any rate till there is a suitable opportunity for a review of the position.

21. Representation - (a) Adult Franchise : The Partially Excluded Areas are already represented in the Provincial Legislature. In the Garo Hills and Mikir Hills the franchise as already stated is a restricted one. The Excluded Areas have no representation at present. So far as the Frontier Tracts Tribal Areas are concerned they have no representation and the circumstances are such that until it is declared that an area is or can be brought under regular administration, representation cannot be provided. We are of opinion that examination should be made as soon as possible of this question in view of the very clear desire expressed by the Abor, Hkampti and others for representation. Meanwhile, we are of the view that there is no longer any justification for the exclusion of the Naga, Lushai and North Cachar Hills and that these areas should be represented in the Provincial Legislature. The restriction on the franchise in Garo and Mikir Hills should be removed and, if there is universal adult franchise elsewhere, that system should be applied to all these hills. We should note here that our colleagues from the Hushai Hills expressed some doubts about the feasibility of adult franchise in the Lushai Hills and seemed to prefer household franchise. We do not anticipate any real difficulty in adult franchise here if it is feasible elsewhere but would recommend that the position of the Lushai Hills may be considered by the appropriate body which deals with the question of franchise.

(b) Provincial Representation : As regards the number of representatives of the Hills District in the Provincial Legislature, we are of the view that if the principle of weightage is recognized for any community, the case of the hill people should receive appropriate consideration in that respect. Though we do not propose that there should be any weightage for the hill people as a principle, we are clear that the number of representatives for each of the hill districts should not be less in proportion to the total number than the ratio of the population of the district to the total population even though this may, in some cases, mean a slightly weighted representation in practice. In the Draft Provincial Constitution we find that it is provided that the scale of representation in the Provincial Assembly is not to exceed one representative for every lakh of the population. On this basis, the hill districts would, according to the minimum recommended by us, obtain representation as follows:

	No.	Population
Khasi & Jaintia Hills	2	1,05,463
Garo Hills	3	2,23,569
Mikir Hills	2	1,49,746
Naga Hills	2	1,89,641
Lushai Hills	2	1,52,786
North-Cachar Hills	1	37,361
Total	12	8,58,566

It will be seen that if the total population of the hills is taken, the number of representatives for all the hills will be somewhat in excess of the number which would be arrived at on the basis of one representative for each lakh of the population. We are not only of the view that in the special circumstances of the hills, representatives as recommended by us are necessary to provide proper representation but that the excess should not be adjusted to the detriment of the rest of Assam out of the total number admissible under clause 19(2) of the Draft Provincial Constitution (Vol.II. Doc. No. 24(v)). We have provided accordingly that in reckoning the number of representatives for the rest of Assam, the population and the number of representatives of the hill shall not be taken into account. We contemplate that the Khasi and Jaintia Hills should include the Municipality and Cantonment of Shillong which is at present a general constituency. This will be an exception provision barring non-tribals from election in the hill constituencies.

(c) **Federal Legislature :** The total population of the Hills Districts given above clearly justifies a seat for the Hills Tribes in the Federal Legislature on the scale proposed in clause 14(1)(c) of the Draft Union Constitution (Vol.II.Doc. No. 18(iv)).

(d) **Joint Electorate :** The Hills Districts have this simple feature, that their populations are almost entirely tribal. In the Khasi and Jaintia Hills (a pocket of Mikir excepted) in the Garo Hills, the Mikir Hills (some Rengma and Kuki excepted) the population is uniform. In the Naga Hills, among the different tribes like the Angami, Ao, Sema, there is now the beginning of a feeling of unity. The Naga Hills District has a population of 1.85 lakhs and is likely to get two representatives at least which might enable the allocation of one each to the two main centres of Kohima and Mokokchung. In the North Cachar Hills the position is less satisfactory but in all these areas we consider that the electorate should be joint for all the tribes and non-tribals residing there. In view of the preponderance of tribal people we consider that no reservation of seats is necessary and the only condition which we propose is that the constituencies should not overlap across the boundaries of the district (in the case of North Cachar subdivision).

(e) **Non-Tribals Barred :** We have considered the question of non-tribals residing permanently in the hills. Some of these have been in residence for more than one generation and may well claim the right to stand for election but we find that the feeling against allowing them to stand for election is extremely strong. It is felt that while in a predominantly tribal constituency the chances are all in favour of a tribal candidate, the non-tribal, in view of their greater financial strength can nullify this advantage. We recommend, therefore, that plain's people should not be eligible for election to the Provincial Legislature from the hills constituencies.

22. **The Provincial Ministry :** That the hills can already provide representatives who can take part in the provincial administration is obvious. On four occasions residents of the Khasi Hills have occupied a place in the Provincial Executive Council or Cabinet. The hithertc excluded Lushai and Naga Hills have the same potentiality. With Ministers from the hills in the Cabinet it may be expected indeed that their interests will not be neglected. The doubts raised are : Will there necessarily be a Minister from the hills even when a suitable person is available? If not who will look after the interests of the hills? The hill areas contain close upon a million people and in view of the great importance of the frontier hills in particular, it would be wise of any Ministry to make a point of having at least one colleague from the hills.

It is our considered view that representation for the hills should be guaranteed by statutory provision, if possible. If this is not possible, we are of the view that a suitable instruction should be provided in the Instrument of Instructions or corresponding provision. The development of the hills, however, is a matter which requires special attention in the interests of the province and we feel that if the circumstances necessitate it, the Governor should be in a position to appoint a special Minister who should, if possible, be from among the hill people. In this connection we would refer to the need for a special development plan which we have referred to in para. 16(b).

23. The Services : A good deal of discussion has centered round the problem of providing suitable officials for the hills. The number of suitably qualified candidates from the hill people themselves has been inadequate hitherto and the utilization of other candidates has of course been found necessary. No special service has been considered necessary for the hills. On the other hand, there has been a certain amount of feeling against the plains official notably against inferior staff, who have been posted there. We have considered this question carefully and come to the conclusion that no separate service for the hills is desirable or necessary and that there should be free interchange between hill and non-hill officials, at least in the higher cadres of the Provincial and All-India Services. The District Councils will doubtlessly appoint all their staff from their own people and to prevent interchangeability would be tantamount to perpetuating exclusion as our proposal involved a good deal of separation already. We recommend, therefore, that while non-tribal officials should be eligible for posting to the hills and vice versa they should be selected with care. We also recommend that in recruitment the appointment of a due proportion of hill people should be particularly kept in mind and provided for in rules or executive instructions of the Provincial Government.

24. A Commission : We have referred to the need for special attention to the development of the hills. No statutory provision for the earmarking of adequate funds is considered possible. On the other hand, the Hill Councils recommended by us will have far greater powers than local bodies in plains districts. The hills occupy a position of strategic importance and it is in our opinion of great importance for constant touch to be maintained with the development and administration of these areas. For this purpose we consider that there should be provision for the appointment of a Commission, on which we expect that there will be representative of the tribes, to examine the state of affairs periodically and report. We recommend that there should be provision to appoint the Commission adhoc or permanently and that the Governor of the Province should have the responsibility and power for appointing it. The report of the Commission should enable the Government to watch the progress of the development plan and take such other administrative action as may be necessary.

25. Plains Tribals : The total tribal population of Assam was shown in the census of 1941 as 2,484,996. The Excluded and Partially Excluded Areas contribute to this only 863,248. About 1.6 million tribals, therefore, live in the plains including those who work as tea-gardens labour. The terms of our enquiry are that we report on a scheme of administration for the tribal and Excluded Areas and the question of tribal people in the plains strictly does not concern us. Their case will doubtlessly be dealt with by the Minorities Sub-committee. The population of the plains tribals which is being gradually assimilated to the population of the plains, should for all practical purposes be treated as a minority. Measures of protection for their land are also in our view, necessary. At present certain seats are reserved in the Provincial Legislature. The question of their representation and protection will we hope be considered by Minorities Sub-Committee. We have kept in mind, however, the possibility of there being certain areas inhabited by tribals in the plains or at the foot of the hills whom it may be necessary to provide for in the same manner (see clause A (3) of Appendix A).

26. Boundaries : All the hills people have expressed a desire for the rectification of district boundaries so that people of the same tribe are brought under a common administration. We sympathize with this desire but find that it is not only outside our terms of reference but also that it would necessitate an amount of examination which would make it impossible for us to submit our report to the Advisory Committee in time. The present boundaries have, we find, been in existence for many years and we feel that there is time for a separate commission to be set up by the Provincial Government to work on the problems involved. An exception should, however, be the case of the Barpathar and Sarupathar Mauzas, included in the Mikir Hills which the Provincial Government have already decided should be removed from the category of Excluded Areas and added to the regularly administered areas (see memorandum of Government of Assam). We agree with this recommendation and propose that it should be given effect when the new Constitution comes into force.

27. Non-Tribal Residents : In the Hill District, a certain number of non-tribal people reside as permanent residents. They generally follow non-agricultural professions but some cultivate land also. We have recommended that these residents should not be eligible to stand for election to the Provincial Legislature. It is necessary, however, to provide them with representation in the local council if they are sufficiently numerous. We contemplate that constituencies may be formed for the local councils if the number of residents is not below 500 and that non-tribal constituencies should be formed where this is justified.

28. Draft Provisions : For the sake of convenience we have condensed most of our recommendations into the form of a draft provision in roughly legal form and this draft will be found as Appendix A to this part. The draft also contains incidental provision including finance not referred to in this report.

29. Transitional Provisions : Reference has been made to the constitutions drafted in the different districts for their local councils. This is of course the expression of the strong desire for autonomy in the hill district. Rather more important however are the individualities of the different tribes and the distinctness of their customs and social systems. If the tribes are allowed to decide the composition and powers of their own councils it will doubtlessly afford them the maximum of sentimental satisfaction and conduce also to the erection of a mechanism suited without question for their own needs and purposes. While, therefore, it will be necessary in the existing conditions for the Governor of Assam(as the functionary who will carry on the administration till the new Constitution comes into force) to frame provincial rules for holding elections and constituting the councils, we recommend that the councils thus convened should be provisional councils (one year) and that they should frame their own constitutions and regulations for the future.

APPENDIX A

A. (1) The areas included in Schedule A to this part shall be autonomous district.

(2) An autonomous district may be divided into autonomous regions.

(3) Subject to the provisions of section P the Government of Assam may from time to time notify any area not included in the said schedule as an autonomous district or as included in an autonomous district and the provisions of this part shall thereupon apply to such area as if it was included in the said schedule.

(4) Except in pursuance of a resolution passed by the District Council of an autonomous district in this behalf the Government of Assam shall not notify any district specified or deemed to be specified in the Schedule, or part of such district, as ceasing to be an autonomous district or a part thereof.

B. (1) There shall be a District Council for each of the areas specified in Schedule A. The council shall have not less than twenty, not more than forty members, of whom not less than three-fourths shall be elected by universal adult franchise.

Note: If adult franchise is not universally adopted this provision will have to be altered.

(2) The constituencies for the elections to the District Council shall be so constituted if practicable that the different tribals or non-tribals, if any, inhabiting the area shall elect a representative from among their own tribe or group :

> Provided that no constituency shall be formed with a total population of less than 500.

(3) If there are different tribes inhabiting distinct areas within an autonomous district, there shall be a separate Regional Councils for each such area or group of areas that may so desire.

(4) The District Councils in an autonomous district with Regional Councils shall have such powers as may be delegated by the Regional Councils in addition to the powers conferred by this Constitution.

(5) The District or the Regional Council may frame rules regarding (a) the conduct of future elections, the composition of the Councils, the office bearers who may be appointed, the manner of their election and other incidental matters, (b) the conduct of business, (c) the appointment of staff, (d) the formation and functioning of subordinate local councils or boards, (e) generally all matters pertaining to the administration of subjects entrusted to it or failing with in its power:

> Provided that the Deputy Commissioner, or the Sub-divisional Officer, as the case may be, of the Mikir and the North Cachar Hills shall be the Chairman ex-officio of the District Council and shall have for a period of six years after the Constitution of the Council, powers subject to the control of Government of Assam to annul or modify any resolution or decision of the District Council or to issue such instructions as he may consider appropriate.

C. (1) The Regional Council, or if there is no Regional Council, the District Council, shall have power to make laws for the area under its jurisdiction regarding (a) allotment, occupation or use for agricultural, residential or other non-agricultural purposes, or setting apart for grazing, cultivation, residential or other purposes ancillary to the life of the village or town, of land other than land classed as reserved forest under the Assam Forest Regulation, 1891 or other law on the subject applicable to the district: provided that land required by the Government of Assam for public purposes shall be allotted free of cost if vacant, or if occupied, on payment of due compensation in accordance with the law relating to the acquisition of land; (b) the management of any forest which is not a reserve forest; (c) the use of canal or water courses for the purposes of agriculture; (d) controlling, prohibiting or permitting the practice of jhum or other forms of shifting cultivation; (e) the establishment of village or town committees and councils and their powers; (f) all matters relating to village or town management, sanitation, watch and ward.

(2) The Regional Council or if there is no Regional Council, the District Council shall also have powers to make laws regarding (a) the appointment or succession of chiefs or headmen; (b) inheritance of property; (c) marriage and all other social customs.

D. (1) Save as provided in section F the Regional Council, or if there is no Regional Council, the District Council or a Court constituted by it on this behalf shall have all the powers of a final court of appeal in respect of cases or suits between parties, all of whom belong to hill tribes in this jurisdiction.

(2) The Regional Council or if there is no Regional Council, the District Council, may set up Village Councils or Courts for the hearing and disposal of disputes or cases other than cases triable under the provisions of Section F, or cases arising out of laws passed by it in the exercise of its powers, and may also appoint such officials as may be necessary for the administration of its laws.

E. The District Council of an autonomous district shall have the powers to establish or manage primary schools, dispensaries, markets, cattle ponds, ferries, fisheries, roads and waterways and in particular may prescribe the language and manner in which primary education shall be imparted.

F. (1) For the trial of acts which constitute offence punishable with imprisonment for five years or more or with death, or transportation for life under the Indian Penal Code or other law applicable to the district or of suits arising out of special laws or in which one or more of the parties are non-tribals, the Government of Assam may confer such powers under the Criminal Procedure Code or Civil Procedure Code as the case may be to Regional Council, the District Council, or Courts constituted by them or an officer appointed by the Government of Assam as it deems appropriate and such Courts shall try the offence or suits in accordance with the Code of Criminal Procedure or Civil Procedure as the case may be.

(2) The Government of Assam may withdraw or modify powers conferred on the Regional Council or District Council or any Court or officer under this section.

(3) Save as provided in this section the Criminal Procedure Code and the Civil Procedure Code shall not apply to the autonomous districts.

Note : "Special Laws" of the type of the law of control, company law or insurance etc. are contemplated.

G. (1) There shall be constituted a District or Regional fund into which shall be credited all moneys received by the District Council or Regional Council as the case may be in the course of its administration or in the discharge of its responsibilities.

(2) Rules approved by the Comptroller of Assam shall be made for the management of the Fund by the District or Regional Council and management of the fund shall be subject to these rules.

H. (1) A Regional Council, or if there is no Regional Council, the District Council shall have the following powers of taxation:

(a) Subject to the general principles of assessment approved on this behalf for the rest of Assam, land revenue,

(b) poll tax or house tax.

(2) The District Council shall have powers to impose the following taxes, that is to say (a) a tax on professions, trades or callings, (b) a tax on animals,vehicles, (c) toll tax, (d) market dues, (f) cesses for the maintenance of schools, dispensaries or roads.

(3) A Regional Council or District Council may make rules for the imposition and recovery of the taxes within its financial powers.

I. (1) The Government of Assam shall not grant any licence or lease to prospect for or extract minerals within an autonomous district save in consultation with the District Council.

(2) Such share of the royalties accruing from licences or leases for minerals as may be agreed upon shall be made over to the District Council. In default of agreement such share as may be determined by the Governor in his discretion shall be paid.

J. (1) The District Council may for the purpose of regulating the profession of money lending or trading by non-tribals in a manner detrimental to the interests of the tribals make rules applicable to the district or any portion of it : (a) prescribing that except the holder of a licence issued by the Council in this behalf no person shall carry on money lending, (b) prescribing the maximum rate of interest which may be levied by moneylender, (c) providing for the maintenance of accounts and for their inspection by its officials, (d) prescribing that no non-tribal shall carry on wholesale or retail business in any commodity except under a licence issued by the District Council in this behalf:

Provided that no such rules may be made unless the District Council approves of the rules by a majority of not less than three-fourths of its members:

Provided further that a licence shall not be refused to moneylenders and dealers carrying on business at the time of the making of rules.

K. (1) The number of members representing an autonomous district in the Provincial Legislature shall bear at least the same proportion to the population of the district as the total number of members in that Legislature bears to the total population of Assam.

(2) The total number of representatives allotted to the autonomous districts (which may at any time be specified in Schedule A) in accordance with sub-section (1) of this Section shall not be taken into account in reckoning the total number of representatives to be allotted to the rest of the Province under the provisions of the Provincial Constitution.

(3) No constituencies shall be formed for the purpose of election to the Provincial Legislature which include portions of other autonomous districts or other areas nor shall any non-tribal be eligible for election except in the constituency which includes the Cantonment and Municipality of Shillong.

L. (1) Legislation passed by the Provincial Legislature in respect of --

(a) any of the subjects specified in Section C, or

(b) prohibiting or restricting the consumption of any non-distilled alcoholic liquor, shall not apply to an autonomous district.

(2) A Regional Council of an autonomous district or, if there be no

Regional Council, may apply any such law to the area under its jurisdiction, with or without modification.

M. The revenue and expenditure pertaining to an autonomous district which is credited to or met from the funds of the Government of Assam shall be shown separately in the annual financial statement of the Province of Assam.

N. There shall be paid out of the revenues of the Federation to the Government of Assam such capital and recurring sums as may be necessary, to enable that Government--

(a) to meet the average excess of expenditure over the revenue during the three years immediately preceding the commencement of this Constitution in respect of the administration of the areas specified in Schedule A; and (b) to meet the cost of such schemes of development as may be undertaken by the Government with the approval of the Federal Government for the purpose of raising the level of administration of the aforesaid areas to that of the rest of the province.

O. (1) The Governor of Assam may at any time institute a commission specifically to examine and report on any matter relating to the administration or generally at such intervals as he may prescribe, on the administration of the autonomous districts generally and in particular on (a) the provision of educational and medical facilities and communications, (b) the need for any new or special legislation and (c) the administration of the District or Regional Councils and the laws or rules made by them.

(2) The report of such a commission with the recommendations of the Governor shall be placed before the Provincial Legislature by the Minister concerned with an explanatory memorandum regarding the action taken or proposed to be taken on it.

(3) The Governor may appoint a special Minister for the autonomous districts.

P. (1) The Government of Assam may, with approval of the Federal Government by notification make foregoing provisions or any of them applicable to any area specified in Schedule B to this part, or to a part thereof; and may also, with the approval of the Federal Government, exclude any such area or part thereof from the said Schedule. (2) Till a notification is issued under this Section, the administration of any area specified in Schedule B or of any part thereof shall be carried on by the Union Government through the Government of Assam as its agent.

Q. (1) The Governor of Assam on his discretion may, if he is satisfied that any act or resolution of a Regional or District Council is likely to endanger the safety of India, amend or suspend such act or resolution and take such steps as he may consider necessary (including dissolution of the Council and the taking over of its administration) to prevent the commission or continuation of such act or giving effect to such resolution.

(2) The Governor shall place the matter before the Legislature as soon as possible and the Legislature may confirm or set aside the declaration of the Governor.

R. The Governor of Assam may on the recommendation of a commission set up by him under Section N, order the dissolution of a Regional or District Council and direct either that fresh election should take place immediately, or with the approval of the Legislature of the Province, place the administration of the area directly under himself or the commission or other body considered suitable by him, during the interim period or for a period not exceeding twelve months:

Provided that such action shall not be taken without affording an opportunity to the District or Regional Council to be heard by the Provincial Legislature is opposed to it.

Transitional Provisions:

Governor to carry on administration as under the 1935 Act till a council is set up. He should take action to constitute the first District Council or Regional Council and frame provisional rules in consultation with existing tribal councils or other representative organizations, for the conduct of the elections, prescribe who shall be the office bearers etc. The term of the first Council is to be one year.

GOPINATH BORDOLOI (Chairman)
J.J.M. NICHOLS-ROY
RUP NATH BRAHMA
A.V. THAKKAR

SCHEDULE A

The Khasi and Jaintia Hills District excluding the Shillong.

The Garo Hills District.

The Lushai Hills District.

The Naga Hills District.

The North Cachar Subdivision of the Cachar District.

The Mikir Hills portion of Nowgong and Sibsagar District excepting the mouzas of Barpathar and Sarupathar.

SCHEDULE B

The Sadiya and Balipara Frontier Tracts.

The Tirap Frontier Tract (excluding the Lakhimpur Frontier Tract).

The Naga Tribal Area.

APPENDIX B

COPY OF NOTIFICATION NO. 1-X, DATED THE 1ST APRIL, 1937, FROM THE GOVERNMENT OF INDIA IN THE EXTERNAL AFFAIRS DEPARTMENT

In exercise of the powers conferred by sub-section(1) of Section 123, read with sub-section(3)of Section 313 of the Government of India Act, 1935, the Governor-General in Council is pleased to direct the Governor of Assam to discharge as his Agent, in and in relation to the tribal areas beyond the external boundaries of the Province of Assam, all functions hitherto discharged in and in relation to the said areas by the said Governor as Agent to the Governor-General in respect of the political control of the trans-border tribes, and the administration of the said areas and the administration of Assam Rifles and other armed civil forces.

Part II

The Balipara Frontier Tract

This is the tract between the Subansiri river on the east, Bhutan on the west and the MacMahon Line to the north, with its headquarters at Charduar about 20 miles from Tezpur. It is included in the Schedule to the Government of India (Excluded and Partially Excluded Areas) Order as an Excluded Area, but in practice it is administered by the Governor of Assam as the Agent to the Government of India and is treated in this respect as a tribal area. The portion immediately to the north of Charduar and up to the Inner Line is a plains portion of the area of which is estimated to be approximately 1,000 square miles. The censussed portion of the area was 571 square miles and the population of 6,512 contained only 560 Dafla, the remaining number of 2,323 persons enumerated as Assam tribes consisting of Cachari, Garo, Mikir and Miri. The area beyond the Inner is estimated to cover about 11,000 square miles and contain a population of approximately 350,000. For administrative purpose it is at present divided into two parts, the Balipara or Sela Agency and the Subansiri Area under two political officers. Particularly in the Subansiri Area there are portions which have not yet been explored by our officers, and the details of the tribes living there are still not fully known. In the Sela area administration has been extended as far as Dirang Dzong and this area contains tribes like the Momba, Sillung, Aka or Rhuso, and the Senjithonji. The Subansiri area is inhabited largely by Dafla (Nisu) and Apatani but large areas have yet to be visited and explored.

In the western portions of the tract the way of life of the tribes is influenced a good deal by Tibetan customs and Buddhist monasteries but in the eastern sector the people are much more primitive. Some terraced cultivation and orange gardens exist but people like the Aka depend on jhuming. Literacy among the tribes seems to be very poor in spite of the influence of monasteries.

Except among the Momba there is little demand even for education. For their requirements of cloth and salt notably, the inhabitants depend upon contact with the plains areas or with the Tibetans.

The monastery at Towant exercises considerable influence over the lives of these tribes and put forward claims to monastic taxation. The tribes keep poultry, pigs, goats and mithun. In the olden days some chiefs here apparently used to exercise a kind of right of levying taxes in plains villages. This appears to have been recognized by the Ahom Kings who allowed relief to the people liable to such taxes from other taxes to a corresponding extent. In connection with these levies an agreement* was entered into by the British Government for the payment of annual subsidy, known as posa. Rs. 5,000 are paid to the Talung Dzpngpons and the Sat Rajas of Kalaktang and some bottles of rum and cloth are given. The tribes in return also give certain presents like ebony, a gold ring, two Chinese cups, two yak rails and two blankets. Similar payments of posa are made to the Charduar Bhutia or Sherdukpen Thembangia Bhutia, Aka and certain other tribes. Payments to the Dafla and Miri are, however, made only to freemen and in all cases cease on the death of the present holder. The total payment of posa comes to about 10,000 rupees per year. Maintenance of law and order in this area as well as defence against external encroachment is looked after by the posts occupied by the Assam Rifles.

Though some of the witnesses who appeared before us could speak Assamese and appeared to be intelligent, we are inclined to agree with the Political Officer's view that until the five year plan which provides for an expansion of schools and communications has been given effect, there is likely to be little material in this tract particularly in the Subansiri area for local self-governing institutions. For some time the problems of administration here must remain confined largely to the maintenance of peace among the tribes, prevention of encroachment and oppression by Tibetan tax collectors, extension of communications, and elementary facilities for obtaining medicine and primary education. Tibetan officials are known to have set up trade blocks with a view to compelling trade with Tibet rather than India and the removal of these obstructions is a matter which may involve political contact with Tibetan authorities. As already pointed out large areas are as yet terra incognito to our officers and the attitude of the tribes is one of fear or suspicion which may easily turn to hostility. It is clear however that the southern portions and administration of the political agency type can therefore be gradually shifted northwards. The Political Officer's view is that the time is not yet ripe for shifting his headquarters from Charduar to a place in the hills. The area round Charduar which is in the plains portion is inhabited mostly by non-tribals or detribalized people of tribal origin. The question of bringing it under regular administration needs therefore to be examined in detail

* Class IV of Agreement No.XLIV of 1888 with the Kapasshor or Kavatsum Akas runs as follows : The "posa" we shall receive from Government is in lieu of the due we formerly levied on the Assamese inhabitants of the plains, and that we have no right to receive any food, service, dues or other token of superiority from any raiyat in British territory...." Aitechison Vol. XII.

by the Provincial Government. What we contemplate is that areas over which adequate control has been established should be brought under the regular provincial administration while areas further north remain under the control of the Central Government as at present. The Centre should however administer the tract through the Provincial Government as its agent so that the Provincial Government remains in contact with the administration.

We are also of the view that the steps should be taken as soon as practicable to erect boundary pillars on the trade routes to Tibet at places where they intersect the MacMahon Line.

The payments of posa represent a small amount and the sentimental value attached to it and the probability that any cessation of it concurrently with the coming into force of the new Constitution would have most undesirable consequences on the attitude of the tribes, should be kept in mind. It should clearly not be discontinued for the present.

2. The Sadiya Frontier Tract :

The Sadiya Frontier Tract is the tract between the Subansiri river on the west and the boundary of the Tirap Frontier Tract on the north-east. The latter boundary has been adjusted from time to time. The Frontier area comprising the Sadiya and Tirap Frontier Tracts is somewhat in the shape of parabola which contains the area through which the Brahmaputra river with its tributaries debauches on to the plains. The Sadiya tract may be regarded as falling into two or three distinct portions. To begin with, there is the portion to the west consisting of the Valley of the Dihang or Siang with Abor tribes like Minyong, Bori, Galong, Padam. The Valley of the Dibang in the centre covers the area inhabited by Idu or Chulikata Mishmi, and Valley of the Lohit is inhabited by Digaru and other Mishmi and certain Khampti and Miri tribes. Included in these three broad divisions is the plains portion of the tract (which included Saikhoaghat on the south bank of the Lohit river) which runs up to the foot of the hill (roughly along the Inner Line). As in the case of the Balipara tract, regular administration has yet to be established in portions up to the MacMahon Line, which itself needs to be demarcated by the erection of boundary pillars at least at the points where the trade routes cross into India. The headquarters of the Political Officer is at Sadiya and there is an Assistant Political Officer at Pasighat.

The Assistant Political Officer of the Lohit Valley stays at Sadiya and his jurisdiction includes the Chulikata or Idu Mishmi in the north and the

Digaru and others towards the east and south of the tract. There are no easy lateral communications between the Chulikata area and the Lohit Valley proper.

By inhabitants, the hill tract falls broadly into portions inhabited by Abor (Siang Valley), the Chulikata in the Dibang Valley and other Mishmi in the Lohit Valley, and the Khampti or Shan who are a comparatively civilized tribe following Buddhism. In addition there is the mixed population of the Sadiya portion to the south of Inner Line containing non-tribals and some Miri. Although the Gallong Abor are somewhat different from the Padam and Minyong the languages are practically the same and the whole of the Tract could be regarded as reasonably uniform. The Mishmi area, though it falls into two separate portions along the Dibang and Lohit Rivers respectively, and the tribes do not understand one another's language, could be treated as one. The Khampti area which is the third one is small and the Sadiya population is a mixed one. The area beyond the Inner Line which is not censussed is estimated to contain 250,000 Abor, 40,000 Idu, 25,000 Digaru and Miri and about 2,000 Khampti. The censussed portion is an area of 3,309 square miles with a total population of 60,118 of which 39,974 are of tribal origin.

The total area of the tract may be in the neighbourhood of 15,000 square miles and its development and administration clearly necessitate the Sub-Division of the tract and the appointment of more officials. In fact the Political Officer has already recommended the division of the tract into two portions based on Pasighat and Sadiya respectively. This is roughly equivalent to a division into the Mishmi area, and the Abor area respectively and the proposals under consideration at present seem to contemplate the posting of Political Officer at Sadiya for the Mishmi Agency with an Assistant with headquarters at Walong (Lohit Valley) and a second Political Officer at Pasighat (now the headquarters of an Assistant Political Officer).

The main reason for keeping Sadiya as the headquarters for the Mishmi Agency would appear to be the lack of lateral communications between the Chulikata area in the Dibang Valley and the Digaru area in the Lohit Valley. It is clear, however, that Sadiya and the portion up to the Inner Line are in the plains and contain a mixed population. Cultivation in this tract is also settled and the people of the tract desire that it should not continue under the present system of exclusion.

Moveover, there is the area occupied by Hkampti who are settled cultivators professing Buddhism which has also spread a good deal of literacy among them. Prima facie there is a strong case for treating the plains portions of the tract as well as the Hkampti portions as regularly administered areas, in the form perhaps of a separate Sub-Division or district. The distinctness of the Hkampti must however be borne in mind and the area will probably have to be treated as a separate taluq. An early and detailed examination of the whole question is clearly called for if Sadiya is treated as plain, a suitable headquarters for the Political Officer of the Mishmi area needs to be looked for keeping in mind the difficulties of communications between the Dibang and Lohit Valley.

With the exception of the Hkampti who are settled cultivators, and may be regarded as comparatively civilized, and a few people in the plains portion who also do settled cultivation, the Abor and Mishmi pursue jhuming and appear to exhibit little competence in the art of raising crops. They of course eke out a livelihood by keeping poultry, sheep and mithun. The herds of mithun kept by these tribes are in fact the occasion for disputes between people as raiding for mithun seems to be in this area what head-hunting is in the Naga tribal area. Serious quarrels arising out of raiding for mithun may call for the intervention of the Political Officer. The tribes are generally heavily addicted to opium and attempts to keep the growth and consumption of opium in check seem to be meeting with little success. Though we feel that the Abor and Mishmi are people who can be educated and assimilated to civilized administration in a comparatively short time, there is little literacy or education among them at present, and the depth of the area over which control has been established beyond the Inner Line does not seem to be great. Communications are the urgent need so that greater contact is possible even if the lack of education is regarded as no impediment. By the time the five year plan has been worked out (it contemplates the making of a road to Walong and improvement of communications in other respects also) it may be possible to give effect to the keenly expressed desire among the Abors of a share in the Provincial Administration. It is obvious that the pace of establishment of full-fledged administration in this area should be accelerated.

A beginning should, however, be possible by way of political education of the people, if tribal councils are set up to enable the different tribes to come together to discuss matters of mutual interest and understand the problems of administration.

The forests of this tract can produce a good revenue but land revenue in the plains portions amounts to about Rs.50,000 and the poll tax which is also levied in this area amounts to about Rs.15,000. The forest revenue in 1946-47 was Rs.430,000.

3. The Lakhimpur and Tirap Frontier Tracts

The exact position legal and de facto is not clear. The Lakhimpur Frontier Tract is mentioned as one of the North-East Frontier Tracts scheduled as an Excluded Area. No frontier has yet been laid down between Burma and India in this region. There is an area locally known as the Lakhimpur Frontier Tract which is treated as an Excluded Area with the Deputy Commissioner, Lakhimpur, as the Agent or Political Officer. The Tirap Frontier Tract, which apparently derives its name from the river of that name, is said at present to contain a number of villages added to it from the Lakhimpur Frontier Tract during the war, and the rest of the portion inhabited by Naga Tribes towards the Burmese territory. In addition to the Tirap Frontier Tract the Political Officer, whose headquarters are at present in Margherita in Lakhimpur district, is also in charge of a portion of the Naga Tribal Area which stretches along the boundary of the Lakhimpur district till it touches the northern apex of the Naga Hills district towards its southern projection towards Burma. The area of the Lakhimpur Frontier Tract as shown in the census is about 394 square miles. The area of the Tirap Frontier Tract can of course only be guessed as there is no definite boundary with Burma. It may be in the neighbourhood of 4,000 square miles. In population also the tract differs from part to part. The Lakhimpur Frontier Tract differs "in no way from the surrounding plains; possesses none of the characteristics of the hill areas and need not be considered in relation to the problems of the hill tribes". In the portion of the Lakhimpur Frontier Tract which has now been taken into the Tirap Frontier Tract there are several villages inhabited by Kachins and others who are regarded as tribal and pay house tax. In the Tirap Frontier Tract a number of tribes classed as Naga such as Tikak,Yogli, Ranrang, Lungri, Sanke, Morang etc. reside. The whole of the area inhabited by the Naga tribes could appropriately be regarded as part of india since the economic relation of all these tribes with India and not with any other country. The demarcation of a boundary with Burma is to be taken up therefore on this principle and the question is said to be now under consideration to the Government of India. It is obviously a matter which needs to be expedited.

In the northern portion of the Naga Tribal area (which may be really regarded as part of the Tirap Frontier, since for a considerable distance the boundary of this area runs along with the eastern boundary of Lakhimpur district) there are tribes classed as Konyak Naga and the relations of this area are also with the plains portion of the Lakhimpur district. For instance it is common for tribes from Namsang and Borduria to come frequently to Jaipur for their marketing etc., and a good number of them seem to speak Assamese. The area is thickly populated. The Singtrspho or Kachin are Buddhists and they had chiefs belonging to the old ruling family before the country was taken over in 1839. The agreements entered into in 1826 and 1836 are a dead letter and though the chiefs are consulted by the Political Officer whenever there is any dispute to be settled or other matter to be dealt with, the Political Officer is being looked up to more and more, and the Chief is regarded only by way of being an adviser to the Political Officer.

Agriculture is mostly by the primitive method of jhuming and there are no educational facilities. The economic condition of the tract is pretty poor. The Kachins however are settled cultivators and are in a better position than the Naga. In the Naga Tribal Area head-hunting is still practised and slavery also seems to exist.

For the Tirap Frontier Tract also the five year plan approved by the Government of India contemplates the extension of the benefits of administration. The headquarters is proposed to be moved to a place in the interior called Horukhunma and hospitals and schools are to be constructed. Both in the Tirap Frontier Tract and the Naga Tribal Area the policy is just the same, namely, the extension of administration gradually up to the Burma frontier. This policy appears to us to be the correct one to follow, whatever the legal status of the area may be under the Government of India Act as in the case of the MacMahon Line Frontier, all the portions between the Burmese boundary and the administered area of Assam should be merged in Assam as soon as possible and the distinction between tribal area and administered Indian territory abolished.

The Lakhimpur Frontier Tract need no longer be treated as an Excluded Area. As regards the portion of this tract taken over into the Tirap Frontier Tract the justification for continuing it as a frontier area needs to be further examined and if no difficulty is likely to be caused by the inclusion of the Kachins and other tribes who live there in the Lakhimpur district the area should be merged in the district. In the rest of the area, steps should be taken to organise non-statutory tribal councils, panchayats etc., in anticipation of the time when this tract will be fit for inclusion in the Provincial Administration. For the proper administration of Naga Hills Tribal Area it would appear desirable to provide more officials, and a separate officer with headquarters as close as possible to the area, if not inside it is necessary. It would appear that there is already sanction for a separate Sub-Division Officer at Mokokchung under the control of the Deputy Commissioner, Naga Hills district, but the present arrangement by which the tribal area is shared between the Deputy Commissioner, Kohima, and the Political Officer, Tirap Frontier Tract, needs to be further examined. It would perhaps be best to divide the portion into two districts, one which will in due course either merge with the existing Naga Hills district and form a Sub-Division thereof or be a Konyak district, and another which will form a portion of another district under an officer with headquarters in the present Tirap Frontier Tract.

4. Naga Hills District

The Naga Hills District is an area of 4,289 square miles bounded on the east by the Naga Tribal Area, on the south by Manipur State and on the west by the Sibsagar district. The population was given as 189,766 or 97.4 per cent were tribal, at the 1941 census. The district is inhabited by a number of Naga tribes notably the Angami, the Sema, the Lhota and the Ao. Of these tribes the Angami are the most numerous and inhabit the area round Kohima, their number at the 1941 census being slightly over 52,000. The Aos are the next numerous numbering over 40,000 and the Semas come third with 35,741. These two tribes inhabit the area round Mokokchung which is a separate Sub-Division of the district, and the Sema also inhabit the region to the north-west of the Angami country. The tribes speak different languages and their lingua franca is Assamese or Hindustani. They have also differing customs and traditions. Areas claimed by the tribe or village are jealously guarded against encroachment and to such an extent in the Naga Tribal Area that a villager seldom ventures outside his village boundary. Within the boundary of the district proper there is generally speaking regular administration though during the war a slightly different atmosphere might have been introduced. Though the percentage of literacy among male Naga is about six only, quite a good number of these have received high education. Female literacy among the Naga is however negligible, though in the Mokokchung Sub-Division it was found to be nearly four per cent. Literacy seems to be higher in the Mokokchung area than the Kohima area and the demand for education is also keener here.

As regards economic circumstances a good deal of terracing is done in the Angami areas and a number of Nagas seem to have taken up non-agricultural occupations–the planting gardens etc.

It has been mentioned that the district is inhabited by mutually exclusive, diverse tribes. A movement for unification has however been afoot in the last two or three years and a body known as the Naga National Council (with sub-councils of the different tribes) was formed in 1945. Though a non-official political organisation, many of its leaders and members are Government officials and the organisation has also received official recognition locally. Thus the anomalous position of Government servants participating in political activity exists and in part this situation is due to the fact that the educated, influential and leading elements are Government servants. Though the formation of this council may be taken as an indication that the unity of administration has given a sense of unity to the different tribes it would perhaps be a mistake to suppose that there has been any real consolidation, and the tenacity with which the tribes hold on to their own particular views or traditions is still a potent factor. A notable characteristic of Naga* tribes is that decisions in their tribal councils are taken by general agreement and not by the minority accepting the decisions of the majority. This feature, though perhaps well suited to village areas, may lead to many an unsatisfactory compromise in matters of greater moment.

In June 1946, the Naga National Council passed a resolution expressing their approval of the scheme proposed by the Cabinet Mission in the State paper of May 16, 1946, and their desire to form part of Assam and India. The resolution protested against the proposal to group Assam with Bengal. This resolution and the feeling which prompted it seems to have held the field throughout 1946 and the Premier of Assam who visited the district in November 1946 was greeted with the utmost cordiality. Early in 1947 the Governor of Assam, Sir Andrew Clow, visited the Naga Hills and advised the Nagas that their future lay with India and with Assam. Subsequently towards the end of February 1947, the Naga National Council passed a resolution in which they desired the establishment of "an Interim Government of Nagas with financial provisions, for a period of ten years at the end of which the Naga people will be left to choose any form of Government under which they themselves choose to live." This resolution was of course completely different from the previous one in that it was based on the idea of being a separate nation and country. Subsequently, the Naga National Council sent another memorandum in which they mentioned a "guardian power" without however stating who should be the guardian power, and it was found that they were extremely reluctant to express any choice openly between three possibilities of the Government and H.M.G. It would appear that this was the formula on which a general measure of agreement could be obtained among the Nagas since there were clear indications that many of them were inclined to take moderate views more on the lines of the original resolution passed at Wokha but in view of the intransigence of certain other members probably of the Angami group, they were prevented from doing so.

Subsequent events connected with the visit of H.E the Governor to the Naga Hills on the 26th of June 1946 show that the Nagas have dropped their extreme demands. The substance of the claims made by the Nagas is now to maintain their customary laws and courts, management of their land with its resources, the continuance of the regulations by which entry and residence in the hills could be controlled and a review of the whole position after ten years.

5. Lushai Hills (District) Tract

This district has an area of 8,142 square miles and lies to the south of the Surma Valley. It forms a narrow wedgeshaped strip of territory about 70 miles wide in the north tapering to almost a point at its southern extremity and separates Burma from the State of Tripura and the Chittagong Hill Tracts of Bengal on the east and southeast respectively. With the exception of a small area at its southern extremity which is inhabited by the Lakher tribesmen, the rest of the district is inhabited by the tribes known as Lushai or Mizo and found elsewhere in North Cachar Sub-Division, and Manipur as Kuki. The communication with the main inhabited area of Aija l(headquarters) and Lungleh are difficult and there is only a bridal path connecting Aijal with Silchar. From Serang, near Aijal, communication by river, along the Dhaleswari, is possible and Demagiri in the south is connected with Rangamati in the Chittagong Hill Tracts, by the Karnaphuly river. There is also a bridal path connecting Lungleh with Rangamati. The population of this district is 152,786 according to the last census and over 96 per cent of the population is tribal. The district as a whole is hilly, with a general elevation of between 3,000 and 4,000 feet and the slopes are usually quite steep.

Jhuming, with the exception of certain orange gardens, is the common form of cultivation and terracing and wet cultivation present many difficulties. Spinning and weaving is a common cottage industry, and every woman in a Lushai household spins and weaves for the needs of the family. Most attractive tapestry work is done in these hills and the designs make a very colourful display. Much of the weaving and spinning is done however for personal use and not for sale. The degree of literacy in the area is very high, the reason for it being probably the fact that a large proportion of the population is Christian and the Sunday Schools have assisted in the spread of literacy even among the adult men but, apart from a few Government servants, the number of people following non-agricultural occupations is negligible. The general level of intelligence and civilized behaviour in this area is high and compares favourably with most places in the plains.

There are no local self-governing institutions and village life is to a great extent dominated by the Chief who is generally hereditary.* Formerly the number of Chiefs was small, probably 50 or 60, but on account of the increase in population and the growth of new villages the present number is over 300. The Chiefs settle disputes in the villages, make a distribution of land for jhuming and generally carry out any orders issued to them by the officials including such work as collection of taxes. Of late the relations between the Chiefs and the people have been rather strained, and it would appear that one reason for this is the convening of the so-called District Conference by the Superintendent of the Lushai Hills. The "Mizo Union" was started some time ago by the people (including Chiefs also as members) as a non-official organization, with the consent of the Superintendent. This organization seems to have been without a rival to begin with but in 1946 the Superintendent convened the District Conference with a membership of 40 of which 20 were commoners and 20 were Chiefs. The District Conference was supposed to be elected by household franchise at the rate of one vote for every 10 houses and in the first conference, the chiefs and the people had separate electorates, that is, the people elected their own representatives and the chiefs theirs. The conference apparently created little enthusiasm and the large representation of Chiefs on it must have caused some dissatisfaction. The Superintendent was the President of the Conference. Towards October 1946, this Conference seems to have broken down and was virtually abandoned. Shortly before the visit of the sub-committee however fresh election was held by the Superintendent. At this election a change was made in the franchise so that the separate electorate was abolished and Chiefs and commoners voted jointly. The ratio of Chiefs and commoners was however maintained and on this account the "Mizo Union" decided to boycott the elections with considerable effect on it. In fact it is claimed by the Mizo Union that only two or three hundred voters actually took part in the elections. However, this might be,the convening of the District Conference which was claimed to be an elected body obviously brought it into rivalry with the Mizo Union and since the Conference was supported by the Superintendent, the Mizo Union incurred official disfavour.* The Superintendent being the President of the Conference and the Chiefs being largely under official control and influence, there was apparent justification for the view of the people. In fact the attitude of the Superintendent gave us very good reason to believe that the District Conference was completely dominated by him and was his mouthpiece. The Superintendent himself propounded a scheme before the committee the purport of which was that all local affairs should be managed by a constitutional body elected by the district who would have their own officers appointed by themselves and that the Government of Assam or of the Union should pay only a certain sum of money amounting to the deficit of the district and enter into an agreement regarding the defence of the district and its external relations. To what extent the Superintendent believed that the Lushais could actually administer their own affairs efficiently in every matter other than defence is a matter of some doubt because in answer to a question whether he thought that the whole administration could be managed by them, he replied "I will not guarantee that it could be done". (See Vol.II Evidence). In answer to a further question he gave it as his opinion that it would not be very long before the district could manage its own affairs and that the length of the period would depend upon whether there was interference from out side by bodies that were too powerful or not. The general impressions gathered by us during our discussions with representatives of various interests in the district was that,with the exception of a few people who were under the influence of the Superintendent, the attitude of the rest was reasonable, and it would not be long before disruptive ideas prevailing now completely disappear.

The main emphasis in the demands of the Lushais was laid on the protection of the land, the prevention of exploitation by outsiders and the continuance of their local customs and language.

The district has a revenue of about two lakhs and an expenditure amounting to about six lakhs. A high school has recently been started. The Assam Rifles are stationed at Aijal and Lungleh.

6. The North Cachar Hills Sub-Division

This area is a Sub-Division of the Cachar district whose headquarters is Silchar. It is an area of 1,888 square miles inhabited by 37,361 people of which 31,529 were tribals, the remainder being accounted for by the various railways and other colonies of outsiders. The main feature of this Sub-Division is that it contains a number of different tribes namely the Cachar, the Naga, the Kuki and Mikir; a small number of Synteng or Khasi also inhabit the area. The general characteristic is that the tribes named above, with the exception of one or two villages of Naga inhabited by a few Kuki, live in areas of their own and there is no intermingling of population of the different tribes in the villages. The Zemi Naga are however not in a compact block and live in three different portions with Kuki or Cachari in the intervening portions. The Mikir form a pocket to the north-west of the area and the Cachari roughly inhabit the central and south-west portions. The Cachari are the most numerous of the tribes with a population of about 16,000; the Kuki are about 7,000 and the Zemi about 6,000. Relations between the Kuki and the Naga are said to be unsatisfactory though for the time being relations appear to be good. It may be mentioned here that the Zemi have still unpleasant memories of bad treatment by the Angami of the Naga Hills District and there is not much love lost between them though they showed themselves responsive to instructions given by certain Angami officials from Kohima.

There is little literacy in this area and cultivation is by the primitive method of jhuming. Unlike the Angami areas in the Naga Hills District, the hillsides here are much steeper and apart from rainfall, there is no scope for irrigation. Then again, unlike the Angami, the Zemi live in small hamlets and it is not an easy matter to find adequate labour for the introduction of terracing and wet cultivation. A certain number of orange gardens have been planted and potatoes have been introduced into the district. There is little doubt that with the encouragement of education, for which there is a demand the tribes can be brought up to the others but at present while they are quite capable of understanding the broad outlines of the democratic mechanism and can take part in elections, it is unlikely that they will be able to manage a body like a local board without official aid. The main difficulty in this portion is however caused by the existence of different tribes who have little feeling of solidarity among themselves. Quite recently a sort of tribal council to bring together the different tribes with a view to educating them in local self-government was undertaken by the Sub-Division Officer, but the Mikir influenced as they were by people from the Mikir Hills who wanted an amalgamation of the Mikir area with the Mikir Hills portion, would not cooperate in the jointed council. Then there is the question of choosing a common representative. The Cachari being the most numerous have some advantage and the area is obviously too small for the representation of more than one in the Provincial Legislature. It is likely however that there will be a sufficient combination for the purpose of electing a common representative. Since this area cannot share a representative with plains areas, the population of 37,000 will have to be provided with a representative of their own. If however a local self-governing body is formed in this district it is clear that there will have to be some kind of regional arrangement by which the different tribes have their own separate councils which will then come together in the form of a council for the whole Sub-Division.

Like most other hill districts this area is also a deficit area. The same feeling which exists in other areas about safeguarding land and protection of the land from occupation by outsiders as well as excluding them also from other activities which may lead to exploitation prevents here. One feature of this area is that among the different tribes it is Hindustani which is more of a common language than Assamese.

7. Khasi and Jaintia Hills

This Partially Excluded Area consists of the Jaintia Hills formerly forming part of the Kingdom of the old Jaintia kings and now forming the Jowai Sub-Division, and some 176 villages in the Sadar Sub-Division. The Khasi and Jaintia Hills as a whole consist of a large territory between the Garo Hills on the west and the North Cachar Hills and the Mikir Hills on the east. The Khasi states which consist of 1,509 villages cover the western portion of the Hills and the British villages are interlaced with them. The people of the Jowai Sub-Division are known as Synteng or Pnar and speak a dialect but with the exception of a small number of Mikir on the northern slopes of the Hills, the whole population of these Hills may be regarded as uniform. Unlike their neighbours who speak Tibeto-Burmese tongues the Khasi form an island of the Mon Khmer linguistic family.

The Khasi states,which are about 25 in number, are some of the smallest in India. The largest states are Khyriem, Mylliem and Nongkhlao and the smallest is Nonglewai. The system of inheritance of chiefship is described as follows:

> The Chiefs of these little states are generally taken from the same family inheritance going through the female. A uterine brother usually has the first claim and failing him a sister's son. The appointment is however subject to the approval of a small electoral body, and the heir-apparent is occasionally passed over, if for any reason, mental, physical or moral, he is unfit for the position. The electors are generally the Mantries or Lyngdohs the representatives of the clans which go to form the state.

In Langrin, the appointment is by popular election. In some of the States, if the Mantries are not unanimous in their choice, a popular election is held. The Chiefs are known as Siem in most States but in some they are called Sardar, Lyngdoh in three of them and Wahadadar in one. The functions of the Chiefs are largely magisterial and in the discharge of their duties they are assosted by their Mantries. The relations between them and the Government of India are based upon sanads issued to them.For specimen of these sanads Volume XII of Aitchison's "Treaties,Engagements and Sanads" may be referred to. Under the terms of the sanad, the Chiefs are placed completely under the control of the Deputy Commissioner and the Government of India. Waste lands as well as minerals are ceded to the Government on condition that half the revenue is made over to the Siems. Their criminal and civil authority are also limited. The sanads do not mention the right to levy excise on liquor and drugs and presumably the Siems have that right. Though the states are not in the partially excluded areas, the main interest attaching to them is the fact that there is an understandable feeling among the people of the states that there should be a federation between the states and British portions so that all the Khasi people are brought under a common administration. The position is that in the British areas, though there is now the Franchise and a member is sent to the Provincial Legislature, there is no statutory body for local self-government. The states, on the other hand, enjoy certain rights, as stated above, and the problem is to bridge the gap.

The Khasi and Jaintia Hills have the advantage of the Provincial headquarters, Shillong, being situated among them. Literacy among the Khasi amounts to about 11 per cent with a male literacy of 19 per cent. The district is largely enfranchised and the special features which it is desirable to bear in mind is the matriarchal system prevalent there, the democratic village systems and other special custom and traditions. Cultivation in the Khasi and Jaintia Hills may be regarded as comparatively advanced. There is a good deal of wet cultivation and the culture of oranges and potatoes is common. The Khasi have also taken to non-agricultural professions much more than other hill people.

8. The Garo Hills

The Garo Hills which is the butt-end of the range of hills which constitute the watershed for the Brahmaputra and the Surma Valleys. The Garo who inhabit these hills are people of Tibeto-Burmese origin and are similar to the Cachari. The area of the district is 3,152 square miles and it is inhabited by a population of 233,569 of which 198,474 or nearly 85 per cent are tribals, mainly Garo. The Garo inhabit not only the district which bears their name but there are villages inhabited by them in Kamrup and Goalpara also and portions of the Mymensingh district of Bengal joining the Garo Hills is inhabited by thousands of Garo.

The Garo are a people with a matriarchal system like the Khasi. The tribal system of the Garo is highly democratic and the whole village with the Nokma as the head or chairman takes part in the council if any matter is in dispute. The district as a whole is pretty backward with only about five literates in a hundred and lacking in communications. Christian missions have been active and there has been a certain amount of conversion but on the whole the Garo even while being able to produce a fair number of intelligent and literate people have yet to come up to the degree of the Khasi or the Lushai. Franchise at present is restricted to the Nokma but it is unlikely that there will be any great difficulty in working a franchise system based on adult franchise than in most other areas.

In the Garo Hills also the sole occupation is agriculture and though garden crops are grown round the huts sometimes, the method is largely that of jhuming. The people weave their own clothes but there is no important cottage industry. The area is however much more in contact with the plains on either side of it than areas like the Lushai Hills or the Naga Hills.

The Garo are keenly desirous of uniting all the villages inhabited by Garo whether in the plains of Assam or in the Mymensingh district of Bengal under a common administration. The Bengal district of Mymen-singh seems to be the home of about 48,000 Garo most of whom are on the fringe of the Garo Hills, and the question of rectification of the boundary to include this area in the Garo Hills district of Assam definitely deserves consideration. A similar examination is necessary in respect of other Garo villages in the Kamrup and Goalpara districts of Assam.

9. The Mikir Hills

The Partially Excluded Area of the Mikir Hills with an area of about 4,400 square miles and a population of about 150,000 persons is split up between two districts namely Nowgaong and Sibsagar. The Mikir Hills form an area rather irregular in shape into which there projects an enclave of the Assam Valley. The western extremity of the Partially Excluded Area actually reaches a point in the Khasi Hills and eastwards it extends to a point not far from Dimapur while to the north it approaches Golaghat. It is clear that the irregular shape of this area makes the administration from centres outside the area rather inconvenient which apparently is the reason why the district has had to be split up between two plains districts. Being a rather sparsely populated* area with rather less than 50 persons to the square mile and containing no communications other than the railway passing through it, it has apparently not been considered suitable for treatment as a separate district. The Provincial Government has at present under consideration a proposal for the making of the whole of the Mikir Hills area into a separate Sub-Division, perhaps on the analogy of the North Cachar Hills Sub-Division. Divided between two districts as it is and consisting of inhospitable territory in which jhuming is the only method of cultivation practised while malaria takes its toll, it has been sadly neglected in many ways and special steps are necessary for its development. Very obviously the present state of affairs where it is divided between two districts cannot continue if the area is to be developed and it should be made either a district or a Sub-Division with its headquarters somewhere in the middle of the bend so that it is accessible from both extremities. The area includes certain mouzas Barapathar and Sarupathar inhabited very largely by non-tribals which even at the time of the Constitution of the Partially Excluded Areas were considered doubtful areas for exclusion, and the Provincial Government have since taken a decision that the areas should be added to regularly administered portions as soon as possible.

The Mikir are probably the most backward of all the tribes of the Assam Hills though this backwardness is probably not their own fault. There are pockets of Mikir in the North Cachar and the Khasi Hills like the Garo and Khasi the Mikir desire the consolidation of their own tribesmen under a single administration. Unlike the Lushai or the Khasi Hills, Christianity has made little progress here.

While the special customs of the Mikir, their addiction to jhuming cultivation etc. necessitate that an arrangement must be made by which they are able to maintain their own system, the Mikir Hills at present find representation in the Provincial Legislature although through the restricted franchise of the headmen, and opinion generally is that there is no objection to the extension of adult franchise in the area. The sparse population may give rise to certain practical difficulties in organising elections there but it would appear that these are not insurmountable.

The Mikir Hill are inhabited to some extent by Kachari (about 2000), Rengma Naga and a few Kuki, but on the whole, the population may be regarded as uniform.

In view of the comparatively backward state of the Mikir and the fact that there are no self-governing institutions of a statutory type locally, it is necessary in introducing institutions of this kind to arrange for a period of supervision and guidance. In other words, any local council set up in the hills should at first be subject to the control of the local, district or Sub-Divisional Officer.

G.N. BORDOLOI (Chairman)
J.J.M. NICHOLS - ROY
RUP NATH BRAHMA
A.V. THAKKAR

Summary of Recommendations of the Assam Sub-committee

1. District Councils should be set up in the hill district (see Section B of Appendix A) with powers of legislation over occupation or use of land other than land comprising reserved forest under the Assam Forest Regulation of 1891 or other law applicable. This is subject to the provision that no payment would be required for the occupation of vacant land by the Provincial Government for public purposes and private land required for public purposes by the Provincial Government will be acquired for it on payment of compensation (Paragraph 9 and Section C(1) of Appendix A).

2. Reserved forests will be managed by the Provincial Government. In questions of actual management including the appointment of forest staff and the granting of contracts and leases, the susceptibilities and the legitimate desires and needs of the hill people should be taken into account (para. 10).

3. On account of its disastrous effects upon the forest, rainfall and other climatic features, jhuming should be discouraged and stopped wherever possible but the initiative for this should come from the tribes themselves and the control of jhuming should be left to the local councils (para. 11 and Section C of Appendix A).

4. All social law and custom is left to be controlled or regulated by the tribes (para. 12 and Section C(2) of Appendix A). All criminal offences except those punishable with death, transportation or imprisonment for five years and upwards should be left to be dealt with in accordance with local practice and the Code of Criminal Procedure will not apply to such cases. As regards the serious offences punishable with imprisonment of five years or more they should be tried henceforth regularly under the Criminal Procedure Code. To try such cases, powers should be conferred by the Provincial Government whenever suitable upon tribal councils or courts set up by the district councils themselves.

All ordinary civil suits should be disposed of by tribal courts and local councils may have full powers to deal with them including appeal and revision.

Where non-tribals are involved, civil or criminal cases should be tried under the regular law and the Provincial Government should make suitable arrangements for the expeditious disposal of such cases by employing circuit magistrates or judges (Para.12 and Section D and F of Appendix A).

5. The District Councils should have powers of management over primary schools, dispensaries and other institutions which normally come under the scope of local self-governing institutions in the plains. They should have full control over primary education. As regards secondary school education there should be some integration with the general system of the Province and it is left open to the Provincial Government to entrust local councils with responsibility for secondary schools wherever they find this suitable(Paragraph 13 and Section E of Appendix A).

For the Mikir and North Cachar Hills the District or Sub-Divisional Officer, as the case may be, ex-officio President of the local council with powers, subject to the control of the Government of Assam, to modify or annul resolution or decisions of the local councils and to issue such instruction as may be necessary(Paragraph 13 and Section B(5) of Appendix A).

6. Certain taxes and financial powers should be allotted to the councils. They should have all the powers which local bodies in regulation districts enjoy and in addition they should have powers to impose house tax or poll tax, land revenue and levies arising out of the powers of management of village forest (Section H of Appendix A and Para. 14(a)).

Statutory provision for a fixed proportion of Provincial funds to be spent on the hill districts is not considered practicable. A separate statement for each hill district showing the revenue derived from the district and the expenditure proposed on it is recommended. The framing of a suitable programme of development should be enjoined either by statute or by Instrument of Instructions (Section M of Appendix A and Para.14(b)).

It is quite clear that the urgent requirements of the hill districts by way of expenditure on development schemes are beyond the resources of the Provincial Government and the development of the hill districts should be as much the concern of the Federal Government as the Provincial Government. Financial assistance should be provided by the Federation to meet the deficit in the ordinary administration on the basis of the average deficit during the past three years and the cost of development scheme should also be borne by the Central Exchequer (Section N of Appendix A and Para.14(c)).

The claim of the Hill District Councils for assistance from general provincial revenues to the extent that they are unable to raise the necessary finances within their own powers is recognised (Paragraph 14(d)).

7. If local councils decide by a majority of three-fourths of their members to licence moneylenders or traders they should have powers to require moneylenders and professional dealers from outside to take our licences (Para.15 and Section J of Appendix A).

8. The management of mineral resources should be centralized in the hand of the Provincial Government but the right of the district councils to a fair share of the revenue is recognized. No licence or leases shall be given by the Provincial Government except in consultation with local council. If there is no agreement between the Provincial Government and the District Council regarding the share of the revenue, the Governor will decide the matter in his discretion (Paragraph 16 and Section 1 of Appendix A).

9. Provincial Legislature which deals with the subjects in which the Hill Councils have legislative powers will not apply to the hill districts. Legislature prohibiting the consumption of non-distilled liquors like Zu will also not apply; the District Council may however apply the legislation (Para. 17 and Section L of Appendix A).

10. It is necessary to provide for the creation of Regional Councils for the different tribes inhabiting an autonomous district if they so desire. Regional Councils have powers limited to their customary law and the management of lands and villages and courts. Regional Councils may delegate their powers to the District Councils (Para.18 and Section B(4) of Appendix A).

11. The Governor is empowered to set aside any act or resolution of the council if the safety of the country is prejudiced and to take such action as may be necessary including dissolution of the local councils subject to the approval of the legislature. The Governor is also given power to dissolve the council if gross mismanagement is reported by a commission (Paragraph 19 and Section P Q and R of Appendix A).

12. The Central Government should continue to administer the Frontier Tracts and Tribal Area with the Government of Assam as its agent until administration has been satisfactorily established over a sufficiently wide area. Areas over which administration has been satisfactorily established

may be taken over by the Provincial Government with the approval of the Federal Government (Section P of Appendix A and Para. 20(a)).

The pace of extending administration should be greatly accelerated and separate officers be appointed for the Lohit Valley, the Siang Valley and the Naga Tribal Area (Para.20(a)).

The Lakhimpur Frontier Tract should be attached to the regular administration of the district. The case of the portion of the Lakhimpur Frontier Tract recently included in the Tirap Frontier Tract should be examined by the Provincial Government with a view to a decision whether it could immediately be brought under Provincial Administration. A similar examination of the position in the plains portion of the Sadiya Frontier Tract is recommended. The portion of the Balipara Frontier Tract around Charduar should also be subject to a similar examination (Para.20(b)). Posa payment should be continued (Para.20(c)).

13. The excluded areas other than the Frontier Tracts should be enfranchised immediately and restrictions on the franchise in the Garo and Mikir Hills should be removed and adult franchise introduced (Para.21(a) and Section B(1) of Appendix A).

Weightage is not considered necessary but the Hill Districts should be represented in the Provincial Legislature in proportion not less than what is due on their population even if this involves a certain weightage in rounding off. The total number of representatives for the hills thus arrived at (See Para.21(b)) should not be taken into account in determining the number of representatives to the Provincial Legislature from the rest of Assam (Para.21(b) and Section K of Appendix A).

The total population of the Hill Districts justifies a seat for the hill tribes in the Federal Legislature on the scale proposed in Section 13(c) of the Draft Union Constitution (Para.21(c)).

Joint electorate is recommended but constituencies are confined to the autonomous districts. Reservation of seats, in view of this restriction, is not necessary (Para.21(d) and Section K (3) of Appendix A).

Non-tribals should not be eligible for election from hill constituencies except in the constituency which includes the municipality and Cantonment of Shillong (Para.21(e) and Section K(3) of Appendix A).

14. Representation for the hills in the Ministry should be guaranteed by

statutory provision if possible or at least by a suitable instruction in the Instrument of Instructions or Corresponding Provision (Para.22 and Section O(3) of Appendix A).

15. Non-tribal officials should not be barred from serving in the hills but they should be selected with care if posted to the hills. The appointment of a due proportion of hill people in the service should be particularly kept in mind and provided for in rules or executive instructions of the Provincial Government (Paragraph 23).

16. A commission may be appointed at any time or permanently to enable the Government to watch the progress of development plans or to examine any particular aspects of the administration (Paragraph 24 and Section O(1) of Appendix A).

17. Plains tribals number 1.6 million. Their case for special representation and safeguards should be considered by the Minorities Sub-Committee (Para. 25).

18. The question of altering boundaries so as to bring the people of the same tribe under a common administration should be considered by the Provincial Government. The Barpathar and Sarupathar Mouzas included in the Mikir Hills should be included in the regularly administered areas henceforth (Para. 26).

19. Non-tribal residents may be provided with representation in the local councils if they are sufficiently numerous. For this purpose non-tribal constituencies may be formed if justified and if the population is not below 500 (Para. 27 and Section B(2) of Appendix A).

20. Provisional councils should be set up by the Governor of Assam after consulting such local organisations as exist. These provisional councils which will be for one year will have powers to frame their own constitution and rules for the future (Para. 29 and Transitional Provisions of Appendix A).

---

*The framing of Indian Constitution: A study. Editor B. Shiva Rao.

CHAPTER IV

Gandhiji's Letters to Gopinath Bordoloi

Wardha, 1st October 1934

Dear Friend,

I have your letter for which I thank you. It is essentially a domestic matter which the local people should settle. In any case I dare not interfere. You can act up to the formula that I have presented–he who has the least chance should retire.

Yours sincerely,
M.K. Gandhi.

Sevagram Wardha
6.5.41

Dear Bordoloi,

I was delighted to have your letter. You are certainly making the best use of your time. I am glad too that you are all spinning.

I do not mind your writing about me. But you will offend all orthodoxy by bracketing me with the avatars or prophets and I think rightly. You cannot write of a living man in the same way as of the dead who by common consent, have been acclaimed as great teachers.

Your second question is difficult. I believe with those Muslims who think that the Prophet's years in Mecca were the years in which he taught and lived pure non-violence. He became an administrator in Medina and thus ceased to be a pure teacher. In any case the net effect of the Quran is that non-violence is one obligation but violence is permissible. We are bound to accept as authoritative the interpretation generally given by the Muslim world and not the one I have prepared.

As to Krishna's advice to Arjuna you should read any introduction to Anasakti Yog. If you have not read it, you will tell me and I shall send you a copy.

I would advise you all to learn well both Urdu and Hindi. Then only shall we evolve an all India speech.

Yours
Bapu
(M.K.Gandhi)

Sevagram
Wardha
30.6.41

My dear Bordoloi,

I replied to your wire there and then. I had a note from the Telephone office that you had left and that the wire was posted to you. You must have got it. In view of the notice given by you, I suppose you must court imprisonment but if the Govt. had good grounds for releasing you, it would be violence to court imprisonment. But you are best judge. Please keep me informed of your movement and doings. This is a long drawing struggle in which there will be no waste. Everyone will have all the opportunity he needs to show his mettle.

Yours
Bapu

Sevagram
20.11.44

Dear Bordoloi,

I have your letter with enclosures concentrate on producing a solid scheme for villages and the names of and qualifications of those who would work it. If you can do that, there might be no difficulty about funds even if you extend your allotment. But you must be prepared for a stiff test. Don't take a full bite at once and face disaster.

Yours
Bapu

Malki, Shillong
1.2.48

Dear Mr. Bordoloi,

May I be allowed to thank you for yesterday's most beautiful and impressive gathering especially for your address? It made me feel more strongly than ever what I have often felt before–namely, what a tremendous task you, who are Gandhiji's friends and followers, have taken upon your shoulders in trying to carry his way of life into the political world. To do it while he was still here to turn to for guidance and strength must have been difficult enough; to face the future without him, a burden almost too heavy to bear.

Please do not trouble to answer this note. On pondering today over what you had said I suddenly felt I must write and assure you of my deep sympathy and for what it is worth of my unswerving support in your heroic attempts to give life and reality to Bapu's ideals in this province.

With warm regards and deep respect,

Yours very sincerely,
Margaret Ban*

*Margaret Slade was called Margaret Ban by Bapuji. She was a PA to him.

Jorhat Jail
Bapuji,

I am thankful for your kind letter.

I am grateful to you for the permission given to me to "write about you." I am surely not "bracketing you" with the recognized teachers of the world. To me such teachers are "bracketable". But the entire object of my book would be frustrated if I could not show by your life and your teaching how among many other truths Ahimsa practised and taught by you, how toleration is one which is examined by all the religions and can be practised by their followers. As your life and teaching only interpret the fundamentals of all religions I have no option but to put your life in the same book. In the presentation I will surely take every care not to hurt the "orthodoxy".

I am deeply grateful for your advice reg. the Ahimsa practised by the great teachers. I am sorry that I have not got Anasakti Joga or its preface by you with me.

Do kindly have a copy sent to me.

Yours respectfully,
Gopinath Bordoloi

We are trying to translate into action, your advice regarding the study of Urdu, Mr. F.A. Ahmed has volunteered to teach us. None of the 1st ever know the alphabets. We would like to make an attempt to be able to read Urdu while in Jail.

Jorhat Jail, Assam
26.4.41

Revered Bapuji,

I was cherishing for sometime the desire of writing to you on the subject noted below. But the apprehension that I might encroach on your valuable time prevented me from writing to you earlier. I now hope I have your indulgence to disturb you for a short while.

While considering, if I could be of any use to anybody while in Jail, it stuck me if I could be of use to the growing children by letting them know something about the lives of Avatars and religious teachers of the world–the underlying idea being developed in the youthful mind, the idea of toleration generally, and communal unity in particular. I accordingly decided to write the lives of Raja Ramachandra, Buddha, Christ, Mohammed and your life. In order to make it interesting reading, I am presenting them in the nature of discourse, with as many stories and Kahinis as it is possible to do for illustrating their great virtues. I have tried to show that in reference to sacrifice, and their suffering for the poor and the downtrodden, in the observance of truth and their faith in God, their lives and teaching gives the same moral. I have also tried to analyse in as simple a way as possible for me the fundamental teachings of Hinduism, Buddhism, Christianity and Mohammadanism to show that they agree essentially; and that all controversy, strife and bloodshed that have occurred in the world over religion are due to selfish and ignorant people giving undue stress on non-essentials of religion. In presenting your life and teachings my attempt will be to show that although a Hindu, you sympathize in your life and teachings the fundamentals of all the religions. But before doing so, I thought it would be proper to obtain your permission to do so. Have I your permission? I would even be happy if you say no permission is necessary; but refusal will surely hurt me. I need tell you that the book is being written in Assamesse for boys of say 13 to 17 years of age. It is not known whether I shall ever come to print, although I now feel that I should do my best to do so.

The script that I am troubling myself about is the difficulty of reconciling the life of Md. Rasul at Medina (where he took up arms–and abreast in aggression in last 3 years) and the great saying of Sri Krishna to Arjuna (in Bgt. Geeta) to flight. With the doctrine of Ahimsa, so far as the life of Mohammed is concerned, I have already stated the historical arguments, viz. that although Ahimsa might have been fully understood and practised by Buddha and Christ, its application was restricted to individual lives and barring a few recent exceptions, never has it been used by or against the State until now by you. Would it be now too much if I requested you to give your opinion in this matter as briefly as possible? I have been compelled to make this almost impartial request having failed to your opinion on the subject from the small tolerance that is now with me here in Jail.

I am quite at peace and with the life we are leading, there is nothing to disturb our tranquillity or even equanimity. Three other friends of our Assembly Mr. F.A. Ahmed, Ex. Fin. Min., Sjt. B.R. Medhi, Ex. Pre. P.C.C., Sjt. Deveswar Sarma, our Chief Whip are staying in a high walled compound which was meant for detenus. But the place is good nevertheless, and the ground spacious for 4 persons. We have 2 M.L.As. in another ward far away from us. We are thus a small party of congress M.L.A supposed to be functioning even now; for all the proceedings and papers connected with the Assembly come to us. I feel we are all making good use of our time. I spin about 4 hours a day and my average output is never below 1000 yds. Sj. Sanker Barua, M.L.A. spins about 1500 to 2000 yds. daily possibly a good record for any Satyagrahi. In presenting the best of Satyagrahi M.L.A. before you, instead "indifferent spinner" against some of us here, and not a "habitual spinner" even against Sj. Bishnu Ram Medhi, my joy knew no bound, in the heart of my hearts,when sending them for competition at Wardha. Most of us are spending 5 to 6 hours in reading and take additional 2 hours in writing. I feel I am not less busy in important matters that when outside.

The Jail and the Supdt. particularly are all considerate to us. But sometimes I am troubled by the thought as to whether all this is not due to our previous position–Minister and legislatures of the state. I have otherwise nothing to complain. But I definitely wish that the C Dns. prisoners of whom there are 20, in all, were given equal status with us. I hear they spend about-/8/-p.d. on our account, whereas they do not spend more than - /3/- on them. But the rules–inexorable-are there and you know about the Jail rules and their observance so well.

As I will suspend writing your life till I hear your advice,I naturally do wait an early reply.

With respectful regards.

Yours in reverence,
Gopinath Bordoloi

Nehru's letter to GNB on Sylhat disturbances (correspondence between Nehru and Maulana Hussain Ahmad Madri on Sylhet)

19-9-46

My dear Bordoloi,

I enclose a letter addressed to you from Maulana Hussain Ahmad Madri. If you cannot read Urdu you had better get it read out to you. I have not myself read this letter, but I have had a talk with the Maulana. He is very worried at occurrences in Sylhet recently when he was there and he is anxious that something should be done about them. I understand that the Muslim Hotel there was sacked and looted and that the behaviour of the Magistrate was far from satisfactory.

About the live system I read a report prepared by a committee of the Jamiat-Ul-Ulema. The report was a good one generally speaking though Fakhruddin pointed out some minor errors. I understand that some affect has been given to the recommendations in that report.

Yours sincerely
Jawaharlal Nehru

G.N.B.'s reply to Nehru–

(1) Bureaucratic machinery including the forum.

(2) I.C.S.,I.P.S.,I.M.S. officers role.

(3) Necessity to decide policies on the above through Premier conference.

Express

Gopinath Bordoloi
Gauhati (Assam)

On reaching Calcutta Saturday morning staying there two days stop would like visit Gauhati meet workers also, if possible refugee camps stop please send representative meet me Calcutta.

Jawaharlal Nehru

16/4/42

CONFIDENTIAL

10th October, 46

My dear Panditjee,

Your letter of 19th September enclosed with Maulana Madri's letter reached me sometime ago. We are no less serious about the occurrence at Sylhet than Maulana Saheb. As a matter of fact we had to rush to Sylhet from a cabinet meeting to see what we could do on that quitened down. But some mischief was done in the meanwhile to Jamiat-u1-Ulema friends and to some Hindus by the rowdy elements among the Muslim League people. It will not recur in the future although tensions on both sides seem to inhibit themselves on occasions, and section 144 of Police guards is yet being maintained.

As regards the conduct of the Dist. Magistrate little police force at his disposal (his version) public version failure to take adequate steps: action taking transfer of the Magistrate to relieve the people from fear and pain and put another officer.

It is necessary to inform you in this connection that bureaucratic machinery in which the Governor also comes to the picture is causing delay, if not obstruction, in the matter.

In this connection it becomes very necessary for us to know what action you are proposing in ref. to I.C.S., I.P.S. and I.M.S people. In the apprehensive of a change from the 1st of January next they do not seem to move for any action at all. They are biased for the Muslim League and although not perceptible in action, the matter is too patent to escape our intelligence. They desire to have a set up in which the hands of the British elements of the administration which as you know are now being maintained through the assistance of the Governor. The elderly of these people are entirely shown of ideas of representative Government. I can never think of anything else but a sort of a police rule. The result is a great handicap for the administration.

Things have been rendered worst on the face of the coming changes. We have refused recruitment of I.C.S. and I.P.S. people although in fact we have not been able as yet to set up a proper machinery for selection of personnel for the superior post. With big works before as in the matter of development and planning and also in all other branches the question of appointment of proper personnel must be very great. Don't you think that a meeting of the Prime Minister of the provinces is urgently called for to decide these important matters of policy even if their deliberations were to be confidential and private?

With best wishes to you,

Yours sincerely,
G.N.B.

Shillong
24th March 1939

My dear Panditji,

I am ashamed of myself for not having replied to your letter earlier. The fact is that I wanted to be more economical about my time, for I thought I would be getting the information that you wanted in your letter in the meanwhile and then let you know the whole thing. But in spite of all my efforts, I am afraid that my information may not be as correct and accurate as I wanted it to be.

I had in the meanwhile met several Naga students, two particularly, belonging to a neighbouring village to that in which Rani Guidelieu lived. The information given by them does not seem to be very accurate and I am waiting for further information from other Nagas. The information received by me so far seems to indicate that an elder brother of Rani Guidelieu Jadunang Kacha Naga, led a kind of movement the object of which was to assert himself as a king among Nagas. This leadership, he said, was given to him by powers from above and that therefore no one should question it. The movement spread among a certain section of the Nagas. This was interpreted by the British Raj as a revolt against their authority and he was therefore charged with treason and conspiracy and sentenced to death. His sister Rani Guidelieu took up the cause for which her brother was executed. She was supposed to have instilled into the minds of the Nagas that she was really sent from heaven. It is stated that when search for her was made in places where she was seen a minute before, she could not be found. She was supposed to have appeared like a spirit of the dawn in certain place and to have disappeared soon after. She was found to be roaming from place to place, and although the whole British soldiery was after her, she could not be traced or arrested. In the meanwhile she continued to preach that she was the queen of the Nagas and that the whole Naga tribe should follow her. After some time, however, she was arrested and sentenced to transportation for life.

It is learnt that she read in some missionary school. What she preached was independence for the Nagas with a stress on the purity of the people. It is also stated that she got her inspiration from her brother who was near about Silchar and had come to know something about the Satyagraha movement of 1930. It is also said that a copy of 'Gandhi Vasys' was found in his possession before he was put under trial.

Any further information I get I will let you know when received. I once more request you to excuse my delay.

Yours sincerely,
Sd/-(G.N.Bordoloi)

Pandit Jawaharlal Nehru,
Allahabad

23rd Nov. 1945

Revered Sardarji,

Shri Gopinath Bordoloi has written to you in detail about the position in Assam.

I went over the whole of Assam valley and met a number of workers and other members of my community and other communities. The report of Shri Gopinath Bordoloi is fairly accurate. The Labour seats should also come to us. On the whole we should have a very clear majority in the whole house. I have discussed the matter with Shri Brajmohanji and would request you to give him standing instructions to pay as and when required, within the maximum limit fixed. When I was in Bombay I was feeling to contest all the seats about 5 lacs would be needed; but there might be saving and I think an advance of 3 lacs from the centre should be sufficient. We have not been able to raise much on account of the fact that Sir Md. Saadulla is very much in power and all sorts of means are being adopted to coerce and frighten people.

As regards Musalman Constituency, my report is that even Sir Md. Saadulla is feeling different in his own constituency, and so also Mr. Abdul Motin Choudhury. It is likely that both of them will succeed, but only after a very tough fight and good deal of election campaign and canvassing.

I have advanced money for the present and I shall arrange it with Shri B.M Birla. I shall be sending you periodical reports.

In Bengal, the Mahasabha authorities are feeling very funky and we are trying to have all the seats made uncontested. I will not be surprised if they agree to withdraw from the contest. The only question is about Dr. S.P. Mookherjee himself. We shall see what can be done.

Yours sincerely,

Sd/- P.D. Himet Singha

Sardar Vallabh Bhai Patel,

Marine Drive,

Bombay.

Copy to Shri G.N.Bordoloi,

Gauhati.

Premier's Secretariat
(Seal)

Gauhati
3rd July, 50

My dear Sir,

I understand with surprise that you left a letter withdrawing from Kamalpur in favour of Sjt. Jogendra Nath Bhattacharya with somebody here, to be submitted before the returning officer immediately after you are declared elected in the Gauhati East Constituency and before the counting in the Kamalpur Constituency.

Evidently they procured this inconsistent piece (inconsistent with your previous withdrawal from the Gauhati East Constituency) from you to spite me and by misrepresenting me. They did not however produce it before the R.O. because they could not be sure of its result. They will now advise you to resign your membership of the Kamalpur Constituency and not of the Gauhati East Constituency so that I may not get in into the P.C.C. It is the elementary duty of any sensible man to hear both sides before he decides upon such a case. But it appears that even sufficiently balanced people have lost their equilibrium in their craze for power.

Yours sincerely,
Sd/-Harendranath Barua

To
Sjt. G.N.Bordoloi
Shillong

This is a confidential letter found in the personal portfolio (made of pure leather) of Gopinath Bordoloi addressed to and from Harendranath Barua (an eminent journalist and editor of Natun Asamiya).

CONFIDENTIAL

Chief Minister, Assam

Camp Gauhati
July 6, 1950

My dear Barua,

Your letter of 3rd July, 1950. I feel that there is nothing to be surprised that I should withdraw in favour of Shri Jogendra Nath Bhattacharya, after I was declared elected in the Gauhati East Constituency. It is not however true that I decided to do so before the "counting of Kamalpur constituency". It is obvious that I could not afford to be defeated in any of the constituencies where I was contested; and I had to make that clear to my supporters and friends who were desiring that I should be elected. According to their advice also I am resigning from Kamalpur constituency. The plain fact is that I could not launch any canvassing campaign, nor could I have any time to choose even my constituency. I had to leave all these matters naturally in the hands of my supporters and friends who knew the situation best.

I did not expect that a member like you having known very well the constitutional position of the leader of the Assembly Party should have thought it desirable to contest me. On the 26th of June, I told you at Gauhati that I did not want to withdraw from this constituency–may be due to the fact that I am a man who came from that place as also because my supporters decided that I should continue to be a candidate from that constituency.

I do not know to whom the last two sentences of your letter are meant. I could certainly tell you that if I had to agree to contest any seat, it is simply because I had to maintain the prestige of the leader of the Assembly Party. It is perhaps only the Congress Committee like that of ours and with leaders like you, that think of contesting the leader of Congress Party in the Legislature. In the normal course of thing also, after the contest was declared, I could not allow myself to be defeated just for the same reason.

I hope I have made myself clear.

Yours sincerely,
Sd/- Gopinath Bordoloi

Shri Harendranath Barua,
Gauhati

Circular letter to the members of the Congress Party in Legislative Assembly

Member, Legislative Assembly

Dear Friend,

You have no doubt learnt from the summons issued to you that the Budget Session of the Assembly starts from the 1st of March 1945. As decided last time we continue the policy of giving importance to and attend the House only on matters that vitally concerns. After consultation with the party members I had given indication of the line of activity to be pursued by us in my speech in the last Assembly. For further clarification I repeat them.

1. To see that freedom of speech, of association, of movement, of the press etc. are assured. This means that the question of security prisoners, and of those under restrictions outside, should form the most important item of our work. To this may be added the question regarding the revival of the Congress Organisation, removal of ban on meetings in the various districts etc. Questions, resolutions, and motions may accordingly be submitted.
2. The present distribution of seats in the Local Boards and principles underlying the same, must also be taken up by us for questions, resolutions and motions. The injustice done to particular districts must be taken up by the members representing those districts.
3. Food scarcity in oil, of consumable articles such as dal, ata, etc. must also form part of the programme. In this connection, the question of distribution and procurement may be taken up. It should be the attempt of all of us to expose all corruptions, wherever they are found.
4. Land settlement questions must be particularly dealt with by the members of Nowgong, Kamrup and Darrang districts in a searching manner and all must take part in it. All informations of encroachments, their validity by Government orders, and all departure from the policy enunciated by government in the past and the present, should particularly be made the target of attack.

You may also put up local questions of importance, but how far they may be made the subject of the party attendance in the Assembly, will be decided later on.

As regards the attendance of members under restrictions, I repeat Mahatmaji's advice to the effect that members should not generally apply for permission, but if exigency so demands, they may do so in consultation with their leader. I did accordingly ask both Mr. Chanda and Sj. Purna Chandra Sarma to apply for dealing with the land settlement question and the procurement scheme in the Surma Valley districts. I do think even now that those members, whose health is well enough should attend the Assembly by all means, and do their duty by their constituency and the country on the most vital questions. But I would not go the length of asking such members as may have conscientious objection to apply. I hope to discuss this point with Gandhiji, I get a chance of meeting him in the meanwhile, but at present, I am communicating my attitude in accordance with his previous directions.

Mahatmaji's advice in this connection runs as follows:-

" *Duties ofLegislators:* Members of the Assembly outside jail should attend the Assembly in order to register their views on important matters such as Land Settlement, Food, Evacuation etc. Internee M.L.As should not apply for permission to attend the Assembly but if the gravity of the situation so demands, they may do so. In cases like these, exigency is the governing factor and that is to be decided by the Party or its leader."

Yours sincerely,
Gopinath Bordoloi

Respected Maulana Saheb,

I did not write a separate note to you as it would be only repeating what I have written to Bapuji. The matter is both urgent and serious. I hope you will be pleased to give it the consideration it deserves. I feel that the Working Committee should take up this matter.

Yours sincerely,
Gopinath Bordoloi

TELEGRAPH

To	To
Mahatma Gandhi MADRAS	Maulana Azad DELHI

BUREAUCRATIC SCHEME SECRETARY HATCHED FOR SEPARATION OF ASSAM FRONTIER HILLS WITH NORTHERN BURMA AND POSSIBLY ALSO KHASI AND GARO HILLS NOW PARTIALLY EXCLUDED AREAS SEEMS TO BE RUSHED THROUGH STOP LAST MONTH VICEROY MET SOME HILLS PEOPLE AT BALIPARA AND SADIYA SPECIALLY SENT TO HIM IN SUPPORT OF BRITISH DOMINATION OF THE HILLS STOP GOVERNOR IS TOURING INTERIOR OF THE EXCLUDED AREAS APPARENTLY CANVASSING SUPPORT OF THE SCHEME WHICH IT IS FEARED INCLUDE ALSO AMALGAMATION OF ASSAM IN BENGAL THIS GIVING VIRTUAL EFFECT TO COUPLANDS SCHEME STOP THE DISTRICT OFFICERS IN EXCLUDED AREAS ALL BRITISH ARE SIMILARLY PREACHING ANTI-ASSAMESE PROPAGANDA STOP WHOLE PROPOSAL SIMPLY SHOCKING TO PEOPLE OF ASSAM ALSO TO PEOPLE OF THE HILLS STOP THEIR LEADERS HAVE OPENLY EXPRESSED AGAINST THIS SINISTER MOVE AND PEOPLE OF ASSAM WOULD NOT AGREE TO ANY SUCH SEPARATION BUT WOULD HELP HILLS PEOPLE GROW THEIR FULL STATURE ACCORDING THEIR GENIUS STOP THE PEOPLE OF ASSAM WOULD UNDER NO CIRCUMSTANCES AGREE TO GO TO BENGAL IN ORDER THAT A

PROVINCE WITH LINGUISTIC AND CULTURAL BASIS IN TERMS OF THE CONGRESS MANIFESTO MAY BE PERFORMED STOP PRAY DO THE NEEDFUL TO PREVENT THIS GRAVE MISCHIEF TO ASSAM AND INDIA STOP.

Sd/- G.N.bordoloi

NOT TO BE TELEGRAPHED

Srijut Gopinath Bordoloi,
Gauhati, ASSAM

Copy to Srijut Sarat Bose, Delhi

Letter to Daughter

Jorhat Jail
29/8/43

My dear Lily,

I am very sorry to learn that you are not cured of cold and cough. Write to me as soon as you receive this letter. Could you recognise me when I came to you? Ask God if he allows me to go soon. I am quite alright at present. If you can write letter yourself, please do write.

With love,

Yours affectionately,
(Father)

Jorhat Jail
12/8/43

My dear Punu,

Pooja is nearing. You must be having weekly test. If your exams are over please let me know. If you have woven any other cloth for your dress to wear in Pooja, let me know. Do you cook sometimes? I feel very sad when I think of you all about the Pooja. But the war havoc and the ill condition of the people could not make one hope to enjoy the Pooja. I am quite alright. God bless you all.

With love,

Yours affectionately,
(Father)

Congress House
Gauhati
18th February, 1946

Revered Sardarji,

The whole subject of having a joint parliamentary board for advising the Ministry was discussed with us, some members from the Surma Valley districts and the Secretary of the Bengal Provincial Congress Committee. Maulana Sahib, in the beginning, was not in favour of it, and thought that the Assam Provincial Congress Committee might do the function of advising the Ministry on matters of policy, leaving the Ministry free to carry on day-to-day administration. It was pointed out, however, on behalf of the Surma Valley districts (Sylhet and Cachar) that being under the Bengal PCC and having problems of their own, (they would like to have some say in the enunciation of policies, etc.). Ultimately I was told by the Secretary, Bengal PCC, that he had spoken to Maulana Sahib about the establishment of a sort of joint parliamentary committee with functions as described above and consisting of the following members:

(a)	Two members from Sylhet DCC	2
(b)	One from Cachar DCC	1
(c)	Secretary of the BPCC	1
(d)	Leader of the Party	1
(e)	Secretary, Assam PCC	1
(f)	Four members to be elected from the Assam PCC	4
		10

To such an arrangement, the Bengal PCC Secretary has already agreed and signed, but so far as the Assam PCC is concerned the matter is awaiting consideration of the Working Committee. My own reaction to the proposal is that while I have no objection to the setting up of any machinery of advice or even control, I am not quite sure how smoothly it will work. The success of the Congress in the general seats has brought the Surma Valley feelings to the forefront and, I am sorry to say, to the extent of causing bitterness among some members. The Surma Valley friends have chosen to criticise the Government, and even the Congress Government of 13 months, on grounds, which from the point of view of population, revenue given to the Government, etc., and all other considerations, are absolutely untenable. Maulana Sahib has learnt it first hand and I am not quite sure whether establishment of such a Committee will really not keep this jealously alive. I should keep you informed that every action of mine, beginning from the formation of the Ministry, giving 3 (seats) to either valley, where the population between Assam Valley and Surma Valley is 6 to 4 roughly, distribution of important portfolios, etc., are being adversely criticised by a considerable section of the Assamese people. Maulana Sahib seemed to come to the conclusion that the only alternative to this state of things is to separate the Bengali districts of Sylhet and a portion of Cachar from Assam and join these with Bengal–a consummation to which the Assamese people are also looking forward for the last 70 years,when this district was tagged to Assam for "administrative reasons". He said he would take up the matter as soon as it is possible; my prayer to you also is to have it as soon as the Congress assumes power in the Central Government and is in a position to do so.

Maulana Sahib's meeting with Sir Muhammad (Saadullah), and his offer to the League, became the subject (of) criticism among a large number of people. I am afraid my statement on a former occasion may have to do with it wherein I followed you in saying that after having given the last Government (primarily a League one) the chance to run it with our support, and the deplorable condition to which we are subjected, I strongly protested against any Government but on party lines. The Maulana addressed a meeting of the Party members and explained that if the League accepted the offer of the Congress to join on the basis of work according to the Congress manifesto, the whole moral of the League would break down. The League, however, has chosen to turn a deaf ear to it and the Government vacancies in the Central Cabinet yet remain so. The non-inclusion of a tribal in the Cabinet left room for propagandas and the Governor himself showed interest in the subject, but the Maulana's statement to the effect that if a properly efficient man was available a tribal would also be taken in may help to remove the fear that was fanned by interested tribal leaders. I need inform you in this connection that in our province the following are the constituent population (1) Hindus, with schedule castes, 45 lakhs schedules castes, 7 lakhs); (2) tribals, about 20 lakhs, and (3) Muslims 34 lakhs (in the included area).

Thanks so much for your inquiry about my health, which continues just as before with blood pressure.

Yours sincerely,
Gopinath Bordoloi

Government House
Shillong,
Assam

PERSONAL & CONFIDENTIAL

April 12, 1950

My dear Mr. Bordoloi,

I am very grateful to you for your kind letter to Fakhruddin. I thought it may be possible for a seat to be found for him within six months; but if the official campus is not likely to favour his nomination there is nothing more to say. It is a pity. We allow various extraneous considerations to usurp our judgement and spoil public work. However, it is not for me to criticise the attitude of the Congress Committee.

You will have received the copies of the telegrams of Jawaharlal and Gopalaswamiji that I had sent earlier today. That takes away a great load from my mind. You should, I think, now proceed with the appointment of a Minister. We can have him earlier than May 1, if you should have no objection. I have no doubt that in the interest of public duty, either of the colleagues mentioned by you, would undertake the extra burden at whatever personal inconvenience that may involve. You will, of course, I fear, have to consult non-official Congress leaders. I do hope they will take a sensible view of things, appreciate the seriousness of the position and let you have a free hand. In any case I am at your absolute service for whatever I might be able to do.

With kind regards and good wishes.

Yours sincerely
Sri Prakasa

The Hon'ble
Shri G.N.Bordoloi

SECRET & PERSONAL

Government House
Shillong
5th May 1947

My dear Mr. Bordoloi,

I hope that you have not had a very tiresome journey back from Delhi and have returned safe and sound. I missed you greatly yesterday, but was much read out at the Assumption Ceremony. I hope that you liked my reply which you may have possibly seen in the press. If not, I will show you a copy when we meet.

I would very much like to see you tomorrow over the eviction issue; and in this connection I have put down my thoughts in the attached note which I have discussed with no one. It is at present meant for your eyes alone. I would be grateful if you will consider the note and discuss it with me. You will notice that I have entirely dropped the idea which I mentioned to you in Delhi and which you felt would, in the present circumstances, be a dangerous one to pursue.

Provided you give me sufficient notice I can free myself from other interviews between 9.30 a.m. and 11.20 a.m. tomorrow by postponing the interviews fixed for that period; or if the morning is inconvenient I shall be free any time in the afternoon that suits you.

More when we meet.

With kind regards,

Yours very sincerely,
A K Hydari

The Hon'ble Srijut Gopinath Bordoloi, M.L.A.,
Prime Minister of Assam

SECRET & PERSONAL

A settlement of the eviction question in Assam is one which will become progressively more difficult of solution the longer it is delayed. That was, I presume, the reason which led H.P.M. to make the recent statesmanlike but unfortunately infructuous attempt. I have read the correspondence between H.P.M. and Mr. Saadulla. I have also had the advantage of talks on this subject in Delhi when H.P.M. met me last, and with Sir Andrew Clow before he left Assam. As a result I have dropped some of my pre-conceived notions in this regard and have been casting about for a possible fresh line of approach which, if acceptable to H.P.M. and to any of his colleagues whom he may wish to consult, after H.P.M. and I here had a talk might form the basis of a fresh discussion with Mr. Saddulla. Needless to say, I have not so far mentioned this topic to the latter.

2. It is greatly in the interests of the Ministry to settle this eviction trouble. While it continues it distracts their energies which, I am sure, H.P.M. and my other colleagues would like to apply towards measures of development for the uplift and prosperity of the people of Assam. Apart from this positive aspect there is a negative aspect also. If the present unlawful movement continues and gathers strength through the further incitement of communal passions and assistance from our next door neighbour we may find that the armed strength at our disposal at present or which may be placed at our disposal by the Central Government, who are themselves pre-occupied with grave troubles in certain other provinces, insufficient to cope with the situation.

3. From the point of view of Mr. Saadulla also a peaceful solution is highly desirable. He must realize, being the man of affairs that he is, that the continuance of the present illegal activities is bound to bring an increasing measure of hardship in terms of life and property on the Muslim elements concerned, in whose behalf he is waging this struggle; he must also realize that in the long run he is bound to lose the fight even if the Muslim League succeed in their objective of Pakistan; for, I think we may take it as settled that Assam, with or without the district of Sylhet, will form part of the proposed Indian Union or Federation by whatever name the future Government of India may be called; and, therefore, it follows that the Government of Assam will be able to rely on support from such a Government should the security of its administration be gravely assailed by unlawful activities within the territories of the province or without or both. Mr. Saadulla's trouble, I imagine, comes from the more hotheaded of his lieutenants who may have support, though we have no proof of that, of certain elements in the Muslim League High Command. On the other hand, it would, I think, be correct to say that there is considerable feeling in Assam League circles that the present activities are leading the mass of Assam Muslims nowhere except into trouble. Our problem, therefore, is to offer terms to Mr. Saadulla which, given his known desire for a settlement, will strengthen his hands in bringing the majority of the Muslim League Committee of Action to support something which he accepts. It is with this background that I place the following possible terms of settlement for H.P.M.'s consideration.

4. My tentative suggestions are:

(1) The Assam League should call off the Civil Disobedience movement.

(2) It should agree that there should be no further immigration for purposes of land settlement into Assam for the next 5 years, no undertaking being given that it will be allowed after this period, as that will depend upon the circumstances then prevailing to which reference is made later.

If the League agrees to the above and offers co-operation in implementing the above, the Ministry on its side would

(i) agree not to evict those who have filtered into Assam up to the 15th of May 1947;

(ii) The Government of Assam would immediately undertake a scientific survey of the land available for settlement in Ministerial Assam i.e. outside the tribal areas, after allowing for sufficient land to be earmarked for the people of Assam of all communities in case the survey shows that there are landless agriculturists in Assam who need land for cultivation. This survey implies that if there are immigrants who have settled on land which it would be injurious in the public interests to cultivate, Government would have the right to shift such squatters to other land which the results of the survey might show as being capable of being brought under cultivation. In this context Government would undertake to build such roads and markets and give such temporary revenue remissions as may be found to be necessary.

(3) To ensure that no further illicit immigration takes place Government would establish posts at all the possible points of entry to check this. In case persons from the areas from which illicit immigration is now taking place wish to visit friends or relatives among the immigrants who have already entered Assam, they would only be allowed to do so by permit which would be valid for a short period. If the permit-holder exceeds the period of stay allowed he would be externed from the province. This is a system which is not unknown in European countries.

To

The Honourable Prime Minister, Assam
Shillong.

Dated, Dibrugarh, the 8th August, 1949

THROUGH THE PRINCIPAL, ASSAM MEDICAL COLLEGE, DIBRUGARH

Honourable Sir,

We, the students of the Assam Medical College, are touched by your fatherly solicitude conveyed to us through our Principal. As true sons of Assam we send our filial affection and respect to you, our God father and beg to assure you that we feel not only happy but proud in our new habitation, and pledge ourselves in all earnestness to be good and disciplined students. We further assure you that we shall spend our time in so moulding our destiny that we make ourselves fit for the service that is expected of us.

Yours faithfully,
Benu Borgohain
President,
Assam Medical College Union
on behalf of the students

Government House
Shillong
8th April 1947

My dear Mr. Bordoloi,

Many thanks for your letter of this morning. I welcome your readiness to have an inquiry made with the co-operation of the Muslim League party, if that is forthcoming. As you feel that in view of your previous statements, you cannot issue another, I feel that in order to make sure that Saadulla and his followers are under no misapprehension as to the situation, I should make it clear to him myself. I therefore propose to send him urgently the enclosed letter which makes the Ministry's position in this respect clear and invites him to make an approach on the subject. Would you be so good as to let me know by return if I have put your attitude correctly in this matter? I sincerely hope that this will lead to his making a definite request.

Yours sincerely,
A. G. Clow

The Hon'ble Sjt. Gopinath Bordoloi, M.L.A.,
Prime Minister of Assam.

DRAFT

In our discussion last night you said that you considered that the Government had, in certain respects, not carried out the policy in respect of evictions announced by your Government and which it is their declared intention to implement. And you indicated that if they were prepared to examine specific allegations of failure in this respect, this might prevent a breach for the time being, with the hope of reaching a satisfactory settlement between the parties later. I communicated the substance of our discussion to the Prime Minister. Mr. Bordoloi has informed me that the Ministry has many times declared that they are willing to have any such question examined by Government with the co-operation of the Muslim League Party, if the opposition is willing to co-operate. I suggest, therefore, that if your party is willing to co-operate, you might send him a statement indicating, as precisely as possible, the points in respect of which the policy accepted by both ministries has not been carried out and which you desire to be examined, so that an inquiry in a manner satisfactory to both sides can be instituted.

Maulvi Muhammad Saadulla, M.L.A.

Shillong
8th April 1947

My dear Sir Andrew Clow,

I have not the slightest objection to your writing to Mr. Saadulla in the manner you have suggested in your draft. In view of the tension that is being created in the country and the processions and meetings held in different parts of Assam for starting civil disobedience don't you consider it advisable to add a line to the draft asking Maulvi Muhammad Saadulla to use his influence against these tendencies?

Yours sincerely,
Sd/- G.N. Bordoloi

His excellency
Sir Andrew Gourlay Clow,
K.C.S.I., C.I.E., I.C.S.
Governor of Assam,
Shillong

Government House
Shillong
8th April 1947

My dear Mr. Bordoloi

Many thanks for your letter. I enclose (1) a copy of the letter you sent this morning and (2) a copy of the letter I sent to Mr. Saadulla. In this the words added have been underlined, and include a sentence to meet your suggestion.

Yours sincerely,
A.G. Clow

The Hon'ble Srijut Gopinath Bordoloi M.L.A.
Prime Minister of Assam.

Shillong
8.4.1947

My dear Sir Andrew Clow,

I am glad to hear from your letter of last night that Maulvi Md. Saadulla's reason for the Civil Disobedience is only our failure to implement the Clause regarding settlement of protected encroachers. We have said many times, that we are prepared to have the same examined by Government with the League party (in the Opposition) if League would co-operate in the effort. In spite of the threatened C.D. I said in my last statement that whether the Muslim League co-operated or not, we shall continue to deal most humanely with the protected immigrants; and that if the C.D. movement was not a plea for extension of Pakistan, the League was bound to co-operate with Govt. for this purpose. I have not heard anything from Maulvi Md. Saadulla, as to what response he will be prepared to give. But it seems to me quite clear that without some response from their side, we cannot go on seeking their co-operation, while they say that they would carry a C.D. against Govt. for its overthrow and in that process hold daily processions, meetings, hoist M.L. flags in Govt. buildings, surround an armed force to destroy it and what is worse insult

H.M.Rev. for having explained the land settlement agreement to the people in Surma Valley. I am therefore of the opinion that if Maulvi Md. Saadulla does not give me chance of acting as you have wished (and I wish it no less) by deploring some of these excesses and wish to give co-operation to Govt. if Govt. wish I cannot issue a second statement so soon after the one I have issued. It would submit Govt. to ridicule if I did it. On the other hand, if I found any conciliatory attitude on the part of the Muslim League, I should most surely seek their co-operation on the points mentioned by you.

I understand Maulvi Md. Saadulla is giving an interview to the Associated Press this morning at 9 a.m. I feel it is on that statement the future relation of Govt. and League would depend.

Yours sincerely,
Sd/- G.N.Bordoloi

CONFIDENTIAL

8th April 1947

My dear Mr. Saadulla,

In our discussion last night you said that you considered that the Government had, in certain respects, not carried out the policy in respect of evictions announced by your Government and which it is their declared intention to implement. And you indicated that if they were prepared to examine specific allegations of failure in this respect, this might prevent a breach for the time being, with the hope of reaching a satisfactory settlement between the parties later. I communicated the substance of our discussion to the Prime Minister. Mr. Bordoloi has informed me that the ministry has many times declared that they are willing to have any such question examined by Government with the co-operation of the Muslim League Party, if the opposition is willing to co-operate. I suggest therefore, that if your party is willing to co-operate, you might send him a statement indicating, as precisely as possible, the points in respect of which you consider that the policy accepted by both ministries has not been carried out and which you desire to be examined, so that an inquiry in a manner satisfactory to both sides can be instituted. *I know that the great majority of people of all communities in Assam would welcome an easing of the present tension and feel sure that, as you said last night, you will do all you can to resolve the differences which have arisen in a peaceful manner.*

Yours sincerely,
Sd/- A.G.Clow

Maulvi Syed Muhammad Saadulla, M.L.A.

The Legislative Assembly of Assam

To

The Hon'ble Srijut Gopinath Bordoloi, M.L.A., and
Member, Indian Constituent Assembly.

GREETING.

The "A Group of Members" of the Assam Legislative Assembly referred to in the Announcement of His Excellency the Governor- General dated the 22nd July, 1947 reposing especial trust and confidence in your integrity, wisdom and ability, have at a meeting held on the 12th August, 1947 elected you the said Hon'ble Srijut Gopinath Bordoloi as a representative of Assam for the purpose of framing a new constitution for India.

In testimony whereof the seal of the Legislative Assembly of Assam is hereunto fixed.

Speaker,
Legislative Assembly Of Assam

GOVERNMENT OF ASSAM

OFFICE OF THE SECRETARY, LEGISLATIVE ASSEMBLY, ASSAM

Shillong, dated 12th August 1947

To

The Hon'ble Srijut Gopinath Bordoloi, M.A., B.L., M.L.A., and Member, Indian Constituent Assembly, Shillong.

Sir

I am directed to send herewith for necessary action, a letter of credentials duly signed by the Hon'ble Speaker.

Your obedient servant,
Secretary, Legislative Assembly, Assam

Prof. G.D. Kapur,
M.B.,M.S.,M.Sc.,F.R.C.S.,F.I.C.S.,
Principal

Assam Medical College
Dibrugarh
Dated 10th August, 49

My dear Shri Bordoloi,

I am grateful to you for your letter of 4th August/49. I conveyed your wishes to the boys and waited anxiously to know their reaction. I am glad the reaction was a healthy one, and I am sending you a copy of it. The building up of a grand hostel under conditions so depressing and forbidding, has been phenomenal, and is the result of personal interest taken by the God father, in the welfare of his charge.

Welcoming H.E. the Governor, in his recent visit I said, "Two eminent accoucheurs have been responsible for bringing forth this fine institution to see the light of the day. Shri Bordoloi, the beloved Premier inaugurated the College on 3rd November 1947 and your Excellency opened the Hospital on 27th February 1949. I would however be failing as a nurse if I do not press for your assistance to avert the dangers your infant is going for. Finance is the sustaining milk and the springs of finance are drying up. A child who has grown for some years developed a measure of immunity but an infant who has not developed its first milk teeth, will succumb moribund of inanition. The Premier and your Excellency are the God fathers and it is only fit that you look ahead to secure your infant, abundance of life and of strength."

My daughter is in Delhi, 21, Barakhamba Road and has only to be informed of your address in Delhi. She writes to me "Your Premier certainly has an inner being and his depths are deeper than ordinary human beings. Contacts with him certainly would be very 'Nirvanic'." So you see both father and daughter are enamoured of your personality.

I am worried about your health. I have a competent physician friend in Delhi and I am writing to him to give you a look up.

With kind regards,

Yours sincerely,
G.D. Kapur

Jorhat Jail
4-2-41

My dear,

Accept my love and affection for the Bihu. Convey it to the small children. You did not write anything about Lily in a single letter, if she is keeping well, ask her about me and write what she says. Are the children in the Doctor's family OK? Although I am not worried to learn that Sarughaynee and Numali are sick. I am a bit concerned. Except to depending on God, there is nothing else for me to do. But it is better to consult Doctor Bhubaneswar and examine Sarughaynee and Numali. Tell Numali that I want him to be examined by Dr. Bhubaneshwar. Please inform about Tarun and Ananda. Now I am writing about myself.

(1) We have started taking vegetarian meal. We have decided not to bring anything but medicine from outside. Other friends of mine are in want of cotton balls. To send us Naveswari type of cotton balls, I had informed Thakkar Bapa, but till today we haven't received. I have not complete seer of yarn. Probably it will be only $3\frac{1}{2}$ powa. In this state, to complete two dhoties, at least another two powas will be needed. I think there are about half a powa of fine yarn at home. With that amount it may be a seer and a half powa. Had I another 1 powa, you could have easily woven three dhoties. Therefore try to get Naveswari cotton balls about one or one and a half seer from Jogeswar Hazarika, address 15 No. Armherst Street, Calcutta. Or, send it to me through VP Parcel to me to the Jorhat Jail address. With this cotton ball you may get your blouse. It will take some time for me to get those yarn. Hence, as soon as you receive this letter, send at least a seer of yarn through Bapa or somebody for any panjabi (Shirt).

(2) Regarding reading books, I did not get any useful books. I have started writing lives of Prophet meant for boys of Bapa's age. As I did not get good books on Buddha and Mahammad, I have purchased some books. But because they were no good ones I need some nice books. Ask Numali to fetch them from the college library or some other place.

(1) Edwin Arnold–Light of Asia

(2) Dr. Rhys David–Buddhism and some other writing of Buddha by this author

(3) Amir Ali's Spirit of Islam

(4) Life of Mohammad by some Muslim author

(5) Asoke–Bring it from Karmavir Nabin Chandra Library.
I shall be able to send books when Bapa comes here.

At present I work about 12 hours daily. $3\frac{1}{2}$ hours in spinning and winding, 1 hour in Geeta recitation, $1\frac{1}{2}$ hours in reading newspaper and Journals and the rest 6 hours I read. Sometimes I stop it. So the time I am spending in such a way that I can't say how it is fleeing.

Sri Gopinath Bordoloi

N.B.: Don't forget to send a box of soap, 3 bottles of coconut oil, 6 strings (mal) of spinning wheel. Be sure that with license I shall not send the gun for less than Rs. 250. Today I have received 1/2 seer of cotton from Bhandari of Burma. Therefore you need not write to Calcutta for fine quality of cotton. If you send one seer of local cotton for me would be enough.

Sri Gopinath Bordoloi

Jorhat Jail
27-3-41

My dear,

Received your letter four days back. As there was nothing to write, I did not reply. On the other hand it will probably be a fortnight of your writing the same.

The other day Dr. Das[1] and Sriman Umesh Chowdhaury[2] must have told Numali that we are fine here. Actually, we are very well. You have written that you are anticipating my release from here ; but I don't wish to go before any negotiation with the British Government. Otherwise I shall have to come back again. To me, we shall have to continue the movement till we achieve full independence. And in that case, whether we stay in or outside the Jail makes no difference. Thinking of all this, I am not so keen to come out of the Jail, so don't think that you will be relieved of the responsibility which has fallen on you. Even if I am released from the Jail, I have no wish to take any responsibility of the duties. Frankly speaking, after I complete my duties to my children, I do not wish to lead a worldly life. But I cannot shirk from the responsibility and therefore I need your help. Although you are uneducated, I cannot but appreciate and love you for the way you have been managing the family till today. Numali and Saru Bapa[3] are always indifferent. But that doesn't mean they are disobedient. Please don't worry over it.

Actually being so far away from home, I have been receiving whatever I wanted. Please don't feel sad. Ask Bapa[4] to do bits of household works and you too think about it. God will guide you properly.

I have about a powa (quarter of a seer) of fine yarn and with rough cotton rolls another powa with me. If possible I shall send it through Dr. on the 27th instant. In another 15 days time, I shall be absolutely without cotton roll, therefore send me another locally made cotton rolls.

Alongwith our dresses, send about $1\frac{1}{2}$ seer of cotton rolls before Bihu. Preferably finer rolls that the ones you have sent now. If you have woven three dhoties, send me two, and if you have woven khadi towel type of Gamochas send me two, because I wish to give one to Fakhruddin Saheb[5]. We will all be wearing new dresses and probably no one will give him because of his religion. I don't know how I am going to change the sacred thread during Bihu. Regarding Phukans[6] biography herewith I am sending a letter to Dina Sarmah[7] after reading the letter if 200 copies can be sold, then ask Numali to send it. If not then Numali will bring the amount of copies he can sell.

There is no comment if Gosainghar is not constructed. I had suggested for a Gosainghar thinking it would be necessary for sacred thread ceremony of Bapa and Monola[8]. If Suru and Numali can do without it, I can also go without it. I shall decide after going home.

Why did you reply to my letter without the children's letters? I enjoy their letters, I keep so busy that there is no time to think of any one. Probably because of this sometimes I see you in my dream. It is in this way. In my dreams I feel myself an outsider as I have only come to enquire about you and will soon be going away from you. But you also want to come alongwith me. Please send the reply with the children's letters.

It is quite natural that Bapa will quarrel. Don't try to change boy's nature, keep an eye on him so that his mind is absorbed in good things. If you can guide him for about four years from now, he will be able to look after himself later on. Boys should be properly guided from this particular period.

Try to sell the car if you get the price at Rs. 475.00. If it gets out of order by parking it in the Company's yard then bring it here. After hearing from Jogesh Dutta[9] send it through Numali's letter as soon as possible. I shall decide it. Umesh also wants to buy the car. I doubt whether I shall be able to write letters to you for the Bihu. Remember me to Dharani,[10] Surya[11], Nila[12] and Hema[13], also Saru, Numali[14] and Saru's wife. Convey my love to the children and also love to you.

I wonder why you are so much worried of thinking that you are ignorant.

How many women are there who know more than yourself? Everybody in the world is busy comparing oneself with another. There are many learned than myself but they are ignorant also. In the same way there are thousand of wretched people who need sympathy and love from you. Therefore whatever you have is the mercy of God and therefore make proper use of it. Then only you are obeying God. Have courage and go on.

With love

Sri Gopinath

N.B. Send Rs. 15 in the next month.

Sri Gopinath

1. Dr. Das—Late Jyotish Das, a noted Congressman and associate of late Gopinath Bordoloi.
2. Sriman Umesh Chowdhaury—Nephew of Bihagi kabi Raghunath Chowdhaury. He was just like a younger brother to Bordoloi.
3. Saru Bapa—Ganesh Chandra Bordoloi, younger brother of Lokopriya Bordoloi.
4. Bapa—Brig. Dhiren Bordoloi VSM, eldest son of late Bordoloi.
5. Fakhruddin Saheb—Fakhruddin Ali Ahmed, Ex President of India.
6. Phukans—Deshbhakta Tarun Ram Phukan.
7. Dina Sarmah—Ex-Editor, Awahan.
8. Monola—Late Girin Bordoloi (nephew of late Gopinath Bordoloi).
9. Jogesh Dutta—A reputed Bengali businessman.
10. Dharani—Dr. Dharani Kanta Baruah, brother-in-law of Lokopriya Bordoloi.
11. Surya—Surya Kanta Baruah.
12. Nila—Nila Kanta Baruah, brother-in-law of Lokopriya Bordoloi.
13. Hema—Hema Kanta Baruah, brother-in-law of Lokopriya Bordoloi.
14. Numali—Ratneshwar Bordoloi, youngest brother of Lokopriya Bordoloi.

Jorhat Jail
30-10-42

Dear Bapa,

Because this space is left, I am replying to your letter. Learn horse-riding and mind that you ride well. As you should not be present in the school, you must be having enough time. Bring tools for carpentry and learn from Numali Khura. You will develop intelligence if you learn to do craftwork. Regarding horticulture read Sutton's book of horticulture so that you learn both theory and practical work. Be sure, that God guides you in all your work. Therefore think of him specially during the period of 'gayatri'. I hope all you children sing the Stotra and songs in the Gosaighar together. During these days of trial look after your brother and sisters with special care. God bless you. Give my love to Babul.

Yours affectionately,
Father

N.B. In my address, you always type Ex-Premier. I dislike it. I shall receive my letter even if you do not write all these.

Sri Gopinath

Letter to his second son Prof. Birendranath Bordoloi

My dear Babul,

On the 9th while I was travelling someone stole away my yellow-coloured attache with all its contents including the punjabee and my old Endichaddar given to me by your mother. Gandhiji's presentation of Anasakti Yoga and late Kamala Miri's bag prepared by himself are the valuables which I have lost. I have been feeling very sad.

You have given me some sizes for shopping–I have lost everything. Please send them again and tell your mother to talk over telephone. Inform Mai Baidew immediately.

Apart from all these, I have faced much trouble because I have lost the medicine.

(1) Tell Numali Dada to prepare an ointment and send me immediately.

(2) Protargol 4% for my eye. Ask Dr. B. Baruah for another medicine like Borotax and send me immediately.

With love

Deuta

6, Ferozeshah Road
New Delhi

CHAPTER V

Articles by Gopinath Bordoloi

A Case for a University in Assam

To be inside the jail gates and to think of the world outside as well all go together; and yet that is the function which I am undertaking today in submitting my opinion on the question of a University for Assam in general, and of the University Bill sponsored by the Government in particular. This should not, therefore, be mistaken for the view of any political party or even of an individual belonging to any party but as one coming from a prisoner who has only made an attempt to study the subject. In a humble way I associated myself with the movement for an independent University in Assam since the very beginning of the movement and hence I feel tempted to express my opinion of it.

It is no doubt true that this movement is a very old one. The whole subject took a concrete shape during the University Commission which functioned sometime in 1915. The late Nabin Chandra Bordoloi was a great advocate of this movement. I well remember an incident which throws some light on the character of a University, the Great Tiger of Bengal, Sir Ashutosh Mukherjee wanted. While coming back from a trip to the Auniati Satra on the North Bank of Gauhati, where his Holiness resided, the late Bordoloi was discussing with Sir Ashutosh Mukherjee about the necessity of establishing a University in Assam. After he had heard the late Bordoloi at length Sir Ashutosh Mukherjee enquired of him whether he would like to have an official University with the Superintendent of Police as its Vice-Chancellor. Things are surely very much different now from what it was then. We have today a vast number of graduates and probably sufficient number of academicians to be able to run a University without creating an officialdom. In the existing subjects which are taught, I am afraid, neither too many nor sufficient to meet the needs of the young man, it is probably possible to create Faculties, Board of Studies and so on. A new University may also be in a position to take charge of Secondary Education. But the fundamental question as to whether (1) A University is at all wanted, and if so (2) whether it should be completely Government controlled or should be as autonomous as possible is yet a subject to which we address ourselves.

In trying to answer the first question we have to satisfy ourselves as to how far such an institution will be beneficial to the people. There can be no doubt that the bulk of the revenue for running this institution shall have to be found from the toiling masses of the villages. It is also true that University Education, as it is today, hardly affects the villages, and if it at all does so indirectly it creates more evil than good. The educated man instead of keeping in touch with and improving the village has left it to indulge in the comforts of the town. The whole outlook of the so-called educated man has been one of self-indulgence and self-aggrandisement with neglect of and often times at the cost of the interests of the villagers. This is of course an indictment against all modern higher education. But it does not mean that we should perpetuate a recognized evil, or any rate should not take it into serious consideration when we are out on venture of higher education. To me, however, it is quite possible to bring into our society a new outlook–an outlook of service and duty to our fellowmen, with a properly constituted educational centre. Sacrificing leadership is as much necessary for this service of our masses as it is necessary to feed and clothe men. It is very necessary that our educated youngmen should be men with full knowledge of the needs and necessities of the masses and of the means to satisfy them. They should be the fountain-head of the basic culture of communal unity and should represent a common meeting group where all communal differences have found their settlement.

They should be able to breathe freedom and exhibit character in all that they would feel, think and will. We can expect such youngmen to lead us and guide us and any institution that would train them should receive our support. Does the present University Bill satisfy this test; the production of this type of men to be of service to the masses so that they may note the money necessary for the institution? I am afraid the answer will be a most disappointing 'no' after all the Bill seems at nothing more than the establishment of a replica of an ordinary Examining University with all the worst features (which I discuss below) added to it. It may undoubtedly be argued that the University Bill must necessarily contemplate only a form and that such a consummation will be possible only by the character of the people working it. I have only to say in reply that the Calcutta University has that form and, I believe is worked by eminent men of character and learning; why should we then pay for another institution–apparently one–much worse every way? I am not also unmindful of the fact that the Calcutta University is going to be deprived of control of the Secondary Education in High Schools. But the Bengal Secondary Bill has not yet been passed; and if it is passed its power over Bengal Schools alone will be taken away. In any case, we might ourselves have a good Board of Secondary Education for Assam High Schools pending the establishment of a real University. Should we, for the mere apprehension that we will be deprived of the control of the Calcutta University which is being in turn controlled by the Government of Bengal, be in a hurry to accept any form of University that is proposed? My opinion is that I would prefer to wait for a year or two if necessary to bring in a real University rather than accept now a body which may be a source of more evil than good to the country at large.

I cannot, however, agree with some of the deputationists from Sylhet that there should not be any University in Assam simply because some population of a district is against it. And that leads me to the discussion about the origin of the University Movement in Assam and the location of the site for a University in Assam.

The Hon'ble Education Minister has stated in his introductory speech that the province has been after this matter for the last 25 years. It has been free from incubus of party politics. He would have to say that the Movement is entirely confined to the people of Assam proper with the Hill districts till about a decade after when it was taken up by Hon'ble Moulbi Munawar Ali. The object of the whole Movement, till it was side-tracked by Cunningham's report, was the establishment of a residential University at Gauhati with the Cotton College converted into a University.

The exigencies of the situation viz, the establishment of many of the colleges and educational institutions in the Province may lead to some change in the proposed character of the University, viz from one of entirely residential nature than proposed to one of a teaching and affiliating University. In my opinion it is even today possible if the people of Sylhet would agree to a new University in Assam, to convert the two colleges in the Province to be made into a constituent college of the University, with the University controlling the teaching of the colleges. It may even be possible to allow private colleges to be such constituent colleges provided Managing Committees make them over to the University under such terms and conditions as may be agreed upon. In the alternative,we may have a Board of Examination and affiliation, for colleges whose teaching would not be undertaken by the University. But in any case, the public opinion for the University has been that it cannot be the any other centre but Gauhati which should be the seat for the University.

I am disposed to think that the people of Sylhet have as much right to remain under Calcutta University as the people of Assam to have University of their own. The same principle of selfdetermination which would give Sylhet the right to remain with the Calcutta University, should also give Assam the right to have her own University. This is perfectly consistent with the Congress principle of distribution of provinces under linguistic and cultural basis. I, therefore, feel that if Sylhet or even Silchar want to be outside the jurisdiction of the new University they should be free to do so. But the opposition of Sylhet or Silchar cannot be an adequate reason for the rejection of the University as a whole. This alternative may be the surrender of fee receipts of the University so for as the examiners of those areas are concerned but Government should be able to find this amount if it feels the necessity of establishing a University for those who want it.

The conclusion, therefore, is clear that if a right type of University is to be established in Assam it must have its seat at Gauhati.

The answer to the second question will depend on the nature of Government, that would guide a particular society. A totalitarian state whether pseudo-democratic or otherwise would like to control every activity inside a state whether governmental or otherwise. The finished products, whether goods, chattel or human being must be according to the pattern sought for by a few leaders of the society and any deviation would be surely put down by providing for state interference in all details. The fundamental outlook of these states being achievement of a particular object e.g. the maintenance of domination or acquisition of the same by evil means, they would harness all the resources of the state towards the fulfilment of that object. In the sphere of education they would shape the policy in such a manner as to create educated youths who should know nothing but the views of the state as conceived by their totalitarian leaders, and all their initiative, education and character would be directed to nothing else but what their leaders would want of them. In such a state the higher education must be guided by such people as Government would choose, and in order to see that the body corporate does not go astray the state would preserve the right of interference in details at every stage.

The defect of such a system, whatever might be thoroughness and efficiency of their products in some particular direction, is much too obvious. In concentrating upon a particular like of study, and in attempting to develop a particular type of character, other finer subjects of perception and understanding are lost by non-use or misuse.

Freedom of thought, the highest gift of God to a human being, is bound to go, by Government which cannot be anything but derogatory for anybody of respectable people. It provides for interference in all details of the University by (academic and administrative) governmental direction. I don't find such provisions even in the local self Government and Municipal Acts. Analogous provisions in other University Acts (e.g. the Delhi University Acts) leave this power of interference with the Chancellor of the University : but even there, the ultimate power is out of "advice" only. There is no question of forcing the University Authority of whom the Chancellor also is one, to adopt a line of action determined by the Government of the day. I cannot think of a worse interference into the administration of a self-governing institution than that provided in Clause 8 of the Bill.

Another provision that passes my understanding is in reference to the affiliation of colleges. The University, according to the bill, is only a recommendatory body: it is the Government of the day which apparently would accord the final sanction. It is clear that Government would not be satisfied with the opinion of the University experts for the maintenance of which they are going to deprive the poor rate-payers of the countryside of fair portion of state revenue, but would consider the Education Minister fitter persons to do this job. This provision is probably one which is absent in any other University Act and which only shows to what extent, the sponsors of the bill wanted to subordinate higher education to their sweet will.

It may be argued that much of these powers are enjoyed by the Government of Bengal after amending Act in 1923. Those who know anything about the history of this legislation know also the protest of the Calcutta University in this matter, and the roar of the Tiger of Bengal Sir Aushotosh Mukherjee in that great, unique and dignified utterance, which appeared in the shape of an open letter to Lord Lyttons and which drew the unstinted admiration from all, throughout the length and breadth for its advocacy for freedom of the University.

Another evil, that is apparent to me, is the recognition of communal representation in the authorities of the University. I quite recognize the importance of teaching or creating Board of Studies for subjects like Persian and Arabic through learned persons and Arabic Scholars, but I don't see any reason why is it necessary to reserve any quota of members from any particular community in any academic body on any body which will be concerned with academic administration. In order that I may not be misunderstood, I want to make it clear that I should not have the slightest objection to have all the fellows from the Muslim Community or from the Scheduled or Tribal Communities provided the cause of higher education is properly furthered. Personally, I feel that in the Government University no discrimination of caste, creed, colour or race should be maintained; an attempt should always be made to secure the best men to serve and advise this body. I also think even without legislative enactment a fair representation of qualified persons of all communities in that body will be possible. I am afraid under the enactment by Government, the membership of the senate has been understood more as conferment of rights and privileges than as one of responsibilities and service. If I object to the introduction of the principle of communal representation in University, it is for the only reason that we may transfer the atmosphere of Assembly politics into the sacred abodes of learning and that we might be responsible for injecting into our youths the virus of communal poison. I feel the bill is vitiated by the recognition of a principle which has till now I worked to the detriment of communal harmony in our body politic.

I am definitely of the opinion that with these two great evils viz. the complete affiliation of the body and the communal representation, embodied in the bill, a University brought into being under it is likely to do more harm than good.

As against such grave evils there is not one little thing to be spoken in its favour at present at least so far as Assam proper is concerned. Although the Bill provides for teaching, it gives no indication of adopting of any college as the basic institution for University teaching. In view of severe Government control provided for in the Bill, it does not seem that the present Government will at any times surrender their prestige of governing these colleges to an autonomous body. I personally feel (as a tentative scheme drawn up by me for the Assam Association indicated) that it would not involve much additional expenditure to do this with M.A. classes in all the Science and Arts subjects now taught in the Cotton College. Today I would even make some selection in the subjects taught, the expenditure will be lesser than what is now spent in the college, although more initial expenditure will be necessary for equipment and library. Then again although mention of subjects is there in the enumeration of the various faculties, there is hardly any indication in the Bill that any subject that will be suitable for study according to the circumstances and needs of the Province for preservation of its culture will be taken up in the near future. I do not know if the Education Minister in his speeches gave any indication of his desire to initiate any course of study or technology, consistent with the peculiar needs and culture of the people.

One grave omission in the Bill, and a circumstance, which casts grave reflection on the author of the Bill is its silence regarding the site. I have shown that if the University is at all wanted it is for the people of Assam proper. In modern India, Assam is the only Province and Assamese are the only people without a cultural centre for higher education; and yet it is not known why a site, which was selected by the University Committee, is hoary with antiquity, and the modern seat of learning could not be fixed upon as the abode of the University. It is obvious that party politics is at the abode of this move. Already there seems to be an attempt to fix its location in Shillong. I do not propose to dilate this point. Then with the existing powers of the siems, there is hardly any independent territory for the site of a University unless of course it was to be an affiliating and examining University only. The only first grade college is surely not good enough for the provision for teaching higher sciences and degrees being only a private college under the management of the missionaries. It, therefore, surpasses my understanding how and why such a site could be seriously thought of for the seat of any University. Shillong, therefore, could be anything else but the seat of an examining and affiliating University and the opinion of the people who vote for this as a site can have no room for misunderstanding.

I do not know whether the Bill could be so altered by the legislators as to make it acceptable to those who require this University, and in the lines pointed out above. But if it were not possible, the best thing for any right thinking person would be to oppose the Bill. We should be no party in inviting evil. I personally feel that the Government would do well to drop such a Bill.

On Gandhiji's Birthday

Gandhiji is completing his seventieth year and his birthday falls today. It is worth our while to ponder over the greatness and glory of this unique life.

In the midst of this devastating war, with the political make-beliefs and diplomatic intrigues, the simplicity and directness of Gandhiji's methods are making a stronger appeal to the minds of all thinking people. The impending destruction of mankind as a result of the pursuance of the former methods is forcing on us the truth and reality of the latter. It is becoming clearer every day that the old order where countries and nations must not only live as equals to one another but must also cease to think, speak and act in terms of materials exploitation of the weaker by the stronger.

The difficulty of attaining this ideal will be readily realised from the fact that in theory this ideal was supposed to have been guiding the League of Nations, all the time when this impending catastrophe was in the making, and how feeble its voice has been in preventing it. Russia was indeed experimenting on a new ideology, and not a few thoughtful people of the world turned their eyes to the land of the Soviet Republic for the ushering in of a new era of peace and contentment into this world. The recent activities of the Russian Government, however, have disillusioned many; and although as politicians we may have been wise enough not to be too critical about its present activities in Poland and elsewhere, the fact probably remains that the Russian ideology cannot be the basis of a new world order.

It is quite patent that the basic reason for this failure is that there is in the minds of all the modern nations an inherent belief in violence, exploitation, race-hatred and many other evils, which, if they existed in any degree in any society of individuals, we would have been living in a "state of nature". It has never been realised fully that what can be evil in a society of individuals can be equally an evil in a society of groups of individuals. It is undoubtedly recognised in all civilized societies that a man must not steal; must not covet his neighbour's property and not do any other things which will wrong his neighbour's interests. May we believe in loving our neighbours as we do ourselves. But so far as nations are concerned not only the principle of an eye for an eye and a tooth for a tooth, of five bombs in one would continue, but it would also never be considered wrong to deprive a nation of all its wealth and prowess by means of force or hold a nation in subjugation by force against its determined will to be free. It seems that nations need not have any conscience for doing the right thing by its neighbours and that, as there is no power or force behind to create such a conscience, the world must live in this conflict of carnage and destruction.

Does the Gandhian ideology furnish any answer to this question? Surely it does; and however difficult the solution may be an immediate objective, it is quite clear that nothing but the recognition of such ideals will be able to remove from this world this great evil of world catastrophe. It is quite clear that a thing like "national conscience" based on the consciousness of equal rights of all nations of the world–big or small-must come to all nations; and as by the nature of things physical force cannot achieve it–for it would mean only the installation of another superior state in arms–the basic sanction for developing this conscience must be moral. Mahatmaji, like all the other greatest religious preachers of the world, has rightly placed the moral stimuli in individuals on a higher plane than the physical. But his sense of the practical has led him to travel beyond the domain of the world alone. It has made him launch many schemes the adoption of which might develop in individual as well as in the nation the moral sense necessary to rid them of any tendency towards exploitation. The individuals of India and the nationhood of India are his immediate concern; but that does not mean that, subject to such variations as the climatic conditions and culture of any particular nation may necessitate, the ideals experimented upon by him cannot be held to be good for other nations also. If he could forge a weapon for the independence of India at Shegaon, he could as well create the moral force for the emancipation of the world from its present day annihilating and barbarous tendencies.

Truth and non-violence are simple enough words in themselves and their dictionary meaning is easily available. But what is not available and will not be available to many is their implication in the realities of life, even of individuals. How many of us have been able to follow in life all that these words stand for in their full implication? But, while this training in non-violence and truth is so very difficult in individuals, the difficulty of creating a moral "national conscience"is still greater. But that is also exactly the reason why we must have such a conscience in the nations, that they may cease to live the brute life that they are living.

It is no doubt admitted that the present day economic order in Europe is one factor which is more responsible for existing mentality of the European nations than anything else. Exploitation of the non-mechanised and the less mechanised nations by the mechanised and the more mechanised ones has led to the installation of what is known as "capitalism". Under this order the world must be made to exist for those nations who have been imbued with capitalist conscience, in other words, Imperialism. The standards of life of some have been raised to a so-called high level resulting in the lowering of many others to a state of starvation and nakedness. But while these capitalists of different nations reduce three-fourths of the population of the earth to that abject condition, can they remain in any state of peace? The answer has been furnished by the present day war. Russia did give some exhibition of its intolerance of the above methods; but such are the evils of a mechanised State that, in spite of its anti–imperialistic ideology, it is probably falling into the same pit from which it wanted to extricate itself.

A new economic order must therefore be brought into existence, where any kind of exploitation would not be possible. The moral conscience of man must be so trained that in place of the idea of unholy competition and exploitation of his neighbour, service to him and society must find full scope. Mechanisation should be avoided or atleast the evils resulting therefrom should be reduced to the lowest limit. Man must live by the sweat of his brow, and such leisure as is available must be utilised for the culture of the spirit, which alone would make the existence of a real non-exploiting mentality possible. It is only in an atmosphere of this kind of non-exploiting and non-violent national conscience can grow, resulting in world peace.

In his village home at Shegaon Mahatmaji is trying to solve the riddle of the world. May God give him long life to bring up to the unthinking and unconvinced nations of the world the great truth of his great doctrine, and to usher in a new world order of peace and good will among the nations of the world.

Our Hills Brethren of Assam

While the whole of India buzz with the talk of the Pakistan or its antidote, very few seem to cast any thought about the surroundings of a Province which in itself comes for so little consideration for the rest of India in any connection excepting perhaps for showing that the Province as the Eastern Frontier of India should come within the sphere influence of some rival "Sthan" or "Dom". The authors of the nauseating partition schemes display how vague are their ideas about the country they want to include in their schemes and the people who inhabit it. It is no doubt true that there is not much in the frontier Hills of Assam to catch the news of the day: there are no frontier raids and no mysterious kidnapping and no attempt to extort sensational ransom from captives, and no Fakir or Ipi to break the monotony of a placid British ruler and no connecting link between various independent and semi-independent tribes to revive in anybody the vision of a great communal kingdom. Yet if our minds could be unburdened of these communal consideration, and all our ambition not confined to the distribution and redistribution of only the British possessions in India in terms of what our relations should be with the independent and semi-independent clans and tribes living on the North Eastern Frontier of India as much as with those who are living on its North Western Frontier. The question, it seems to me, is rapidly becoming a live one.

Japan seems to have obtained a permanent footing in Indo-China, and with her avaricious eyes rivetted on the mineral and other natural wealth of Burma and Upper Assam, Assam may cease, in the near future, to be quite the land of oblivion, that has hitherto been her lot to be in reference to her relation with the rest, Indian India. It is not known how long Thailand or even British Burma will continue to play the buffer states for the safety of India; but danger would be nearer home if the Japanese were to occupy the South-Western strip of China, which borders Assam. But apart from the question of international politics, a living and growing State must take serious note of her neighbours, however insignificant they may be, and must be able to determine its policy in reference to them. The fact that all this thinking is done for us now by our imperialist rulers is not only not a sufficient reply to the question itself, but would only indicate our apathy for the great movement for Independence; for no independent nation can do without giving serious thought to the question of her relationship with her neighbours.

The importance of the question to the Province itself can well be understood by a study of the map of Assam. A relief map of Assam would show that the mighty Brahmaputra having scooped down to a depth of several hundred feet in several places majestically flows through various altitudes to the sea with a bed, which lay in places from one to five miles in the winter and to fifteen to sixteen miles in some places in summer. Many rivers both big and small again through various altitudes run from the Northern Hills to the South, and from the Southern Hills to the North to meet the main river Brahmaputra. It will be seen that the actual valley of the Brahmaputra from North to South is not even more than forty-fifty miles in breadth, in most places. Beyond this valley in both the South and the North range after range of hills rise interrupted only by small plains in between till in the North the Himalayan range is reached and in the South an altitude of 6000 ft. is reached. The hills in the South, however, again run down quite steep to meet the valley of the Surma below only to reach in the East and the South other ranges inhabited by hill clans and strange tribes up to the borders of Burma. In the slopes of these hills and sometimes at the tops have lived for centuries, people with varying degrees of civilization and progress, and who through the ages in remote left some impression and at other times even shaped the civilization of the more civil and less hardy people of the plains of Assam.

Not to speak of being able to describe the particular character of all such tribes and sub-tribes and clans and their mode and outlook of life separately, it is difficult even to name all of them, such a wide variety of them inhabit these hills. You have among them ferocious head-hunters, who even indulge in toxicating drinks and would dance the dance of death before starting for their orgies of murder and cruelty. You would, on the other hand, also meet docile and shy semi-nudes, who would shun even the sight of people other than their own clans-men, just as any deer in the hills would do. You have among them fastidious "moderners" draped in varieties of colour; elsewhere you will meet people the major part of whose wardrobe yet consist of nothing else but barks of trees to hide their nakedness. Their customs and manners and their mode of life are so various and different that we should leave this interesting subject to the anthropologists to whom the Hill Tribes of Assam have presented most interesting study. The British civilians among whom men like Lyall, Dr. Hutton and Shakespeare also encouraged by fat grants from the Government of Assam have written beautiful monographs on about fifteen or sixteen such tribes, all of them of absorbing interest to any student of human race. But even these works are not at all exhaustive of all the tribes and clans; e.g. we do not know of many good books on the tribes living on the Northern ranges of the Brahmaputra Valley. The complete absence of interest of the Indians of the plains, particularly of the Assamese, is evidenced by the fact, that beyond a few stray and inaccurate articles in journals appearing from the pen of some adventure travellers there is hardly any literature worth the name written on these brethren of ours.

For a broad understanding of the location of these tribes, without any pretension to the knowledge of the sub-tribes and clans which compose them, one has merely to have agreed the relief map of Assam before him. To the North of the Brahmaputra beyond the plains or the valley portion, we have the following tribes from the West to the East. The Bhutias who extend from Bengal border to the Western portion of the Darrang District of Assam, then we have the Akas, and the Daflas, who occupy hills North of the Darrang Districts, the Miris of the hills and then Abors occupy the North portion of the District of Lakhimpur, and then lastly by the Mismis who occupy the Sadiya frontiers and the Northern hills.

We should, however, remember that each of the above named tribes include many sub-tribes and clans, the above mentioned divisions, being more or less only epithets which have been traditionally handed down from the time of the Assam Kings to represent clusters of tribes having some affinity and occupying some kind of geographical boundaries. Similarly, to the South of the Brahmaputra we start with the Garos from the borders of Bengal, then Khasias (with scores of clans), then we come to the Jaintias, then the Kacharis, the Nagas of various tribes, then Kuki Nagas. Further south of the Kacharis are the Lusheic Kukis, and their east and South are the famous Manipuris.To further East and South are probably tribes who are known as Singfous, nearer to Burma than Assam. Speaking for all these tribes it can be generally stated that the Bhutias in the North and Khasias and Jaintias and the Kacharis in the South of the Brahmaputra did consolidate themselves as to be recognized on status with either kings or ruling at some period of time or other. The rest, led by various clan leaders and chieftains had hardly acquired the status, which we generally associate with suzerainty.

Most of these people live a sub-human life. The more primitive of them live only on roots and on hunting. Others carry on "jhum" cultivation, but they hardly grow cereals enough to carry them for the year. The Nagas carry on terrace cultivation with small spades–a task which appears almost impossible to us. The yield is scarcely sufficient for a whole year. Yet they are not on the whole a complaining lot, and pass their time in apparent contentment. Excepting the Khasi, the Garos and some Nagas who seem to adapt themselves to some change, they remain as they were ages ago. Their main crops are cotton, lac, red pepper and other minor produces. One can well imagine how difficult life must be with these people who from the earliest dawn to the evening twilight like the fowls of the air and the beasts of the jungles.

The old rulers of Assam and their Hindu priests knew, as our present British rulers and Christian Missionaries know, very much more about these tribal people than most of us choose to know. As rulers they had and have to maintain a certain policy in relation to the neighbouring and frontier tribes however difficult the task might be. In the earliest period about which some authentic history can be constructed some of these tribes must have acquired solidarity over larger area and must have formed kingdoms extending far and wide into the plains. The elephant army that was Kamrupa's contribution to the war at Kurukshetra is supposed to be a gift from a great kingbelonging to the Kachari tribe the hill habitat of the race of which is Cachar Hills, which as pointed out above, extended from the borders of Sylhet and Jaintia Hills on the West to the Naga Hills and Lumding on the East and the North; modern Silchar lies in the Southern boundary of these hills. That the Kacharis had considerable supremacy throughout the whole of Assam is borne out by the fact that representatives from that stock are found in large numbers in all the districts of Assam except perhaps Sylhet. Other tribal Kingdoms with tribal kings of ancient times about which we read, are King Ban of modern Tezpur, Bhismak, King of Kundilnagar (Modern Sadiya–one of the easternmost British possessions), of Ghatatkacha and so on. It is, however, clear that the all embracing power of Aryanism had brought these Kingdoms with their mighty kings under the magic of the Aryan civilization in the same manner as it was doing in the Southern India. The existence of a pilgrimage known as Parashuram Kunda in the far east corner of India with the legend connected with it only proves that the whole province of Assam came within the Aryan region from the most ancient time.

Coming to more historical times we find the kings of Assam carrying on detailed negotiations with the tribal Kings in the South of the Brahmaputra for their protection, as well as for the protection of these Kings against the invasion of the Muslims engaged in the extension of the Muhammadan Kingdom of Delhi. Thus, we read very interesting stories of embassies being sent by the Ahom, Raja Rudra Singha to the Raja of Tripura, the King of Jaintia, the King of Khyriem (Khasi) and so on, with a view not only to cultivate friendship with these brother chieftains, but also to create as it were a league of these powers to fight the common enemy. We read how various presents were exchanged between these royal families, how sometimes daughters of the royal families were given in marriage to the princes of the royal blood including those of Manipur. The Ahom Kings were indeed astute politicians–a few with a stamp of Machiavellianism in them. In order to protect their subject in the borders of the tribal kingdom, they established (what they called) "Kouths" or forts in all important places, where they stationed troops under properly qualified commanders. Occasional allies by these hillmen, who generally resorted to them either for failure of crop or for epidemics among their cattle were not quite rare in those times and these soldiers had sometimes hard times to beat off these hillmen engaged in lifting cattle and granaries from the more peaceful subjects of the plains. The work done by the Vaishnava Satras, which were supported by big grants from the Kings for more cordial relationship with the tribes and for their ultimate conversion to the worship of a loving God, was even greater. These Vaishnava Satras had as they have even devotee- celibates trained in the religion and culture of Vaishnavism and they sent out these devotees as missionaries to the borders and oftentimes to the hills to preach the religion of Bhagabat and create converts. Lakhs were thus converted and today they form part of the Hindu society of Assam. The vigour with which this missionary work was pushed from Sylhet can well be understood by the conversion to the religion of Chaitanya Dev of a whole race like the Manipuris who live within the impenetrable fortresses of hills, for a hundred miles from the plains on any side. It should be noted that the process employed either by the Kings or the devotees were never violent, coercive or aggressive. The Assam Kings did hardly think of extending their kingdoms into the hill regions; we do not hear of any expedition that characterize the British regime, and the lure of riches in forests and minerals did not trouble the self-contented Kings of Assam. The Vaishnava missionaries were as selfless as they were painstaking. They taught them cleanliness and hygiene, made them give up intoxicating and unwholesome food, sometimes, taught them letters and some even lived with them. Is it any wonder, therefore, that practically the whole of the Miris numbering more than a lakh and a half that had come down from the hills, thousands of Kacharis who had lived in the plains from time immemorial, practically all other hill tribes living on the borders of Assam should embrace Hinduism and that we should find among these brethren of our faith and devotion to the cult they adopted than in the skeptical educated Hindu. And to those, who value a common culture and communal unity among the people, no less pleasant is the voice of persistent protest that is being raised by this lovable lot against the attempt of the present Government to snatch them away from the bosom of an ancient culture which had nurtured them for ages by giving them the new name "Tribals" with a view to create disruption, isolation and strife among the people that had formed and was gradually forming part of a unified and united community.

The policy of the old Assam rulers in reference to these tribes underwent a thorough change with the establishment of the British rule in Assam. The non-aggressive attitude of the Assam Kings is immediately followed by a systematic policy of aggressive territory-grabbing of all places which might yield immediate or ultimate profit. The hill people, always afraid of the white man and his followers–the Gurkha soldiers would not easily give any cause for conflict, but it is not difficult for a powerful ruler to find excuse to bring them into such. These excuses may not be as ridiculous as those found by Hitler or Musolini before they launched their attack; but more often than not, they bear the same impress. Sometimes the cause is insult to and murder of missionaries, the attack on an "ally" of the British Government by an alien chief is oftentimes another, encroachment of the boundary erected by the British Government is a third cause, and maladministration by such chiefs over their subjects, and many others are other causes. In a rare case like that of Rani Gaidalu, a social revolution is set up as a plea for interference. A clearer analysis in each case would, however, show that expansion of possessions, consolidation of prestige or avarice for the unknown wealth were the root cause of such activities. The method pursued to attain these objects is quite simple. The political agents, often young officers, who are statisticians in the frontier strike up friendship with some tribal chiefs, with whom gifts in cigars and opium from the British side and rare gems and decorated articles from the other were exchanged. The friendly chief probably to harm or subdue one of his rivals, satisfies the agent about the harm done to an ally; the result is an expedition and murder of some of the tribesmen, and gradual expansion of British possessions soon follows. It may be an information to many that during the last twenty years an area of about 20 miles by 180 miles have been ceded to the British territory (Balipara Frontier Tracts) from the possession of the Akas, Daflas, Miris, Abors and Mishmis by a process similar to the above. In the Northern and Eastern portion expedition against the Abors and Kukis were undertaken some twenty three years ago, with similar result in pushing the frontiers. We do not propose to mention here the expedition that were led against the Bhutanese and the Manipuris fifty years ago nor the manner in which places like Shillong came to be the British possessions. The British frontier boundaries are, therefore, a yearly expanding commodity, and all this is happening at the cost of the poor brethren of ours living in the hills. By now all our neighbouring tribesman have been so cowed down in their morale that it is only because the British Government think that no more territories are necessary that some of these tribes have been able to retain their independence.

And it has been quite convenient and easy for the British Government to do so. The Central Government is maintaining a mobile regiment known as the Assam Rifles, the cost of the maintenance of which are shared between the provincial and Central Government. A proposal of making over this whole unit to the control of the provincial Government matured in 1939, but with the continuance of the war the power of control has entirely been kept with the Central Government by an Act of the Central Legislature in the beginning of this year. The large portion of this regiment remains in the frontier to maintain the morale of the tribes and the smaller portion remains in the labour districts to guard the moral of the labourers, and we can be sure that their effect upon either is the same.

A further examination of the British policy in reference to these tribes would show that the British would not allow any outsider to go and meddle with these tribes. These even casually conversant with the Government of India Act, 1935 know how the Viceroy through the Governors maintain irresponsible control over these tribes by creating what are now technically called "Excluded Areas". In Assam, we have also, what are known as "Partially Excluded Areas". The latter areas are indeed an anomaly, there the people have representation in the legislatures; but yet Governor retains certain irresponsible powers said to be necessary for the protection of the tribes. Thus the Garo Hills, the Khasi, the Jaintia Hills and the Mikir Hills are Partially Excluded Areas with five representatives in the Provincial Legislative Assembly in a house of four hundred and eight. But so far as the powers of the Government in reference to immediate ejectment of an outsider is concerned they are equally alike in the fully or Partially Excluded Areas. Besides these, there are the frontier tracts which as we have already seen, are nothing more than tribal areas under the control of the Government of India. All these areas are close preserves for the British officers and possibly their Assistant. They rule there undisputed over all they survey, and none is allowed access into these areas except through some passport. It is difficult to understand all the reasons that lie behind this policy of exclusiveness; but protection of these tribals themselves are put forward as an ostensible plea. It is no doubt true that they do require protection, and our Indian merchants and traders, mostly drawn from other Provinces do indeed exploit them. But who will protect them from the exploitation, if any of the rulers themselves ? The Indians hardly know anything as to what is happening to these people within the hill fortresses either under or outside the administration of the British rulers.

The Missionaries, however, are exceptions to this close surveillance by the British officers or the British political agents. I think it is for this reason that people associate missionaries as precursors of British rule in any savage country. It is true, however, that they have done great service to these people. The Khasis and the Lushai, (Kukis), the Garos and the Nagas, the Mikirs and the Kacharis have all enough reasons to be grateful to them. Yet they develop in these tribes a culture, which is not only alien to their nature, but actually prevent their association and unification with the world of the Indians, in which, in course of time, they must live, more and have their being. A deplorable isolationism is developing in these Christian tribals, so much so, that in spite of all that the Missionaries have done for their moral, educational, and economic uplift, their activities have hardly become sufficiently popular among the rest of the tribals.

But the great pity is that we, the Indians, whether of the Province or outside it, have not, with a few solitary and notable exceptions, thought about these brethren of ours. Those of us, who think about them, think only as to how cheap we could purchase the cotton, the lac, the red pepper etc. and other raw materials they bring out to the market. And yet there is so much to be thought about them. The dreamer of an independent India must also dream how they are going to deal with these tribals, whether they would continue the policy of aggression by working on the fear, envy, and hatred of these tribes and develop isolationism in them, or whether they would adopt and try to raise the moral and economic standard of these people and concede to them equal rights with the rest of the people of India. The humanitarian organisations have even now vast fields for their activity; for no less than a million of these brothers living as they do in a most primitive stage cry for education, sanitation, medical relief, economic uplift and what not. Will India now think of them?

Assam Looks Ahead

Assam, the Easternmost province of India, has been recently much in the news on account of the political controversies centred round Sections and Groupings arising out of the British Cabinet Mission's recommendations in the well-known State Paper of May, 1946. The controversy has led to curiosity, which in its turn has evoked keen interest among largely scattered circles about Assam's past, present and future. People with a sympathetic interest and looking at things from a wider point of view are anxious to know more about the historical, social, cultural and economic aspects of this North-Eastern province of India which, so to say, gate-crashed' into the arena of publicity since the Japanese invasion of 1944 and has ever been looming large in the context of political and defence considerations.

Assam with an area of over 67,000 sq. miles and a total population of nearly 11 million people has in the course of a century developed into a territory with distinctive geo-physical features and characteristics of its own. These are apparent even to the most superficial tourist and casual visitor who is struck by the mighty and bounteous Brahmaputra and the imposing arrays of foothills of the great Himalayas in the Northern and Eastern parts of the Province. Dense forests and rich vegetations with almost tropical monsoon climate and a number of small rivers watering the broad valley, have been a striking physical feature of this part of India for ages gone by.

Looking back beyond the centuries and scores of centuries and even farther than that, into the historical and mythological past of Assam, the references in the two Epics and the much later chronicles after the Christian era,.provide ample material to any dispassionate student about the ancient and highly flourishing civilization of the Brahmaputra Valley which was largely co- existent with the Kingdom of Kamrup in its glorious and mighty days. Even before the Aryan races entering through the North-West spread over and settled down the broad expanse of the Indo-Gangetic Valley, Assam had developed distinctive culture and civilization with peculiarities of its own. Later on the Aryan and Tibeto-Mongolian cultural fusion produced a synthesis and rhythm and gave a distinct shape and colour to the racial, cultural and linguistic development to the later generations of the people of Assam dwelling on the highlands and in the valleys as distinguished from the predominantly Aryan, Dravadian and other racial and cultural evolutions in other parts of India. The shape of things in Assam and the adjacent territories from the Karatoya to Patkai has been largely determined by the impact and influence of the Tibeto-Mongolian and Aryan people and their gradual evolution into a particularly distinctive type not to be seen in any other part of India. The fruits and features and the rich heritages of this fateful fusion in the dim historical past persists till today and give the broad masses of the Assamese people a typical and unique personality within the broader ambit of India's four hundred million.

Historically speaking Assam had throughout ages resisted conquest from the West and defeated waves after waves of invaders. The farthest of penetration by any foreign invader was done by Mir Jumla, the Moghol General, who however ultimately met his Stalingard at Gohigaon. During the peak of the Assam's monsoon weather he and his soldiers most of whom were stricken with malaria diseases had to beat hasty retreat after exacting a few face saving devices. During the long and glorious Ahom rule Assam became the valuable link between the Eastern and Western territories of her flanks, while her orientation was on the whole a balanced one without leaning too much on either side. This position was maintained over a long period of Ahom rule which gave the country stable administration, peace and prosperity until early in the 19th century. Internal squabbles, dynastic dissensions and internal revolutions invited Burmese invasions from the East and the British interventions from the West, since the Treaty of Yandabu in 1826 Assam has been an integral part of British India but despite many changes in the administration, in the political, economic and other fields she has been maintaining most of her tradition mentioned above which have naturally given her a recognised position in the new policy of India.

The growth of modern political, economic and social thought in Assam may be traced to the early years of the current century though this is in no way comparable to the more advanced sister provinces of the three presidencies. The Gandhian era and the Non-Cooperation Movement in 1920 give a fillip to the dormant energies of the Assamese masses who gave a splendid response to the call of the country. Ever since then, Assam has been in the forefront of all national struggles for political, economic and social emancipation.

It should be mentioned here that there was never any communal problem in Assam uptil the mass immigrations from a neighbouring province in recent years. As a matter of fact the liberalising and unifying influence of the Assam school of Vaishnavism as propounded and preached by the great teachers like Sree Sree Shankar Dev and Sree Sree Madhav Dev and the deep and abiding effect of the rich literature that developed about five centuries ago and which form the rich heritage till today largely governed the social tendencies and religious outlook of the people of Assam as a whole, irrespective of any faith, dogma or denomination. And it is no exaggeration to say that social foundations of Assam were largely and firmly laid on those democratic ideals of justice, liberty, fairplay, tolerance and brotherhood. Innumerable new force and new factors have no doubt entered into the arena and are still entering it to create fresh problems in the daily changing context of a modern India in a modern world. Nevertheless, the rich heritages handed down to us from generation to generation still influence Assam's variegated life and its multi-coloured landscapes.

Today Assam as an integral part of mother India is at the threshold of new Dawn. Along with the rest of the country she is looking forward to a new life–a life which must be better, richer and fuller and more useful not only to herself but to India as a whole. She has many problems to solve economic, industrial and educational and also to tackle the basic problem of the standard of living of her citizens particularly the cultivator of the plain and the high-lander of the hills. She has to provide for the education of the backward brethren of the tribal area and the partially excluded territories. She has to develop her immense natural resources that lie scattered throughout the length and breadth of the territory, with unity and faith and the spirit of selfless and integrate economy of her own within the federal ambit of India for the progress, prosperity and well being of every citizen of Assam irrespective of any class or community, the religion or tribes. Pressing problems and urgent calls to duty are beckoning the Assamese youth today, but the most urgent of all is maintenance of Assam's existence today as an autonomous unit in the body politic of India shaping her own destiny without dictation or imposition from any sister province or community.

Last Prayer

The curtain rings down on the drama of life,
The wreath is snapped and the flowers are scattered,
Lost in my lonely path in the deep encircling gloom.

Where from after your tuneful notes
Came flowing and touched a vibrant chord
In my Veena, silent so long ?

Darkness creeps slowly up the limitless blue,
The western sky is aglow with the red of the departing sun,

My woodland is without a flower,
Hushed is the song of life.

You have sprinkled beauty in myriads of stars
In the wavy bossom of the ocean blue
The Moon in a deluge of light has added hue,
The soul of the lotus blossoms anew.

That day your flute with a fare of tuneful melody
Lent a vision of beauty,
Roused the dying petals of life of,
With its flowerly touch;
Dreamy languor left me,
The rhythm caught on;
And the lamp in my gloomy cot
Burnt again.

Where from a distant woodland,
From the shore of dreams
Came flowing the melody
Of your flute?
My soul in slumber, and a thirst
Woke up;
Dream unfolded
A heaven of beauty

And a mirror of bewitching splendour
My Veena picked up the tune again.

Darkness descends and weaves a nest of dreams,
Withering flowers spread fragrance around.
With the flame in my eyes shining bright
I compose my song of dreams.

At the root of my life
Forlorn and deserted
You'd find poignant misery
And extremes of negligence.

I will seek for you on the desert path
Burning and unbearable to plod on,
Will go forward with the rapturous zeal of "Deepak" tune
And will lift the tune, and make it a fire
Worth a hundred flames.

I will reach beyond the Havana fire
That flames the torch of life,
Will soar over the world of dreams,
That fill the cup of life.

My last Arati, a song of resignation
Will be at your feet
An offering of sacrifice sublime.

By Late Gopinath Bordoloi,
1948

(Composed probably between 1948 and 1950 at some Dak Bungalow during a tour in a rural area)

Shri Gopinath Bordoloi–A Study

By Dr. L.K. Barooah

Gopinath Bordoloi the second premier of Assam is one of the rare personalities of Independent India on whom has fallen the task of building a very strategically and administratively different and difficult part of the Indian Dominion. Though paradoxical, it is true he is one of those little published leaders of the country who did play a very vital role in shaping the destiny of the new India, a fact which the page of history will not fail to record. Notwithstanding how the historians of free India record Bordoloi's role, it is certain that to the people of Assam, old and young alike, he will remain as the idol for the very simple reason that but for his efforts, this province, with all the past history and culture, glory and traditions would have been wiped out of existence as part and parcel of India, if the events in India prior to the attainment of freedom would have had their own way.

Born in June 1890, Gopinath Bordoloi matriculated from the Gauhati Collegiate School. He graduated from the Calcutta Scottish Churches College and took the Master's degree in Arts and Bachelor's degree in law from the Calcutta University in 1914 and 1915 respectively. Having attained some academical distinctions as a student, young Bordoloi's earlier aspiration was to become a professor, but the University of Calcutta under which the Colleges in Assam had remained till recently, would not have him as a professor, because he was a second class. He was therefore compelled to join the Bar and had his practice for about five years after which his career took the turn it was destined for.

Non-Cooperation Movement

In 1921 came the call of Non-Cooperation Movement which virtually shook the country from one end to the other. As a matter of fact, Bordoloi did not know till then much of the Messenger of Truth and Non-violence, because he was too young to appreciate fully the noble life which Gandhiji was unfolding in South Africa a few years previously. But when Gandhiji called upon his countrymen in 1921 to participate in the first direct phase of the struggle for Independence against the British Raj it had a strange fascinating effect on the mind of young Bordoloi. In one of his writings on Gandhiji, Bordoloi himself has stated "......To me it appeared as if I got back a track of life which was about to forget; and that even we were not to obtain Swaraj in a year which Mahatmaji promised on the fulfilment of certain conditions the inner soul in us would receive a training in the process which would be all for our good. To me his appeal was a sort of call to the spirit in man which sometimes becomes irresistible." So Bordoloi yielded to the call of his master and accepted Gandhiji as a spiritual as well as political "Guru" the former having in fact a stronger and deeper hold on him. He was one of the first few who suspended practice and as the Secretary of the District Congress brought the message of Non- Violence and Truth to the remotest villages in the interior; and with active help of others organised the Congress Committee and also collected a substantial amount to the Tilak Swarajye Fund. For the first time in August 1921, Bordoloi met Gandhiji. When late Sj. T.R.Phookan and Sj. N.C.Bordoloi the two veteran leaders of Assam were arrested in the wake of the Non-Cooperation Movement, young Gopinath proceeded to the Ahmedabad Congress Session and gave an appraisal of wholesale arrest of all the Congress leaders of the Province and was himself arrested while returning to Assam.

He was subsequently imprisoned for one year in 1922-23. The successive events in Bordoloi's life were now the inevitable results of the close association with Congress organisation which he was having since 1921. His second meeting with Gandhiji in 1926 when the Congress was held in Gauhati deepened his devotedness to the leader of the Nation and as a matter of fact Bordoloi resigned himself to do whatever was possible for him towards the realisation of Gandhiji's ideals. In 1934 Gandhiji came to Assam for the third time and especially for Harijan work, Bordoloi has been a believer in constructive work and not in parliamentary politics of that time. Of this he gave sufficient evidence when Bordoloi was unanimously elected the Chairman of the Gauhati Municipality in 1934 and he took up the cause of the Harijans in right earnest.

Parliamentary Life

Then came the General Election of 1937 under the Government of India Act, 1935. Bordoloi was not offering himself first as a candidate but subsequently he was prevailed upon to stand as Congress candidate to the Assam Assembly and was returned accordingly. The Congress Assembly Party chose Bordoloi as the Leader of the party even though he had then for the first time entered parliamentary life. But the composition of the Assam Legislature then was such that, with 31 members only of the Congress party in a House of 108 it required all the resources to cut through the meshes of the imperialist Government of Assam and their stooges but it did not take any long time for the Congress party under the captaincy of Bordoloi to gain strength soon and to come to a tussle with the resourceful and strong League Ministry of the time. The Muslim

League Ministry in spite of its strong support of the vested interest suffered as many as eight defeats in the Budget session alone in 1938. It needs to be mentioned here that at the time of Congress acceptance of office in other provinces, a live controversy was going on whether coalition ministry should be formed in those Provinces in which the Congress party did not have a majority verdict. Congress High Command was, however, against the principle of coalition ministry and therefore for the Congress party in Assam, there was no other alternative but to array itself against a very strong League pre-dominated Govenment that did little good to people. In many ways Government had wrought positive harm to the interest of the province which it was very difficult for the successive Governments to amend later. It was a surprise that though the press criticised strongly the Saadulla Ministry it saw no wisdom to resign till November 1938 when a no confidence motion was tabled in the Assembly. The burden of forming a ministry now fell on Bordoloi and he became the first Congress Premier in the difficult Province of Assam and formed a coalition Government. After a span of 18 months only in office, Bordoloi Ministry had to resign on the war issue. Bordoloi was imprisoned again for joining the Satyagraha Movement in 1940-41.

In January 1944, Bordoloi was released on grounds of health, the condition in Assam in that period caused by the impact of the war and of the Muslim League second Ministry and distributing all the available cultivable land to outsiders was such that Bordoloi could hardly remain as an idle spectator. He therefore renewed his contact with the initiator and author of Quit India Resolution seeking for direction as to what he (Bordoloi) should do to fight the evils let loose by the war and the Ministry unhindered and unchallenged. As a matter of fact, Gandhiji's constructive programme was both a truthful method of fighting the evils of foreign rule as well as laying the foundation of non-violent society. As a monitor Gandhiji, through his correspondence from prison in the Aga Khan Palace and later from outside imposed on Bordoloi certain duties and the latter discharged them as faithfully as he could. Gandhiji's fourth and last visit to Assam in 1946 too had given added responsibilities. The burden of building Assam was entrusted to Bordoloi by the Father of the Nation.

The year of 1949 was a year of test not only for Bordoloi but to the people of Assam as a whole: plan to place the Provinces on the basis of "Grouping" was announced. Bordoloi in the plan saw the germ which threatened to wipe out Assam as an independent unit. He therefore met the members of the Cabinet Mission and put to them the proposal under which Assam could enjoy an honourable place among the Provinces. But the British statesmen instead of agreeing to it were adamant in their attitude and practically threw Assam's destiny in the hands of brute majority of Muslim League of Bengal to force an unwilling Assam and her people to the grouping proposal. The heart of Gopinath was indeed bleeding for the land of his birth where he participated in the battle of freedom; where he also felt the first bitterness of illusionment and the impact of struggle that is life. He foresaw that in the exceptions of the grouping proposals lay the very germ of the effacement of the Province of Assam. His first impulse was therefore to approach the Congress High Command for rejection of the grouping clause in the plan and thus save Province. It appeared at one time that the arguments of the leaders who were shaping the destiny of the millions were different from those of Bordoloi and it seemed to him that there was no hope left for him but to seek Gandhiji's advice. It is no secret that Bordoloi was in some quarters erroneously judged as one tempting to sabotage the Cabinet Mission plan, which had virtually obtained the acceptance of the leaders of the political party in India. But Bordoloi stood bold and firm in what he considered to be in the best interest of Assam and would not rest till this obnoxious clause of grouping was rejected. How Gandhiji subsequently came to the help of Assam and a leader Bordoloi leading to the rejection of the grouping clause, in favour of the division of India is known to all. Superficial critics of that time hold the view that Bordoloi was one of those persons responsible for partition of the country. But to the men who took a detached view of men matters it was the intransigence of Quaid-e-azam Jinnah which caused the division and non else. Perhaps history too will recall the verdict. But whatever the merit of Bordoloi critics might be it was he who saved from the octopus of grouping the Province. He must be regarded as the virtual saviour of Assam.

The results of the general election in 1945 unlike that of 1937 turned the political scale in favour of Congress Party in Assam dominated by the Muslim League and their allies so long. The responsibility of forming the ministry in the "Problem Province" of India fell on Bordoloi and he successfully undertook it. It has been agreed that in Assam the problems are peculiarly complex and even multifarious. Few could grasp them appropriately much less administer them properly. In spite of his health which has given constant trouble Bordoloi has been discharging his responsibility ably and creditably which has earned for him no little reputation among the administrators of the time.

Bordoloi's rise to power and fame is neither sudden nor meteoric. It is the result of sustained work. A sense of righteousness and justice in him pre-dominate considerably. That is why it is difficult to find a substitute for him in Assam. He is not a silver spooned man, he has known the bitter pangs of life, its difficulties and chaos. He is an instance at the point that fortune favours the brave, although material fortune Bordoloi has had little. He is brave; but his bravery has never been cherished, he is silent and lives a deep-toned spiritual life. He is one who believes in work, hard work, and not to emotional expression of ideas and this perhaps he has learnt from Gandhiji. His stamina for work is inexhaustible and he works at his desk for twelve hours a day. His engagements in the public meetings and villages are also not small. A keen student of history he reads books too. He has a deep intellectual mind.

Bordoloi is essentially a man of peace and of spiritual equipoise. His judgement is neither illusory nor lopsided. He is steady genuine and possesses a searching vision into the vitals and details of men and matters and also the problems that face this province. He is a good writer, but his phrases are not other's phrases nor his views borrowed plumes. He has been capable of original approach to things and problems. Bordoloi is mentally alert but not a publicity monger. He is unassuming and sometimes taciturn too. He carries with him the burden of authority with the least show of ostentation. The qualities of head and heart add a splendour to the crimson of his character. Dignified and unimpeachable in his character, Bordoloi is rightly regarded as the pilot of his men and the intricate problems of Assam. Gopinath is a sportsman and he was himself a cricketeer. Before he joined politics his preoccupations were sports, study and music. He is democrat and believes in democracy. He is a cricketeer in politics, he does not believe in bodyline bowling and underhand balls in politics and in the conduct of his life. A great trait in his character is his regard and sympathy for his opponents point of view. That is possibly why few of his opponents dislike him. He is a teacher in true sense of the term and a great lover of devotional songs, even in the midst of his heavy work which is inevitable to the premier of a complex province, Bordoloi does not miss to teach his little children in the evening and to attend to the evening prayers which his children hold daily. Genius and yet stubborn, Bordoloi is the most loved and respected man of Assam and one of most trusted leaders in India.

Today Bordoloi is a happy man, for, he has the opportunity before him to build up "Lovely Assam" of Gandhiji according to the pattern the latter has set before us all.

[This article was published in the Times of Assam on 27th March 1949. The author Dr. L.K. Barooah was the founder of Sankar Mission Hospital of Nowgong and a noted freedom fighter.]

The Man Who Saved India from Disaster

By Satish C. Kakati Padmashree

In his controversial memoirs, India Wins Freedom, Maulana Abul Kalam Azad blamed Jawaharlal Nehru and Lord Mountbatten more stringently than any other person for the partition of India on August 15, 1947. Maulana Azad did not spare Sardar Vallabhbhai Patel, either, for joining the Nehru-Mountbatten combine in the rejection of the British Cabinet Mission Plan of May 16, 1946.

Significantly, Maulana Saheb did not apportion blame to the proponent of the two nation theory, Mohammad Ali Jinnah; on the contrary, the author of India Wins Freedom was all praise for the Muslim League supremo for his support to the British proposals, particularly Jinnah's interpretation of Clause 5 in the Scheme relating to formation of Groups about which Assam was most concerned. Maulana Azad says in his book: "In fairness I have to admit that in this point Mr. Jinnah was on the whole right. Both justice and expediency demanded that the Congress should have accepted the plan unequivocally".

The fundamental difference over the interpretation of the grouping clause between the Congress and the Muslim League led to the collapse of the British Cabinet Mission plan. It was substituted by an alternative scheme, generally known as the Mountabatten plan, to partition the country into two States, initially dominions, as a prelude to independence for the two countries. This is the Attlee Government of British endorsed, leaving its operation to Lord Mountbatten as the Viceroy at the time.

It needs to be remembered that Maulana Azad was the Congress president when the Cripps Mission was sent by the Churchill Government in 1942 to negotiate transfer of power to India and also during the preliminary stage of talks on the British Cabinet mission plan of May 16, 1946. When Britain proposed the plan, Jawaharlal Nehru succeeded Maulana Saheb as the Congress president. But the Maulana did not lose the initiative in negotiating with the Cabinet Mission and endeavoured to ensure that the British Cabinet Mission plan was accepted in toto. He was very happy when both the Congress and the Muslim League accepted the Mission's proposals which, according to him, was a glorious event in the history of the freedom movement in India and meant, that the intricate question of India's freedom would be settled by negotiations and agreement. Maulana Azad later recorded in his book that he had committed a mistake by handing over the presidentship to Nehru as he noticed the latter's ambivalent stance on the British proposals. Azad Saheb called his mistake as one of "Himalayan Dimension" thereby suggesting that had he been in the office of the Congress president at that crucial stage of negotiations, the Cabinet Mission Plan would have survived and the partition of the country averted leading to the emergence of a united independent India. It is also possible that Maulana Saheb was mentally hurt that the British proposals, which were formulated on the basis of a note submitted by him earlier to the Cripps Mission in 1942, had been rejected by the country.

True, Maulana Azad has not specifically blamed Gandhiji for the partition of India, but he was extremely sad that the Mahatma who earlier said that any division of the country would be "over my dead body" somewhat changed his mind, still he hoped that despite the critical attitude of Nehru and Patel towards the British plan, he would be able to secure Gandhiji's support in its favour. But he received the greatest shock of his life, as the Maulana himself put it, to find that Gandhiji too lent his weight to Assam against the proposals and asked the people of Assam to resist the grouping part of the scheme.

In the face of mounting opposition from Assam leaders to the British Cabinet Mission's proposals, Nehru felt that he was not sure if the plan would eventually be accepted by the Congress. In fact, in a statement to the National Herald (July 11, 1946), Nehru said "Obviously, Section A will decide against grouping."

Speaking in betting language there was a four to one change of NWFP deciding against grouping. There the group collapses. It is highly likely that Assam will decide against grouping with Bengal, although I would not say what the initial decision may be, since it is evenly balanced. But I can say with every assurance and conviction that there is going to be finally no grouping there, because Assam will not tolerate it under any circumstances. There you see, this grouping business approached from any point of view does not get on at all.

This press statement of Nehru indeed sounded the death-knell of the British Cabinet Mission Plan. In a message to the people of Assam sent through two Congressmen who met him on behalf of Gopinath Bordoloi at Srirampur in Noakhali while he was on his epic peace mission, and asked for guidance in regard to "grouping," Gandhiji said that "Assam must not lose its soul. It must uphold it against the whole world, else I will say that Assam had only manikins and no men". It drove, as it were the final nail into the Cabinet Mission Plan's coffin. Needless to say that Gandhiji's message to Bordoloi encouraged the people of Assam to resist the British proposals which finally, to the utter disappointment of Maulana Abul Kalam Azad, fell through. This led on to Lord Mountbatten's plan for the partition of India which the Labour Government of Britain okayed and the country was divided into India and Pakistan.

Two pertinent questions in this regard arise: first, who indeed was the man behind the partition of India ? And second, was the Mountbatten scheme to divide India into two separate countries (thereby enabling the British to quit India on schedule), a better alternative to the proposals for a united India as envisaged in the May 16 plan and strongly supported by Maulana Azad?

Several historians, India-watchers and writers have since given their opinions on the story of India's partition.

H.M. Seervai a former advocate-general of Maharashtra, for instance, in his book The Partition of India - Legend and Reality, points out that the responsibility for the partition of India was not of Jinnah, but of Gandhiji, Jawaharlal Nehru and Vallabhbhai Patel. Seervai does not include in the list Lord Mountbatten who sponsored the scheme and executed it. Then there is the veteran politician and commentator, Minoo Masani, who also supports the Maharashtrian lawyer and Maulana Azad.

However, even a cursory study of how Gopinath Bordoloi ran from pillar to post while the hectic discussions on the British Cabinet Mission Plan were on to plead for its rejection, will point towards the fact that the man behind the partition of India was Gopinath Bordoloi. When the plan was unfolded, he saw in the grouping clause the future of Assam endangered in every way, politically, economically, even culturally. He lost no time and pleaded with the Congress Working Committee to save Assam from the impending disaster as the province a Hindu majority one, would be at the mercy of Muslim-majority Bengal once grouped with it. Except Sarat Chandra Bose, none of the CWC members supported Bordoloi. In a state of desperation, Bordoloi finally met Gandhiji at the Bhangi Colony in New Delhi, and implored for his help to save Assam. In Gandhiji's Emissary Sudhir Ghose, a close associate of the Mahatma narrated this event as follows : "In the North-East Assam was not a Muslim majority province, but it was to be grouped together with Bengal, a Muslim majority province. In order to create a substantial area over which the Muslim League could be defacto rulers, Mr. Gopinath Bordoloi, eminent Congress leader of Assam, shed tears before Gandhiji on behalf of the people of Assam. It seemed to him immoral and unjust."

Notwithstanding Assam's unrelenting opposition to the Cabinet Mission plan so far as Clause 5 in the grouping was concerned, neither the Congress Working Committee nor even Gandhiji at first was inclined to reject the plan, that is, until the Mahatma told Bordoloi's two emissaries, Mahendra Mohan Choudhary and Bijoy Chandra Bhagavati, at Srirampur, that, "if there is no clear cut guidance from the Congress Committee, Assam should not go into sections. It should lodge its protest and retire from the Constituent Assembly. It will be a kind of Satyagraha against the Congress for the Congress." It was under such circumstances that the British plan of May 16, 1946, was abandoned and the alternative scheme for partition of India was implemented.

Viewed in the light of the developments during the period from May 16, 1946 to December 1946, it would not be incorrect to say that Lokopriya Gopinath Bordoloi was actually the man behind the partition of India, though historically, M.A. Jinnah's intransigence was responsible. Indeed, had not Bordoloi persevered in his opposition to the grouping scheme, the history of India would have been different today.

The other paramount question is whether the partition of the country has proved "ruinous" as Maulana Azad genuinely feared. That a three tier governance of India as advocated by the 1946 plan–one at the provincial level, another at the group level and a third at the central level with powers relating to defence, communications and foreign affairs–and, possibly a fourth tier in some of the 362 native states–was bound to fail was seen in the functioning of the interim Government.

(September 2, 1946 to August 14, 1947). This episode has been graphically narrated by Maulana Azad himself in his book. Liaqat Ali, a Muslim League representative in the interim Government holding the finance portfolio rejected each and every proposal put up by the Congress members in the Government. Referring to it in India Wins Freedom Azad says: "Sardar Patel discovered that though he was the home minister he could not create the post of a chaprasi without Liaqat Ali's concurrence!" This observation of Azad Saheb speaks for the impracticability of a Congress League Government. Surprisingly, however, Azad Saheb blamed Patel for this unhappy situation arguing that had Sardar Patel agreed to Liaqat Ali holding the home portfolio, as suggested by the Maulana, there would have been no conflict. Patel refused to allot the home portfolio to a Muslim representative in the interim Government. As it was a Central Government in the set-up planned under the May 16 plan was not to be a more fruitful exercise either, if the functioning of the interim Government was any guide.

Another question was whether the task of integrating some of the recalcitrant native States would have been an easy affair in a united India if the British Cabinet Mission proposals were accepted. This is a relevant question in the context of the refusal by the Nizam of Hyderabad and the ruler of Junagarh, for instance, to join the Indian Union in 1947. Even an inconsequential ruler, the Maharaja of Manipur, had to be cajoled into signing the instrument of accession at Imphal by the Assam Governor, Sir Akbar Hydari, who had to dash to Manipur under instruction of the Deputy Prime Minister, Sardar Patel, on December 28, 1947. There were a number of such reluctant rulers who were in cahoots either with the newly formed Pakistan or with some members of the Raj who like Field Marshal Sir Claude Auchinleck who forecast India's break-up into several States were not agreeable to the idea of quitting India. All this raises apprehension even now, that a united India as perceived by Maulana Azad would have led to the country breaking up further.

Percival Spear in his book, 'A History of India 1965' analysing the reason why India may now be grateful for the failure of the British Cabinet Mission proposals says: "The price of unity was to have a weak centre, only partially set off by the device of subordinate units. There were several dangers in this plan. One was that the centre would have been so weak and so harassed by communal jostling for power that the big developments which have occurred both in India and Pakistan would have been impossible. The other was, given a weak and wrangling centre, that power would have tended to a division of India, not into two, but several independent units".

Analysing the circumstances at the time of partition it seems that it was Assam's leader Lokopriya Gopinath Bordoloi the preparations for whose birth centenary celebrations are under way (born on June 6, 1890 and died on August 5, 1950) was the man who saved India from chaos and possibly from many further unpredictable divisions.

Going by attempts of several secessionist forces threatening the unity and integrity of India in recent years it stands to reason that had there been the type of Government for the whole of India as planned by the British Cabinet Mission, it would have created more problems than it would have solved. Admittedly, the division of the country into India and Pakistan was not a happy event but the circumstances at the time when the British Government decided on transfer of power were against a united nation. Detractors of Gandhiji, Nehru, Patel and Gopinath Bordoloi may continue to try and hold them responsible for the partition of India but, as Percival Spear says, it has saved the post 1947 India from a partition. Indeed, the partition of India was a blessing in disguise.

(By the Courtesy of The Telegraph, 9th August 1989)

Gopinath Bordoloi A Pen Portrait

By Hem Barua

A deep distress overshadows the country today. Bordoloi's death has plunged it into a void; 15th of August this year will be bland without him. Bordoloi was a Congressman and yet above it, no sectarian bias ever coloured his vision or judgment. He was above the party. His was a dedicated life. Once he wrote to me: "I would describe myself as one who had tried to do what he considered to be his duty in life".

I remember those hectic days of 1942, the prison and its red walls and our comrade-fighters. The inspiration he gave, the idealism he spread, are the beacon-light in the lives of many. Bordoloi is to me a symbol of strength and determination, his biographical details do not matter. He was like a lonely pine silhouetted against the firmament, stained wine-red by the fire of the rising sun. Often it is said, his features are rough and heavy; they express a robust man, both physically and mentally. Death has nevertheless crept on him; it is work, heavy work that has cracked him.

Bordoloi's rise to power and prestige was not accidental; neither it was inevitable. The sense of right doing in him dominated all other things and spotlighted his virtues. He was essentially human.

Gopinathji was not a silver-spooned man. He had known the bitter pangs of life, its conflict and chaos. He was an instance of fortune favouring the brave, although material fortune he had but little. Bordoloi is brave; yet his bravery was never "doggish" which as Katherine Mansfield points out consists in a mere external "show up" of things. He was not the type that, to use Dr. Pattabhi Sitaramayya's words "creates a disturbance a crocodile causes in thigh deep waters when its prey on whom it has a firm hold makes a gentle attempt to escape from its grip". It was silent and of the deep-toned spiritual variety.

(An article published in The Assam Tribune on 7-8-50 after the death of G.N.B.)

Believer of Work

Bordoloi believed in work, his stamina for work was inexhaustible. He patterned his life on the gospel of the Gita. A keen student of history, he had a vicarious love of books and used to read politics, poetry and philosophy with equal zeal. One hears him discuss H. G. Wells scientific romances or Spengler's Decline of the West as easily as Buddhist philosophy or Assamese, Vaishnavite culture He had a deep intellectual context.

Maybe, because of the blows and buffets of fortune tossing his early life, he was like a bird with be-ruffled plumes" but he was not an ordinary bird. He was neither a penguin nor a jackdaw; he was the nation's eagle and king-fisher. He in his life-time reached a scintillating serenity where storms seem meaningless as wind on dried grass.

Gopinathji was a man of peace and spiritual equipoise; his judgements were neither illusory nor lop-sided. His was a steady genius which possessed a searching vision into the heart of things and problems. Few understood the various problems of Assam as deeply as he did. He could see the menace with which Assam was threatened with because of the open invasion of the Muslim population from East Bengal. He fought valiantly to undo the evil. "The Land Settlement Problem in Assam" an article written by him which was published all over India is a searching analysis of a complex problem. In spite of it he is free from any communal feeling. He wrote well and had a good command of the English language. His style was precise and clear, it was well knit and "edgy".

Bordoloi's bold protestations destroyed the Anglo-League designs to associate Assam with Bengal provided in the Cabinet Mission's proposals. He characterized the Cabinet Mission's proposals on Group "C" as basically a "negation of democracy." It was negative of both democracy and decorum.

Original Approach

Bordoloi's phrases are not catchphrases; his views are not "borrowed plumes". He was capable of original approach. In the Post-August Revolution days under the influence of lukewarm Congressman and of the "peopls war" theorists, the "Quit India" Revolution fell to disrepute. He alone at a time when his compatriots were in prison stood by it, owned it and called the "Quit India" resolution, "our Charter of Liberty". It was possibly the only solitary defence of the movement in public till at last Pandit Nehru came out of prison and raised it to its legitimate claims.

Maxwell utilized the British propaganda machine to dishonour the Congress as a pro-Japanese organization. Tottenham's "Congress Responsibility" was calculated to give a fillip for it. Bordoloi's bold pleas for collective security when Japanese armed forces climbed in Kohima knocked Maxwell to his senses.

Politics was no poet's dream for Gopinath Bordoloi; he saw and understood things in the most correct perspective. His vision of reality had that touch of idealism which raises politics to a higher plane. His methods are always direct and quite behoving of a man whose pre-occupation prior to politics was cricket. He was a cricketer in politics; he did not believe in body line bowling or underhand bowls. That is possibly the reason why his worst opponents did not dislike him.

He did not cater for popularity cheap and evanescent. He knew nothing of the "carefully learnt up trick of the publicman" to use Pandit Nehru's words. Boswell was of the opinion that popularity is a crime from the moment it is sought; it is only a virtue when men have it whether they will it or not." Assam's Chief Minister did not commit this "crime". He was mentally alert, but he was never a publicity monger, like a true physician he provided a panacea to all national ills.

Music and Sports

Music like sports was his forte. While young he played on several instruments as well as he handled a cricket bat, a tennis racket or the draughts on a chess-board.

Bordoloi was unassuming. He was taciturn too, the qualities of his head and heart add a splendour to the crimson of his character. Dignified of mien, unimpeachable in character, naturally enough he was the nation's pilot.

"Have we not men with us royal,
Men the masters of things?"

Gopinath Bordoloi : A True Statesman

By Indira Miri

I believe,–you will all agree with me, if I say–it is a fact that to assess a specialist in any art a greater specialist in that very art is essential. Statesmanship is an art and therefore it is obvious that to assess a statesman a greater statesman is essential. But unfortunately enough I am not a statesman nor even politician to be able to assess Bordoloi. However, as a lay person, I shall try to do as best as I can. The most outstanding and intellectually fascinating contribution of Bordoloi towards Assam is his operational technique in making the plan of grouping. Assam with West Bengal fell in entirety, for which Maulana Abul Kalam Azad blamed Lord Mountbatten, Nehru, Patel and Bordoloi squarely for the partition of the country. It is here Bordoloi emerged as a great statesman. Had it not been for him Assam would have probably been extinct today. The fight against the British Cabinet Mission plan of May 16th, 1946, popularly known as grouping plan, presented by the British Government towards transfer of power to India reveals clearly the true mettle of Bordoloi.

The plan envisaged many things of which the most destructive clause for Assam was to divide the provinces into 3 groups A, B & C and tag Assam with East Bengal in group C. Bordoloi with his keen foresight could at once foresee the fate of Assam if so tagged. He had a very strong apprehension that Assam, a Hindu majority province inhabited predominantly by Assamese Hindu, if tagged with East Bengal, will be at the mercy of the Muslim majority who are mostly Bengali Muslims.

The clause threatened the very identity, language, religion etc. of the people of Assam. But as the plan had already been accepted by the Congress as well as the Muslim League Bordoloi was helpless. The moment was most frightfully critical and chances of affecting any change in the already accepted plan by all concerned was far from remote.

Nevertheless Bordoloi's brilliant technique saved Assam from the jaws of death. By sending emissaries seeking Gandhiji's blessings, Bordoloi played an extremely imporatnt role in causing the plan to fail. It was almost a miracle. It may at first glance seem startling that out of the supposedly backward people Assam could have produced such a champion as Bordoloi who could save Assam from the gallows just at the point when the death loop was about to be slipped round her neck.

Bordoloi succeeded, I believe, not so much because he was extraordinary, but because he was the man of the moment. There are many great leaders who never rose to eminence or power because the time for their contribution to society had not yet come. The man may be right, the moment may be right, but it is only when the two conjoin that an hour in history is struck.

The British Cabinet Commission Plan was presented on 16th May of 1946 and Bordoloi became the Premier of the full fledged Congress ministry for the first time in Assam in that very year. He met Gandhiji at Khazirkhal in East Bengal seeking his advice on Cabinet Mission vis-a-vis Assam's future. The man and the moment conjoined most perfectly to rush in a new era in Assam. Such a miracle can be brought about only by a very wise statesman.

Bordoloi had no ulterior motive like the Britishers and the prominent minister Sir Syed Md. Sa-adullah–one converting in large scale the Hill tribes into christianity in the name of welfare of the other flooding Assamese Muslim immigrants in the field of agriculture. Here was the first sowing of the seed of separatism. The allegiance of men can be won, not merely by the cunning game of political fraud and trickery but through love, justice.

Bordoloi was true to his land and people. He saw the underlying fraud of both welfare and agriculture. The poison seed of separation thus sown has today grown into a robust tree and blowing poisonous wind at every opportune moment threatening the unity and integration of Assam. Today there is ethnic tension everywhere. So much so, that we fear fragmentation of Assam even in her plains area which is the left over after carving out all the Hill areas.

All the aforesaid facts make Bordoloi stand out in all probability the most important and beyond doubt the most prominent statesman in Assam's national field. Centuries hence he will be remembered when of his contemporaries hardly a name will survive. Rightly said Sardar Vallabh Bhai Patel–"It is difficult to think of Assam without Gopinath Bordoloi. He identified himself with the interest of the State, and for years the political life so much mingled with his great personality that we had come to think of these two entities being always synonymous."

Truly Bordoloi is synonymous with Assam. He is much more than a national patriot, he is the personification of a new era in Assam. Bordoloi can easily be used as a telescope through which to view Assam. Because he is without controversy the outstanding personality of this far eastern region of India. Perhaps, Assam would not have been in the map of India today had it not been for Bordoloi.

Bordoloi's relation with the tribals is another outstanding mark of his great character. As Lincoln saw wri large on the face of the Blacks, "you have interest to be our masters, but how can we have interest to be your slaves?" So also Bordoloi saw writ large on the face of the tribals "you have interest to keep us backward but how can we have interest to keep ourselves backward ?" His approach towards the tribals was unique. He never treated them as liabilities but treated them as assets and pride of Assam.

Well, I am sure, you all know about the great Naga patriot A. Phizo–one of the most intellectually clever and mentally alert Naga. Do you know what he said about Bordoloi? His sentiments speak loud what Bordoloi was to the tribals. The Naga leader lamented Bordoloi's death as "with only a few Bordoloi saw years ago amidst gathering storm a patch of blue sky. In that great vision of his, his unremitting contribution towards its realisation will be found truly the impress of his character which neither death nor time can rob away. In life Bordoloi was a friend of the Naga whose friendship they held dear, Nagas have been made poorer today that he has gone." A tribute which only a truly great can claim. Bordoloi was indeed a true statesman of a very high stature which only a virtuous politician can attain.

Lokopriya Bordoloi as I Knew Him

By R. Vanlawma

Perhaps I am one of the few still living who had the privilege of personal contact with late Gopinath Bordoloi. He was known to me as one of the builders of our Indian Union. His name was known to me since my school days in Shillong when by the Government of India Act, 1935 he became the first Premier of Assam.

Mizoram, known at that time as Lushai Hills, was an excluded area. We, the Mizo students, therefore, felt unconcerned and really took no interest in the political change that was taking place in India at that time. In fact, when the Muslim League Government of Assam led by Muhammad Saadullah fell in 1938 and the Congress Government led by Gopinath Bordoloi took over, the change struck me as an interesting news only. But amusingly enough I was nicknamed 'Bordoloi' by the Mizo students of the Earle Hostel in Shillong when there was a crisis over the management of Mizo Students Affairs and the Leadership was thrust upon me, though I was not actually involved in the fray. The outgoing leader was also nicknamed as Saadullah.

The Second World War broke out on September 1, 1939 just after I left Shillong. This was followed by what was known as the Quit India Movement in 1942 led by Mahatma Gandhi. As a sequel to this Winston Churchill came up with the historic announcement that the British would leave India after winning the war.

Immediately after the war the Britishers made plans to leave India as a complete whole. Accordingly, the Constituent Assembly of India was created under the leadership of Pandit Jawaharlal Nehru acting as Vice President of India and Lord Mountbatten, Governor-General of India as the President.

But soon the Muslims of India came up with the demand for a separate Muslim dominion. The British Crown was, therefore, compelled to accede to the demand for two separate dominions in the Indian Sub-continent. The Cabinet Mission was thus sent to India for this purpose. The Sub-continent was then divided into three groups namely the Punjab, Sindh and West of them forming Group A, the middle portions from Kashmir to Cape Comorin forming group 'B' and, finally, Bengal and the North Eastern Area including Assam as Group 'C'.

The Groups A and C were then earmarked for Pakistan and a separate Constituent Assembly of Pakistan was created with Karachi as its new Headquarters.

Bordoloi was appalled by the situation, the prospect of Assam to fall within Muslim Pakistan. He then approached Pandit Nehru, and Panditji advised him that since the Hindu population in the Assam valley did not have clear majority over the Muslim population of Assam Province, the only way to save Assam from becoming Pakistan Territory would be to approach the Hill people who had the right to choose their own destinies.

Thus, one day in 1946, I received a telegram from him requesting me to come down to Shillong urgently.

By this time we in the then Lushai Hills have had set up our own political party known as the Mizo Union of which I was the founder Secretary and the sole spokesman of the party.

Just after I reached his office Bordoloi suggested to leave the office to stroll down the town of Shillong on foot so that we could talk in private without interferences by officials and others. He told me then what Panditji had advised him as to how Assam and its surrounding areas could be brought within India.

He said, "The Nagas are in favour of their own independence, Khasi people are divided into too many factions and the Garos have no political organisation. And as such the Mizo Union is the best and the only organisation to speak on behalf of the Hill people of the North East India. If the Mizo people decided to opt in favour of Indian Union, it will be a very invaluable help for the people of Assam. Pandit Nehru said that if the Hill people opt in favour of Indian Union he may influence Lord Mountbatten, the Governor General of India to review the plans made by the Cabinet Mission. If that is possible, Assam may be connected by slicing some portions near Siliguri as a connecting corridor." He also said that Assam was at the mercy of the Mizos as they can save Assam from becoming a part of Pakistan as he knew that the Mizos have option to choose their own destiny and India needed the Mizos to save their own Assamese brothers and sisters.

I gave an answer "Look here Mr. Bordoloi, do you find any Khasi shop within Shillong town, all the traders are outsiders ; in our capital Aizawl most of the shopkeepers are Mizos. I don't like to make Aizawl a second Shillong. What we fear most is economic exploitation by business experts from other parts of India. I think you have seen some headings of big Calcutta papers displaying "Black Regulation must Go" in their top front pages meaning the Inner Line Regulation which controlled entries of buisness experts to Mizoram. We still require that Regulation to protect us from economic domination." Bordoloi assured me that so long as we need that Regulation, it should not be abolished in case we opt Indian Union. He promised to bring the matter to Pandit Nehru, who had a soft corner for hill tribes of Assam. The regulation is therefore still in force till today to the benefit of the Mizo people.

I further told him that in Section 7 of Indian Independence Act of 1947, it was mentioned that the Treaty between His Majesty's Government and the tribal Chiefs would have lapsed after the Act was in operation, that provision gave us the right to choose our own destiny including the course we are going to take. Our good District Administrator. Mr. A.R.H. Macdonald had advised us to join India as Scotland joined England. India would bear all the expenses for our development programmes leaving our internal administration to us. As for comparison between India and Pakistan, I preferred India, if they were in a position to recognise our characteristics and ethnic differences from the main stream of India. So, I informed him that I would communicate the decision of our Executive Committee to him as soon as possible.

Bordoloi told me that it had to be decided in the next Constituent Assembly of India which was going to have its session soon and there was no time for waiting for the decision of our Executive Committee as he had to go to New Delhi the day after tomorrow. So, I had decided to give option for India on behalf of the Mizo people as provided by the Independence of India Act of 1947 which was given on our second meeting on the next day on the conditions as already stated.

He informed me afterwards that our action saved Assam and its adjoining regions from becoming parts of the proposed Pakistan and I would be included in the committee made by the Constituent Assembly of India.

I hereby dare to mention that his endeavour to include Assam and its adjoining sister States in the Indian Union made Bordoloi one of the great architects and builders of the present India. Without his efforts the North-Eastern part of India might have become a part of Pakistan.

Let me also mention here the fact that the Constituent Assembly of India did not fully endorse our agreements and they made sixth Schedule in the Constitution which gave us only district autonomy for all the hills districts of Assam.

Though Bordoloi could not make the Constituent Assembly of India to endorse our agreement in full, I did not actually put the blame upon him fully, and I still admire him and respect him in my heart as one of the greatest leaders ever produced by India. I remembered his last public speech delivered at Aizawl just before his death. That was the last time I saw him in person. I sent the copy of the full text of his last public speech to the Shillong Times which I hope, many of you read with tears.

Present-day Assam is only a part of what the great leader had built. The challenge for you today is whether you shall create conditions conducive for the growth and strengthening of your state or whether you shall allow her to disintegrate further.

I wish the Centenary year celebration of Gopinath Bordoloi a good success. Gopinath Bordoloi is dead,–long live Gopinath Bordoloi.

Reminiscence of Gopinath Bordoloi

By Mr. Lalmawi.

I had very little contact with late Gopinath Bordoloi, the First Chief Minister of Assam. But in spite of my few contacts with him, I considered him to be among the great politician and administrators of Assam.

During the 2nd World War, while I was serving in the Indian Army as Emergency Commission officer, the Indian National Congress party won the majority of seats in the Provincial Assembly election in Assam; and Gopinath Bordoloi became the Prime Minister of Assam. The very fact that he was elected as leader of the party in the Assembly is a proof of his leadership quality.

On the eve of Independence of India in 1946, Gopinath Bordoloi, Sir B.N. Rao and J.J.M. Nichols Roy arrived in Aizawl to discuss the future of Lushai Hills (as it was then known). They consulted political leaders of Mizoram and persuaded them to join India, and said that in doing so, they would have certain advantages, such as M.L.As and a Minister in the Assam Government. After a few days of discussion, they were able to convince the leaders of the Mizo Union Party, the first political party formed in Mizoram that what they had to offer would be in the best interest of the Mizo people.

Before independence, the leader of the Government of the Provincial Legislative Assembly was known as the Prime Minister. Gopinath Bordoloi being the leader of the House, he was known as the Prime Minister of Assam. Immediately after the Constituent Assembly finalised the Constitution of India, Assam province became a State and Gopinath Bordoloi became the first Chief Minister of Assam.

In 1947, after leaving my service in Burma, I came to Mizoram to take an active part in politics. I joined the United Mizo Freedom Organisation, a new political party, and became its president. Our party's aim was to join Burma. But the Mizo Union under the influence of Gopinath Bordoloi had already decided to accede to the Indian Union.

A Constituent Assembly was formed to prepare the Constitution of India. Gopinath Bordoloi came again to Aizawl and he nominated CH. Saprawnga as a member of the Constituent Assembly representing the District of Mizoram.

A public meeting was held at the Deputy Commissioner's Lawn, and I was to deliver a speech on behalf of the Mizo people. This speech was prepared by four people, H.K. Bawichhuaka of the Mizo Union, Thakur a non-Tribal, Bangliana and I.

At that time the Assam Government was trying to make Assamese the State language and to introduce it in all the schools. They had even posted Assamese teachers some schools. The speech drafting committee was under the in impression that this was Assamisation policy, and if we become a part of Assam this would be the shape of things to come. We included this in the speech. I remember very clearly that while I was reading out this part during the welcome speech, the then Deputy Commissioner J.N. Barkakati showed signs of displeasure. But I am sure that it had made an impact on Gopinath Bordoloi because plans to introduce the Assamese language in Schools in Mizoram was withdrawn.

As CH. Saprawnga was appointed as a member of Parliament to the Constituent Assembly Gopinath Bordoloi expressed his desire to offer me a job as a class I officer. I did not specify what type of post I wanted as I wished to continue to take an active part in politics. However, I mentioned that I could accept an honorary post and later a post of Hony. Development officer was offered which I accepted.

In conclusion, I would like to say that Gopinath Bordoloi is a great statesman who is a man of understanding, and impartial to all, even those opposed to his party and way of thinking. I have a very high esteem for this great leader.

Lokopriya Gopinath Bordoloi's Contribution to Hills Autonomy

By Sonaram Thaosen

The people, the younger generation in particular must know the history of their country and in more details they should know about the area or the region they live in as bonafide citizens. But sometimes the people find it difficult for a study about certain area or region as such historical records of the remote past or recent are hardly available. As for instance, the case of North Cachar Hills District, its history, archaeology or their chronologies, all have been sunk into oblivion. The present composition is an attempt to meet the foregoing queries on the occasion of the birth centenary of a great son of Assam Late Lokopriya Gopinath Bordoloi, the first Prime Minister of Assam (now Chief Minister) as a memoir.

Bordoloi was the first and the last among the Indian leaders who had come to North Cachar Hills for the cause of the public before Independence and ushered in a new era for hope and aspirations. Another Minister and prominent tribal leader of the time Late Bhimbar Deuri also accompanied him. I could still remember the gist of Bordoloi's speech at Maibang sometime in winter in 1946. He declared in an unequivocal terms that–"The British Government was leaving our country very soon. A Constituent Assembly with prominent persons would be constituted to frame the Constitution for free India. There was also a proposal for the formation of a sub-committee of the Assembly to go into problems of the Hill areas and to recommend their findings."

He then advised the people "to prepare a memorandum claiming their demands in the future Government and he will be always at the disposal of the public etc." It is worthwhile to mention that Bordoloi after sometime became the chairman of the said Sub-Committee which was also known as Bordoloi Sub-Committee.

Now in order to juxtapose the story, let me describe some historical accounts of North Cachar Hills before further detailing of Bordoloi's contribution to the Hills autonomy.

North Cachar Hills is a place where all the tribes and communities reside peacefully without the slightest conflict with one another. Originally it was a part of the Kachari or Haidimba kingdom with its headquarter at Khaspur now in Cachar. The southern part of the kingdom i.e., present Cachar district was annexed to British India in 1832 A.D. after the death of last king Gobinda Chandra Narayan. However, the northern part i.e. North Cachar Hills, part of Nowgong and Karbi Anglong districts was retained as a protectorate State under the suzerainty of Tularam Senapati with headquarter at Modunga near Lanka. After the death of Tularam Senapati, his son and their apparent Nakulram took the administration of the territory and after his death the territory was included to the British empire in 1855 A.D. Then the North Cachar Hills was formed part with Nowgong district as Sub-division with headquarter at Asaloo for some-time. Then it reunited with Cachar its headquarter at Gunjung. But in 1882 Sombhudhan, a Kachari rebel burnt the Gunjung headquarter and consequently the headquarter was shifted at present Haflong. After the annexation to the British India North Cachar Hills was ruled as an excluded area under different relevant Rules and Regulations of the Government.

During the reign of the Kachari Kings, N.C. Hills once flourished for its abundance. Apart for its beautiful forest wealth with flora and fauna the agricultural products were plentiful. Maibang which means abundant paddy could boast for its plenty at one time. Paddy with two annas a mound and a milch cow or buffalo was sold at Rs. 2 at that time.

Being originally the plain's people, the Kacharis or Dimasa knew the improved method of cultivation by ploughing soil. They constructed irrigation canals and dams in place of culturable land. The hill streams namely, Diyung, Mahur and Langting etc., were made navigable by removing obstructions for plying country dug-outs. They burnt bricks for house construction. They also knew the art of stone carving. The rock temple of Maibang and image of birds, beasts, flowers and human pictures etc. were the examples of their skill on the line. Their metal workshops located at present Gidingpur village were known for quality products such as daos, swords, axes and even guns. The neighbouring hill areas had to market the products for their household use.

The rulers particularly King Indra Ballabh Narayan was known for his valour. He defeated the Mughal army led by Islam Khan, the Subadar of Decca near Sylhet in early 17th century and adorned himself with the title Shatrudomon. This has been corroborated by the inscriptions of the gold coins which were unearthed at Maibang some years ago. He also defeated Joshomanik, the Jaintia king and took the title Josho Narayan and lastly he defeated Protap Singha, the Ahom king in a battle at Roha and took the title as Protap Narayan. He then performed a grand victorious celebration and renamed Maibang, the capital as Kirtipur.

The Dimasa at that time took the Hindu culture and religion partially without following the Baidik System of worship. They continued their indigenous faith of Animism. (There is an interesting story for non-acceptance of the Brahminism which cannot be told here for want of space.) On the whole in those days the conditions of the people in the Kachari kingdom was higher than other neighbouring hill people in all respects.

The advent of the Britishers has changed the whole atmosphere in the Kachari kingdom. It is known to all that the British i.e. the East India Company came to this country for trade and has nothing to do with the internal matters of the people. They came in contact with the Kacharis in salt trading at Sylhet and later at Badarpur ghat where they had a Kuti or godown. The Burmese depredations in Assam and in Kachari kingdom in 1825 has precipitated the last king and Tularam Senapati to enter into the Treaty agreement with the Company in 1827 only to protect the kingdom from the external enemies. After the agreement they felt secure as the Company had the regular soldiers equipped with better weapons. But the people particularly in the upper stratas of the society naturally could not adjust themselves with the new administration for self-aggrandizement and consequently conflicts took place here and there in the hill areas. After the rebellion of Sombhudban, the rebel, the administration in North Cachar Hills was tightened. Weapons were confiscated, induced to opium addiction indiscriminately. One by name Ramdas, a Dimasa who was barely literate and an opium addict was appointed as a 'Daroga' only to train the people in opium smoking. Thus after two or three generations the Dimasa lost everything. Their cottage industry and artisanship in other trades already been destroyed in the process of dumping. They then began to forget self-respect and self-realisation. They have been lost to themselves.

In fact, barring a 10 bedded Hospital at Haflong, a dispensary at Maibang, an L.P. School and a few bridle paths, no development worth the name was done by the alien Government in the whole period of administration in the North Cachar Hills. The people had to remain in dark with the contemporary political movement in the rest of the country. No relationship or mutual contact with the people outside N.C. Hills was allowed. Under the provision of the 1935 India Act, the provincial Governments were started functioning throughout India including Assam from 1937 but North Cachar Hills and Lushai Hills had to remain outside the purview of the provincial autonomy. They were not entitled to send their representatives to the Assam Assembly and the result which the laws enacted for public benefit such as Opium Prohibition Act and the like could not be extended to enforce in the areas.

In the field of judicial administration, the Magistrates in the excluded areas were not in compulsion to follow the rules of I.P.C., C.R.P.C. but their own. A great Indian leader and a seasoned Barrister Late C.R. Das once attended Haflong Court in connection with a certain Railway case. After completing his pleadings and arguments etc., submitted to the Magistrate for passing the orders as per law. But the Magistrate said that he agreed with Das but he wanted to punish the person concerned, because he need not follow the law by letter but only in spirit and passed the orders according to his sweet will. Das felt upset and left court. These were the brief account of the alien administration in North Cachar Hills.

There is another episode which should not be left out without mentioning. The British Government though conceded India's independence but in the meantime they had a proposal for creating a 'Crown Colony' comprising the areas of Assam's excluded and partially excluded areas, the N.E.F.A. (now Arunachal) and the Chittagong Hill tracts. Some tribal leaders of these regions even a certain Ahom leader at that time were involved in themselves considering the pros and cons of the proposal. The Governor of Assam, Sir Akbar Hydery was also said to have been entangled with the scheme. However, the proposal had to be dropped for good with the adequate handling from the Government of India after the independence. This was also one of the reasons for the concession to the Hill tribals for their autonomy. On the 15th August, 1947 India won freedom and Bordoloi as the chairman of the Sub-Committee of the Constituent Assembly came to visit North Cachar Hills for the second time. Meanwhile we too have finalised the memorandum to be submitted to Bordoloi after series of discussions in the tribal Council which was formed earlier. The demands which highlighted in the memorandum were "Autonomy to protect the trible languages, cultures, customs and way of life, reservation of seats in the Assam Assembly and creation of tribal welfare portfolio in the Assam Cabinet and entrustment of the portfolio to a tribal minister etc." Stressing to the points of demands the memorandum stated that "Because of the deliberate exclusion by the people of the plains and so the hills should be allowed to enjoy some sort of autonomy till they accustomed to mix with the brothers in the plains". Consequently the Bordoloi Sub-Committee on receipt of memorandun from different Hill areas started sitting to consolidate their findings.

It was learnt that the Sub-Committee deputed B.N. Rau, the then Adviser to the Government for tribal areas, to America for an on the spot study of the autonomy for the Negros and Red Indians. On return from America Rau had submitted his report comparing side by side the conditions of the people in and outside of such autonomous or the reservation areas. According to the findings of Rau the conditions of the people who reside outside autonomous area was far better than that of the autonomous areas as they could sail the same with their primitive life. The report from a prominent and experienced officer like Benegal Nara Singh Rau is a debatable one even today.

However, the Bordoloi sub-committee recommended for the District Autonomy empowering the District Council to make Laws and Regulations on land, water, cattle markets, social customs, primary education, appointment of village headman amd chief etc. The recommendation was accepted of its entirety by the Constituent Assembly the result of which the Sixth Schedule was incorporated in the Constitution of India and subsequently the District Councils were functioning in the hills since 1952.The main purpose of the Sixth Schedule was to protect and preserve the tribal custom, usages and develop their traditions and way of life according to their own genius. It has little to do with the economic programme specially, with plan economy which was highly technical and too big for the District Council.

Here was the mistake of the Hill tribal people to understand spirit and objective of the Sixth Schedule. Instead of following principle, the leaders of the District Council started thinking to be involved with the ambitious schemes of Government in which they had neither experience nor the public spirit and honesty to manage the schemes. However, on request of the District Councils, the State Government entrusted the development schemes for execution to N.C. Hills and Karbi Anglong District Councils in 1972. But after 15 years, the entrustment has been proved to be miserable failure. Now the District Councils in these two districts have been turned to a spot for nasty political gambling of unscrupulous people. It is painful to note that North Cachar Hills within its 35 years of existence could not pass a single legislation in the matters of socio-culture or customs for the improvement or eradication of the old age practice or superstitions. It could not introduce Dimasa or other tribal languages even in the primary stage of education. On the other hand, the same tribe, the Bodos, who live in Assam Valley and outside of such autonomy have gone far ahead and introduced their language in the college and university level. It is really an irony of fate that the institution of District Council should turn to be a destroyer rather than the preserver.

Nevertheless, the intention of the framers of the Sixth Schedule had to allow the hill people to develop and to shape the destiny according to their own genius cannot be questioned in anyway. It is a testimony of the large heartedness of the Indian leaders towards backward hills people and for such a generous gesture the credit should go reasonably to Late Lokopriya Gopinath Bordoloi.

Homage to Gopinath Bordoloi

By Surabala Bordoloi

My heart is bemused with past memories whenever I look back.

I am at a loss, what I should write about my husband. But I have decided to write in short about him as the request has come from the Publication Board. Maybe there are many omissions.

It has since been 59 years I got married with my husband Late Gopinath Bordoloi. But the memories of those bygone days are still fresh in my mind. I was then just thirteen years. And my husband was one month short of 28 years. Our marriage was at that time solemnised with much fanfare and musical extravaganza. My father was late Bhumikanta Mazindar Baruah and my mother was late Bibika Baruah. I happened to be the only daughter of my parents. And I had four brothers. I liked being associated more with the religious rituals of our family than with sports since my childhood. I knew how to adore the elders and love the youngers as well as to entertain guests. In autumn I was filled with thrill of joy to see the Sephali flowers spread around beneath the tree, because they were within my easy reach to worship God. I engaged myself in worshipping, even enshrining a piece of stone. Those days are still vibrant in my memory. My parents and my grandmother were always busy with worshipping. A priest was also engaged. Perhaps, so I was so much drawn to religious rituals and I felt that to be averse to worship would be sinful. I took food only after worshipping.

I came to my in-laws household before I was 14. Two maids were sent with me for my assistance. It was so difficult to understand fully my in-laws household. Those days were far different than today. I was quite young. I derived pleasure learning from kneeling before my seniors. And my joys knew no bounds in association with my younger companions.

Before I could understand everything of the household I had to be in the kitchen and to cook, I was really at a loss. Because I was yet to learn cooking. But my husband was an expert in every work. He taught me first how to cook kalia of Rahu fish. With a long veil over my head, he taught me from outside the thatched and bamboo kitchen. My husband was very fond of roasted deer meat, Rahu kalia etc. He also taught me cutting and embroidery shirts, blouses etc. He drew pictures of different flowers on cloths and embroidered them in diverse colours. He taught me Hindi and English. His elder sister late Sashila Devi was an ideal woman. She took much care of her younger brother's studies and she fostered high ambiions for him. She made joke of him if he went for an outing in the evening after the day's study. Bordoloi was enthusiastic in studies as well as sports. So he was always a first rate student in school.

In 1921, the Non-Cooperation movement started. In 1922 he had to be out of station several times in connection with organizational works. He had also to travel around in explaining to the village people the cause of saving the country and he toured far and wide particularly in the villages. He could return home only after several days. On an evening in 1924, Bordoloi was late in returning home after addressing a meeting at Digaru near Panikhaity. He fell down from his bicycle as the road was in a poor condition. Parasu Gaonburha, the village head of Panikhaity saw him there and took him home to nurse him with utmost care. He applied some herbs to his injuries. Bordoloi was overwhelmed with the unthought of hospitality of the family, as well as effectiveness of the herbal medicine applied by the oldman. He also arranged a bed on the ground with some new clothes taken out of wooden boxes (traditionally used by Assamese villagers for keeping clothes etc.). The old woman picked up fishes from the domestic fishery, vegetables from their own garden and served them with cooked Jaha rice which gave a very sweet and fresh flavour. The pain from his bruises vanished with the tender and affectionate care of the family. "We are privileged to nurse you today", they joyfully said to him. Bordoloi returned home by rail next day.

Our house was at that time at Silpukhuri. One day in 1925 Rohini Kumar Choudhary, Jyotish Chandra Das, my husband and some of their friends were putting up in the Palasbari Dak-Bungalow with their wives. I was also privileged to attend a very important discussion on the country's problems. We went out to see the Palasbari locality. Along with me were the two other ladies, i.e. newly married Smt. Nirmala Medhi and Smt. Rajbala Das, wife of Dr. Jyotish Ch. Das. We served tea with tea-pots.

It was December,1924. Bordoloi was walking at 3-30 a.m. with a turban on his head. There were kerosene lamps on the roads at that time instead of electric lights. Bordoloi was scheduled to reach the ferry service at Pandu at 5-30 a.m. The ferry would cross the Brahmaputra at Amingaon where railways terminated. Bordoloi was leaving for Ahmedabad to attend the Congress Session. Bordoloi reached Pandughat to take the ferry to cross over to Amingaon and took the Down train thwarting sharp police surveillance in that dark night. After about 15 days of his return from Ahmedabad the police caught him at Dhubri.

In the year 1924, the police surrounded our residence in the early hours before dawn. The police feigning to be guest started calling from outside. I with my sister-in-law was terribly shaken as to who would call them at 4-00 a.m. Raising the curtain we saw the police cordoning the house. All of us awoke. But nobody knew that Bordoloi was yet to return from the Congress Session. The police was determined to arrest him at the Congress office itself showing him warrant and directly to take him to the jail. Preparations for the nationwide stir was in full swing, he had done many works like copying, cyclostyling etc., at home and normally brought such works home. Police raided and took away some papers. They held him in the office.

He came home and hurriedly had some food and said, "I am going to prison, and you should not feel sad, don't forget to send any khadi clothes like bed sheet, pillow, bedding, handmade dhoti, kurta and khadi tools." Thus he left for jail with the police in a pony-cart. He was discharged after three days. Next time he was imprisoned for one year.The third time he was kept in the Jorhat Jail. Martyr Kushal Konwar, Pitambar Deva Goswami, the pontiff of the Garmur Sattra, Fakhruddin Sahib, Mahadev Sharma, Bishnuram Medhi, Gauri Talukdar, Bijoy Bhagawati, Kamakhya Prasad Tripathi were his jail mates. I am still preserving a letter he wrote to me from the Jorhat Jail. Every month he sent nearly two seers of yarns to weave dhoti, kurta, pillow-cover, bed-sheets and towels for him. I sent bed sheets with wide colour frills to Fakhruddin Sahib also. Bordoloi translated the Anasakti Yoga into Assamese from the Gita. He also wrote on the Gandhiji and the *Hazarat Muhammed* in his prison days. He found leisure to engage himself in the writing on the Upanisads and the Gita during his imprisonment. He was able to discuss on these with Pitambar Deva Goswami, the Garmur Sattradhikar. My daughter Lily made efforts to bring out *Gandhiji* and the *Hazarat Muhammed.* But the *Jishukhrista* (Jesus Christ) and the *Ramchandra* are yet to be printed. Some time back Sjt. Atul Chandra Hazarika serialized the Ramchandra in a journal. Bordoloi was released from the Jorhat jail when he suffered from tooth and eye ailments. He was in Calcutta for treatment. Initially he was treated by Lokabandhu Dr. Bhubaneswar Baruah and then by Dr. B.C. Roy, the former Chief Minister of Bengal and Dr. Hemchandra Baruah.

In the summer of 1924 (months of July-August) a meeting was organized in Dumunichaki at North-Guwahati. People from several villages poured into the meeting. It was dark night by the time the leaders came to take the boats. Siddhinath Sarma and Bhrigu Chandra Das accompanied Bordoloi. My father arranged a big boat with two boatmen for three of them after entertaining them with food. At 12 midnight the currents of the riotous Brahmaputra took the boat against their destination. The boatmen named Khorakaka and Dhatukaka were however experts. In the troublesome waters in the dark night they however managed to save the situation and safely reached the destination. God always saves at the time of difficulties.

I still remember another event. In 1925 the people of Bamundi organized a large meeting. Bordoloi, Lokabandhu Bhubaneswar Baruah and some other friends were invited to the meeting. This time also they got into a big boat with courage and confidence. The boat by any means could not be driven against the current. In the meantime a postalship came from Dhubri. The boat was on the verge of being capsized on the dangerous waves. The boatmen with great intelligence and courage rowed towards Kamakhya and then to Fancybazar ghat. Bordoloi had great faith in God and remembered Him before doing anything. In 1926, the Congress session was held in Assam. Bordoloi and Deshabhakta Phukan were searching for a suitable site. With them were Mrs. Phukan and the elder sister of Phukan Mrs. Giriza Phukan and I. Bordoloi was engaged day and night for organizing the Congress session in 1926. He sacrificed his legal profession for this purpose.

Domestically we had to suffer a lot as we were far from being financially sound. He considered his service to the country as the greatest religion. Whenever he was burdened with thoughts he started telling myths and stories to his children. He taught them never to discriminate among people. In 1944 the Mahalaya came before the Durga Puja. It was a good day in October. At about 1.00 p.m. he sat for lunch after other members of the family had finished. He suddenly got up at hearing a beggar's voice. He saw that a beggar was sitting outside the house. He asked me if food could be arranged for him. When he saw me pensive, he took his own plate, offered it to him and was not in till the beggar was satisfied. Our third son Bhaity started crying to see that his father's plate was sacrificed to the beggar. Bordoloi explained to him, "The Mahalaya is a day when the forefathers are remembered with worshippings. So it is to my great joy that I could give my food to another." The grown-ups should also bear this truth in their minds.

On the Magh Bihu day Bordoloi called youngsters for playing, asked them to break earthen pitchers with a cloth tied on their eyes and enjoyed giving prizes to 1st, 2nd and 3rd holders. He arranged for cooking fish and meat under his own supervision in the previous night (uruka) in our courtyard. He invited the children of our neighbours, particularly a Mikir boy (Kanti) named Huki and a child of a shoemaker. He kept on asking them what sports they liked and enjoyed their association with different games. He was also fond of marble and ring games which he arranged among young boys and gave prizes to the winners. With his encouragement their interest in different sports was doubled. The young boys and girls called him *Maju dada* (elder brother). He was deeply loved by all of them.

Bordoloi was very much interested in fishing. Huki Mikir, Prasad and Mahiram Barua were his companions in fishing. Every Saturday they went to Bonda for fishing. He took interest in games as well. He often went to Digaru, Panikhaiti, Kshetri and Panbari for hunting. He was very much affectionate towards the villagers of these areas. He made arrangements for an orange garden with plantations. But before he tasted the fruit of his labour destiny took him away.

He was an expert hunter with a long record of experience. He went to these areas with prior information to the villagers with Biru Mikir and Ramkrishan for hunting. He was more interested in hunting deers and wild hens than tigers and elephants. He arranged distribution of deer meat and orange in every house on the festive night before the Magh Bihu.

Every Saturday he assembled all the children in the courtyard during the summer evening and taught them to sing Bargit, Brahma Sangit and Tagore's songs. He also taught stories from old scriptures. Huki Mikir who did not know Assamese was taught Assamese and also Bihu songs. On his singing all were overjoyed with laughter.

Bordoloi extended succour to several poor students to continue their study. A Manipuri student was with him who completed his Matriculation and then was employed in his office.

Bordoloi studied in the Calcutta University. In his student days he was reputed for his expertise in music. He learnt to play Organ, Violin and Esraj and sang classical, Rabindra Sangeet and Brahma Sangeet. He was an expert in Bihu songs also. As a student in Calcutta he was associated with theatrical performances and was reputed for his Bihu songs. Wearing the dress of Hanuman, he sang the traditional Assamese folk song *"Kalmau Khaonte burha hanumante nagari karile chan ou gobindai ram."*

In 1938 a scholar and sage came from Bombay to work for preaching Arya Samaj ideals. Bordoloi liked to listen to him. At that time Chief Engineer Ramesh Chandra and others started working for the Arya Samaj. First they organised sacrificial rites. Then in choral voice they sang, *"uth jag musafir bhor bhai, jo shoyat hai wo khoyat hai, jo jagat hai wo payat hai"*. They started their work with this song.

Bordoloi bought two female elephant kids. He named them Madanmala and Sundarmala. Both these elephants were looked after as if they were his daughters. After bathing, they would trumpet. They would come inside, if Bordoloi did not respond to their call. Bordoloi always derived great pleasure feeding them banana, rice etc. Unfortunately once Madanmala died in an accident while she was taken for hunting. Bordoloi was greatly saddened with the incident. Sundarmala with her kid was sold and

Bordoloi was again very sad. The suitcase containing his spectacles, diary, artificial teeth, the Gita (presented by Mahatma Gandhi) and the bag for folding the Gita (stitched by Kushal Konwar) was stolen from a train in Delhi.

Bordoloi frequently dreamt of bad omens. It is as if God sent premonitions. Nobody could think that the bad dreams would turn into reality. The dark moment finally arrived. The weather which was bright with sunshine suddenly turned dark with lightning and thunder.

Bordoloi came from his office and asked about the children. Some of the students of the Lady Keane College who received shocks of the lightning were treated in hospital. He said that lightning and thunder without clouds signified bad omens for country." Do you hear my children death is beckoning me!" Nobody can dispense with the ways of the destiny! How could one perceive that his words would truly be real?

On August 5 (20th Sravan), 1950 Bordoloi, the light of Assam went out. Destiny untimely took away a great son of Assam. Many tasks of the country remained half-done and incomplete. Nature had as if cried in great sadness. A few days later a devastating earthquake had shaken hills, plains and rivers of Assam to their total ravage. Parasuramkunda, the scared site of Sadiya was totally destroyed. In the Duflla hills as well as in the holy sattras of Majuli nature played havoc. River waters plunged the sattras as well as other villages.The memories of deaths and other devastations created by this earthquake are still fresh in peoples' minds. Lokopriya Bordoloi always shared the sorrows and griefs of others. Justice was his religion. He was averse to discrimination between rich and poor. Once a village boy was brought by a middleman to him with the promise of awarding an employment when Bordoloi was a minister, Bordoloi rebuked the man but fed the boy and sent him after paying him the fares. He was deeply pained when he saw any injustice meted to individuals giving false promises.

Bordoloi never disheartened anybody. Once Bordoloi helped a Nepali milkman by carrying the bride's party in his own car to the groom's house. He spent his lifetime without discriminating between high and low. He considered service and benefaction as a great thing. He always loved the Mikirs (Karbis) and Kacharis of the villages for their simplicity.

I hope his ideal and loving nature and his liberal, tolerant character would always inspire the coming generations.

(Translated from Assamese)

Reminiscence of Gopinath Bordoloi

By R. Thanhlira

Gopinath Bordoloi was undisputedly one of the most prominent and distinguished leaders Assam has ever produced. He is still remembered with respect and admiration.

When death claimed him on the 6th of August 1950 while still holding the reins of administration as a Chief Minister, the people of Assam were overwhelmed with grief. So deeply mourned was his death that the honoured title of 'Lokopriya' was ungrudgingly conferred on him as a token of their love for him.

Born in the year1890, he obtained his M.A. and B.L. degrees. After working as a Headmaster of the Sonaram High School in Gauhati, he joined the bar in 1921. As a freedom-fighter, he suffered one year imprisonment in 1922. He was the Chairman of the Gauhati Municipality from 1934 till 1938. When he was elected to the Assam Legislature in 1937, he became leader of the Congress parliamentary party. He then became the Chief Minister (designated as Prime Minister or Premier in those days) for the period 1938-1939. Because of his ardent devotion towards the freedom struggle for India, he offered an individual Satyagraha. He was arrested under the Defence of India Rules and kept in jail from 1942 to1944. He was elected in 1945 as the President of the Gauhati University Trust Board. Again, he became the Chief Minister of Assam from 1946 till his death in August 1950.Thus, becoming the first Chief Minister of Assam in the Independent India. Bordoloi's monthly salary as Chief Minister was Rs. 1,500 and later increased to Rs. 2,000. But, he used to draw only Rs.1000 and surrendered the balance to the Government as a voluntary cut.

Being also a good parliamentarian, eloquent and forceful speaker, Bordoloi in no time, became a prominent figure in the Constituent Assembly, the body entrusted to the framing of the Constitution for India. He was appointed as Chairman of the Advisory Sub-Committee for the tribal areas of Assam. It might be remembered that the tribal areas of Assam at the time consisted of the present Meghalaya, Nagaland, Mizoram, Arunachal Pradesh and Mikir and North Cachar Hills. And it was as the Chairman of this Advisory Sub-Committee that Bordoloi first came to Mizoram in April 1947 with Revered Thakkar Bapa, an eminent social worker and Sir B.N. Rau, Constitutional Adviser to the

Goverenment of India, to discuss with local tribal representatives the administrative arrangements for the Assam tribal areas under the new Constitution, which was on the anvil.

It may be noted here that the provisions for the establishment of Autonomous District Councils in the tribal areas of Assam, as incorporated in the Sixth Schedule of the Constitution of India, had been based, in the main on the recommendation of the Advisory Committee which Bordoloi headed as mentiond earlier. Hence it is safe and only fair to say that Gopinath Bordoloi was definitely one of the major architects of Sixth Schedule. The provisions of this Sixth Schedule have become so popular that they are in use, not only in the State of Assam but in other States also. Another unforgettable achievement of Bordoloi and other representatives of Assam in the Constituent Assembly was the incorporation in the Constitution of its Article 275 which prescribes the quantum of financial assistance the Central Government should provide for the development of tribal areas in Assam.

I had the privilege of meeting Bordoloi for the first time when he visited Aizawl in the capacity as Chairman of the Advisory Sub-Committee. I appeared before him to give a brief evidence and, later, I heard him address a public meeting. He very much impressed me as a sincere and able leader.

I met Gopinath Bordoloi for the second time at the Government House (now, Raj Bhavan) in Shillong on the 10th of November 1947 to discuss about setting up of an elected Advisory Council for the Lushai Hills District (now Mizoram). The Mizo Union party which had more than 76 per cent of the Mizo people within its fold was, in those days, strongly demanding the constitution of a popularly elected Advisory Council. But the idea did not receive the favour of the authority in Lushai Hills and was opposed by vested interests, like the Mizo Chiefs and others. As the heat of the political situation was about to reach a boiling point the Governor summoned a conference of the representatives of the Chiefs and Commoners. The negotiations held in the presence of the Governor, Sir Akbar Haidari, was conducted by Gopinath Bordoloi, the Prime Minister of Assam. To the delight of all concerned, an agreement was reached without much difficulty to set up an elected Advisory Council. It was at this meeting that I personally witnessed with admiration the high statesmanship, diplomatic skill and the broadmindedness in practice of Gopinath Bordoloi for it was solely due to his able guidance that the meeting of warring groups who could hardly ever see anything eye to eye could disperse after the meeting with smiles on all sides.

The last time I met Bordoloi was in the third week of July, 1950 when he came to Aizawl for the first time in his capacity as Chief Minister; and this unfortunately happened to be his last also. On his arrival on the 22nd of July he was accorded a rousing, enthusiastic and elaborate welcome by the Mizos and non-Mizos , the like of which they have not given again to any visiting political leaders till now. During the three days he halted he had occasion to visit a 15 kilometre long jeep road recently constructed with the voluntary labour of the people. This was a completed portion of the Aizawl- Serchhip- Lunglei jeep road project which was targeted to be constructed on the self-help basis. The road was yet narrow, rough, bumpy and slippery, with heavy rains pouring all the time. He was very much impressed with the works done and sanctioned, then and there, a good amount as grant-in-aid for the maintenance.

On July 24, he inaugurated the Advisory Committee, having 14 members who were chosen out of the popularly elected members of the Advisory Council mentioned earlier. The Advisory Committee was to function as a "Shadow District Council". In the afternoon, a grand public meeting, which I had the privilege to preside over, was held. His speech in the meeting was interesting and enlightening. In the same meeting, he announced the nomination of one Mizo leader to be a member in the then provisional Parliament of India. It was deservedly received with thundering applause.

During the three days he stayed in Aizawl, Gopinath Bordoloi could endear himself to the Mizo people so much so that the unexpected news of his death, barely two weeks after his departure from Aizawl, struck the Mizo people like a bolt from the blue. In a heart-felt resolution adopted at a huge memorial service held on the 7th of August at Aizawl, the people of Mizoram expressed their due acknowledgement of Gopinath Bordoloi's love, sincerity, honesty and untiring zeal to serve the country and, in particular, the backward and undeveloped tribal people.

In the death of Gopinath Bordoloi, not only Assam, but India as a whole lost an able administrator, statesman and patriot of high order.

Gopinath Bordoloi and the Battle for Survival

By Dr. Birendra Kumar Bhattacharyya

[Gopinath Bordoloi's calibre as a leader was fully revealed during the critical days of transfer of powers by the British Crown to the Indian nationalists. The Muslim League's demand for inclusion of Assam in Pakistan was rejected by the people of Assam. Bordoloi could sense their mood and came forward to provide the leadership they needed. But before that he had to tackle the difficult political situation created by the world-shaking events of World War 11 which reached Assam's soil and the last movement for freedom of India which was marked by popular violent resistance against inhuman police repression.]

In jail, Bordoloi suffered from eye trouble and high blood pressure. The Government released him on health ground on January 26,1944 but he was kept interned in the city of Guwahati. However, he was allowed to go to Calcutta for treatment provided he refrained from being involved in political activities.

After his return from Calcutta, Bordoloi had to remain interned in Guwahati. He found the situation outside jail very disturbing. The Allied Army stationed in Assam and Manipur recovered from their initial shock of humiliating defeat and was on the offensive on the Imphal front. The 1942 rebellion in Assam, an operational area of the Allied Army, cost Assam heavily. The Congress Committee and *santi senas* were illegal, civil liberties were non-existent, and special ordinances like Penalties (Enhancement) Ordinance,1942, the Special Criminal Courts Ordinance, the Armed Forces (Special Powers) Ordinance, 1942, Subversive Activities Ordinance, 1943 and Defence of India Rules were in force. All those measures had been used to suppress the popular uprising. Out of a total 3531 persons arrested till December 31,1943, 1679 were convicted. The number of those prosecuted under DIR ran up to 3,364 out of which 2,448 persons were convicted. The total number of detention cases was 403. According to the Government 22 persons lost their lives as a result of police firings and 4 received death sentences. Of the four convicted with death penalty, three were later on granted pardon. The total amount of collective fines imposed was Rs. 4,24,661 out of which Rs.2,94,727 were realised.

Immediately after the arrests of Congress MLAs in 1942 the Governor of Assam, Sir Robert Reid, revoked Sec.93, and called Sir Saadullah back to power. The new Ministry was installed on August 25,1942. The Ministry renewed its policy of support to war efforts and became an instrument of suppression of the August movement. In addition, it revoked the order of the Governor scrapping the Land Development Scheme passed on March 6, 1941, and reverted to its old policy of throwing open grazing and forest reserves to immigrants from East Bengal, which led to clashes between the graziers and the immigrants.

The public were agitated over both these issues. Bordoloi felt that both the imperialists and the communalists were acting concertedly to suppress the secular democratic forces. The communal elements, in addition, were pursuing a policy of division of India on religious basis. The Muslim League, to which some members on the Saadullah Cabinet were affiliated, made a determined attempt to include Assam in their proposed Pakistan. Bordoloi, in consultation with his colleagues, decided to revive constitutional politics and constructive work together. His strategy was flawless. He knew that communalism and imperialism could not be fought on the agitational front alone. The harassed people have to be spiritually revived through constructive work and the alliance between the communalists and the imperialists broken through vigorous legislative action.

Bordoloi got a comprehensive report prepared on the Assam situation by some of his released colleagues and send it to Gandhiji for study and advice. The messengers were two veteran Congress workers, Mahendra Mohan Chaudhury and Akhyaya Kumar Das. Gandhiji had been released from detention on May 5, 1944. The messengers met him in Panchagni and then in Wardha. After reading the report, Gandhiji advised the people of Assam to cultivate fearlessness. In answer to a query on the Muslim League's attempt to change the population-structure of Assam through a policy of unbridled immigration from East Bengal, Gandhiji replied categorically that such unrestricted migration to a small province should not continue.[1] He further opined that in the event of a possibility that due

[1]"Gopinath Bordoloi," pp. 129-130, an anthology published by Assam Publication Board. "The Political History of Assam" (vol. III, .p.262) notes how the Saadullah Ministry allotted 1 lakh bighas of land in Assam valley for settlement of immigrants from East Bengal in the period between 1939-41. The magnitude of this influx was so serious that between the years 1911 and 1941 there was a conspicuous increase in the Muslim population in the Assam valley districts (including Garo Hills) as shown below:

Year	Muslim Population
1911	3,55,320
1921	5,85,943
1931	9,43,352
1941	13,03,9620

to such migration the local population were likely to be reduced to a minority, the people had a right to resort to satyagraha. He however made it plain that the issue should not be given a communal colour. The other query was regarding the policy of non-violence. In Assam, some underground workers led by Sankar Barua advised the women to resist military and police atrocities, if necessary, with swords. This raised a moral issue. Gandhiji replied that non-violence was, for the brave, a very potent weapon. Those who could not wield this matchless weapon were free to use traditionl weapons in defence of their honour or dignity.

Gandhiji invited Bordoloi to come and stay with him to recoup his health. But he could not go. However, Bordoloi used to visit Sevagram frequently. In one of his visits to Wardha, he found that Gandhiji was observing silence. So he put some written questions to him. To these, he got written answers. Bordoloi's questions revealed one dilemma in his mind. He was unable to decide whether as *satyagrahi,* he should attend the Assembly or not. "I have read your thing carefully. I am myself in doubt," replied Gandhiji ."But on the whole way my personal opinion is that if I am a member, I should go and attend. Assam is the most peculiar case. What may apply to Bombay ought not to be made applicable to Assam. Hence I say quite seriously, act as the dictate of your heart tells you. If by coming to Sevagram you discover your heart, the visit will have been worthwhile. It will not be so even if you take a readymade opinion from me. It may flatter my vanity, but not serve you." To a further query, Gandhi said, "I tell you, if you are a leader, act as a leader and not as my follower."

Bordoloi also told Gandhiji that some constructive workers wanted to build a centre in the name of Kasturba in Assam. "Why should they wait if they have an action in mind ?" Gandhi asked ."Let them give the lead. Forty is a good number. They can do education work, maternity work, sanitation etc."

Bordoloi's mind was finally made up. With thirteen of his released colleagues he attended the November session of the Assam Assembly. On November 14,1944, he delivered a hard-hit speech in defence of civil liberties. "We reappear as a party to continue the fight from inside the Legislature," he said. "However thinned our ranks might be and however feeble our voice, will continue to be raised against this evil, which has brought in its wake so much misery to us....We shall work for the elementary liberties of human beings, which in the name of the war has been practically nullified. I mean the liberty of free association, the liberty of speech and the liberty of the press."

In March 1945 the Congress strength in the Assembly was increased to 18. Sir Saadullah's Government became unstable due to dissensions within the ruling party. On the other hand, the Congress party's popularity was at its height. So Sir Saadullah changed his tactics to keep himself in saddle. He made a pact with Bordoloi, the terms of which were as follows: (a) two-third of the security prisoners detained in jail would be released before April 30, 1945; (b) convicted political prisoners would be released as early as possible and cases of prisoners sentenced for sabotage would be reviewed; (c) ban on meetings, processions and rallies would be lifted in view of the coming local bodies and Assembly elections; (d) all restrictions orderd on the Congress MLAs and political prisoners would be removed except in the case of those who were engaged in underground activities; and (e) the Land Development Scheme would be scrapped and the Revenue Department would be placed in the hands of the veteran Assamese leader, Rohini Kumar Choudhury.

The agreement was a tactical victory for Bordoloi for it would restore civil liberties in Assam, which was essential for carrying out constructive work and for mobilising public opinion for the elections.

Sir Saadullah kept his word. His policies towards the 1942 movement and the East Bengal immigrants had been very unpopular, and he wanted Congress support to keep himself in saddle. Many Congressmen opposed the whole agreement, as it involved a question of principle. Bordoloi, therefore, sent Mahendra Mohan Choudhury to meet Gandhiji and get his opinion on the subject. Gandhiji treated the case of Assam as an exception and wrote to him to act as he thought fit.

The Saadullah Ministry resigned on March 23,1945 only to resume office again with tacit Congress support. On May 31,1945 the Government lifted the ban on Assam Congress.But its resolution on land policy adopted on January 16,1945 following a decision made at an all parties meeting became a bone of contention. The resolution conceded the Bordoloi Ministery's earlier decision that the Government would only settle those landless immigrants that had come before 1938. It provided for keeping the professional grazing reserves intact and promised to give special protection to the tribal people. But the Government could not implement the resolution in the right spirit. The Muslim League opposed the resolution wholesale. The Congress found that it gave such discretionary powers to local officials that settlements of land with immigrants could hardly be prevented. Bordoloi had to constantly review his position in regard to the Ministry. He had another consultation with Gandhiji on the subject and found that Gandhiji's opinion concurred with his own.

Meanwhile the Government of India announced its decision to hold general elections on August 21,1945 . The Congress decided to contest the elections. Bordoloi was a special invitee to the Congress Working Committee (held in Pune in September) which took this decision. The Assam Assembly was dissolved on October 1,1945 and the general elections took place on January 9,1946. In this election, the Congress and the Muslim League were the main contestants. The Congress under Bordoloi's leadership won big victory this time. It secured the support of 61 members in a House of 103. On February 11,1946, the new Bordoloi cabinet assumed office in Shillong. The Muslim League, however, got the majority of Muslim seats. The objective of the Muslim League at that time could be clearly seen from the statement made by H.S.Suhrawardy, Secretary of the Muslim League Parliamentary Board at a public meeting: "The Muslims of Bengal have awakened from their slumber and are determined to achieve Pakistan in alliance with our brothers in Assam."

The new Bordoloi Cabinet consisted of nine members including Bisnuram Medhi, J.J.M. Nichols Roy, Baidyanath Mukherjee, Ramnath Das, Bhimbar Deuri, Abdul Matlib Majumdar and Abdur Rashid.[1] The Ministry took power at a crucial moment of Indian history. The Labour Government in Britain decided to send a Cabinet Mission to explore the possibility of drafting a future Constitution for India in consultation with the Viceroy and Indian political leaders. The Mission reached India on March 23, 1946 and began discussion with the Indian leaders. According to its plan, the Union of India would consist of both British India and the Indian States. It arbitrarily divided British India into three sections. Assam and Bengal were to be included in Group 'C' while Group 'B' was to comprise the Punjab, Sindh, the North-West Frontier Province and British Baluchistan. The rest of the provinces were to form Group 'A'.

---

[1] Political History of Assam, Vol. III, p. 335 "Bordoloi ventured at this moment to take two Muslims from the Muslim League and approached Saadullah to nominate them. Bordoloi justified this move saying that Muslims had about thirty-four lakhs of population in the Province. And that League Ministry under Saadullah had included two members in the Cabinet of Congress Nomination. But as soon as the news leaked out, it received an adverse public opinion and Bordoloi had to retrace his steps." Maulana Azad however commended Bordoloi's action.

Side by side, the constitution-making process also was to be started. According to the plan, the Provincial Legislatures would elect members to the Constituent Assembly. The Constituent Assembly would be divided into three sections and each section would draft the Constitution of each group separately. Later on, these section constitutions would be integrated and the Constitution of the Union of India would be drafted.The plan did not seem to deny a province the right to come out of one section and join another.

Before announcing their plan on May 16,1946, the Cabinet Mission had a thorough discussion with the Congress and the Muslim League leaders. On April 1,1946, Bordoloi had an interview with the Mission. He made a forceful plea before it for retaining Assam as a Province. He pointed out that it was already a Province formed on linguistic and cultural basis, enjoying provincial autonomy. It should be allowed to continue, he pleaded, in the future set-up as a full fledged unit. He favoured separation of Sylhet from Assam and rejected Jinnah's demand for Pakistan as absolutely preposterous. Sir Saadullah also reported before the Mission and suggested that the whole Province might be attached to Bengal. The Cabinet Mission stuck to its plan of forming groups.

The Assam Congress reacted sharply. The Working Committee dispatched a message to Abul Kalam Azad, the President of the Congress intimating its strong disapproval of and opposition to the Grouping Clause, Bordoloi, who was in Delhi, pointed out to the Congress leaders to mutually contradictory views expressed in the State paper. While the clause 15(5) stated that "Provinces should be free to form groups", the clause 19 (iv) and (v) made the grouping compulsory for the Provinces.[1] Bordoloi's fear about compulsory grouping was confirmed by Cabinet Mission's statement on the question. Lord Pethick Lawrence said,"The Provinces automatically came into sections A, B and C which are set out in the statement." That meant that Assam and Bengal would draft the group constitution together, and the constitution would be more or less binding on Assam. The right to ot after the constitution had been drafted by a majority vote would be virtually impossible, for in the section Assam would have only 10 members compared to Bengal's 60.

Bordoloi submitted a detailed memorandum to the Congress Working Committee in which he stated:

---

[1] **Political History of Assam, Vol. III, p. 346.**

"If the Working Committee do not stand up to safeguard them against the operation of these sinister proposals then Assam and her people will be compelled to think that the Working Committee in their anxiety to think of larger Provinces have given this small Province a go by. It will not be a surprise if many in Assam will consider it to be a great betrayal."

The Working Committee in its resolution of May 24, 1946 interpreted the paragraph 15 in its own way and stated, "The respective Provinces shall make their choice whether or not to belong to the section in which they are placed." The Cabinet Mission did not agree with this interpretation. It asserted that grouping was an "essential feature of the scheme" that it could only be modified by agreement between the parties. It made clear that opting out after the constitution had been adopted would be a major issue in which all eligible voters in the group would have a say. The interpretation favoured the League.

Bordoloi was not sure that the Congress Working Commitee would be persistent in its demand for a liberal interpretation of the clause. He declared on May 19 that Assam would stand by its right to provincial autonomy granted under the Act of 1933. The Statesman criticised the stand saying that it satisfied nobody. Bordoloi then felt that both the press and the politicians might fail Assam at the critical juncture. He had ample confidence in the national leaders like Nehru, Azad and Patel who agreed in principle that grouping or sitting in sections should not be compulsory. But he wanted unfaltering guidance and moral support of the one who would never fail. He turned to Mahatma Gandhi.

On May 26, the APCC wholeheartedly endorsed Bordoloi's memorandum and requested the Congress Working Committee not to accept any arrangement under which Assam will be compelled to go to the Group 'C'. The APCC opposed the European representation to the Constituent Assembly and the League's demand that it alone could elect Muslim members. Bordoloi insisted that the answer to the situation was a strong mass movement. Accordingly the APCC decided to mobilise public opinion, observed 5th June as an "anti-grouping day" and sent a strong delegation to represent Assam's case in the Working Committee meeting due to be held on June 10.

Sylhet did not initially join the movement. Abala Kanta Gupta, the Congress leader from the district, said, "Bordoloi's opinion does not reflect the sentiments of the Bengalees or Surma Valley of indeed of entire Assam. We feel, should there be grouping at all, the proposed grouping of Assam with Bengal is much more desirable." The Hill tribal leader, J.J.M. Nichols Roy at one stage had welcomed the Cabinet Mission plan, but now he opposed the grouping clause. His fear was that it would pave the way for Muslim domination over the tribal people.[1]

While Assam carried out spontaneous and widespread protest movement throughout the province, the Congress delegation led by Maulana Tyebulla went to different provinces to canvass support for their cause. On June 8, the delegation met Pandit Nehru,who categorically assured, "All Congress provinces will be asked to frame their own Constitutions, and on the basis of those, the Congress will draw up its draft Constitution and go the Constituent Assembly". "Who can force a Constitution on Assam in section C, when Assam will not accept it at all ?" he asked. He suggested that the Assam Assembly should pass a resolution giving a clear directive to the Constituent Assembly members on the issue.[2] Sardar Patel also endorsed Nehru's suggestion. The group led by Tyebulla then met Gandhiji, who said, "Congress is at your back. Even if Congress fails to support you eventually, come out of the Congress."

On June 10, the Congress Working Committee categorically stated in its resolution, "The Congress fully supports the Assam case. Assam shall frame its own Constitution." It also called upon the Assam Assembly to give mandate to its representatives in the Constituent Assembly. The Muslim League, however , had a different viewpoint. Therefore, the Assam delegation feared that the formation of compulsory grouping might ultimately lead to the emergence of Pakistan.

The Assam Assembly was summoned on July 16,1946 to elect ten representatives to the constituent Assembly.[3] Bordoloi also moved a resolution which claimed rights for the Province to frame its own constitution and have it settled by its own representaives. The resolution categorically asserted that it will be detrimental to the interests of the

---

[1]Political History of Assam, Vol. III, pp.355-359. Bordoloi sent a telegram to Maulana Azad on June 10 explaining the stand of these groups.

[2]Ibid .p. 36.

[3]The following members were elected : Gopinath Bordoloi, Rohini Chaudhury, Basanta Kumar Das, J.J.M. Nichols Roy, Omeo Kr. Das, Dharanidhar, Basumatari, Sir Saadullah, Abdul Hamid and Abdul Matin Chaudhury.

Province to form any section or sections, or group or groups with any other Province of British India, for settling the Constitution for the Province of Assam." It rejected the very idea of group Constitution for the province and allocation of provincial subjects by it. Then it specified its directives to the Assam representatives in the Constituent Assembly. The directives were as follows: (i) Assam's representatives should frame and settle the Constitution for Assam. (ii) They should not take part in any meeting or meetings of any section or group for settling the Constitution for Assam. (iii) They should resist all or any attempt made to set up a group Constitution for settlement of questions regarding the Provinces subject or subjects or for any such question being dealt with by any group of Provinces on the basis of majority of votes. (iv) They should take part in the meeting of the Constituent Assembly for the purpose of framing the Union Constitution.

"To me the attitude conveyed in the motion is perfectly consistent with the statement of the Cabinet Mission both in respect of the Provincial Constitution as also about matters in which two or more Provinces may be related,"asserted Bordoloi while moving the motion in the House. He elaborated his idea on provincial autonomy in the following manner: "The Cabinet Mission nowhere says that a Province cannot exercise its right to frame its own Constitution and cannot exercise its right to have any relationship with any other province as partners for discussion of subjects which are common to both the Provinces. If any other interpretation is sought to be put I think that interpretation must be wrong and non-worthy of the Constitution. Any other position cannot be consistent with the dignity and prestige of the Province, and who among us are here who would not feel the prestige and dignity of Assam."

Those who supported grouping were equally vehement. Sir Saadullah, himself an astute parliamentarian, argued that grouping was justified on the ground of economic and administrative convenience and interdependence. Bordoloi was not convinced. He asserted that a Province's autonomy could not be sacrificed for the sake of mere economic and other benefits. "It is from this very place that the honourable leader of the Muslim League tried to vindicate the honour of the Province not once but on several occasions," retorted Bordoloi ."Today, however, he talks in a different way. He has no hesitation to surrender the dignity and well-being of the Province to the mercy of another Province. To me, it is a deplorable sight indeed. A champion of the Provincial autonomy is going to sacrifice his best interests for a place of subservience to another Province."

The motion was carried without division, as the Muslim League desisted from participation in voting. Sir Saadullah's gesture in not pressing for a division was significant. Sir Andrew Clow, the then Governor of Assam, remarked while deposing before the Cabinet Mission that Saadullah was "at heart, a believer in Pakistan."

In July 1946, Maulana Azad relinquished his presidentship of the Congress and Nehru occupied his place. Nehru had some reservations about the Assam Assembly resolution and this he let Bordoloi know. "A section may definitely decide not to form any group and may continue as a section to consider Provincial Constitution," wrote Pandit Nehru in his letter on July 22,1946. He felt that the resolution was not happily worded, and was of the view that while making the Provincial Constitution, representatives of the Province need not be out-voted by others. Bordoloi was not convinced. He said that the resolution was meant to enable the Province to function as a unit within the sections and to ensure that they are not compelled to join any particular section.

The Congress stand on the compulsory grouping issue was not acceptable to the League, which in its Council on July 29, decided to withdraw its support to the Cabinet Mission plan. Jinnah questioned the authority of the Assam Assembly to give directions to its representatives in the Constituent Assembly. The League, instead of joining the interim Government for which there was an invitation, called for a 'Direct Action Day' on August 16. The Congress Working Committee on the other hand in its session on August 10 accepted the Mission Plan with its own interpretation and decided to join the interim Government.

The League Direct Action Day took a turn for the worse in Calcutta where several communal riots broke out on August 16 and continued for three days. Lord Wavell, the Governor General, was apparently influenced by the communal violence and became more rigid on the grouping clause. He directed that the provinces must remain members of the sections until the first elections were held under the new Constitution. The Congress Working Committee, faced with a new compulsion, slightly modified its stand on the grouping clause in its session on August 27. It decided to refer to the Federal Court for any interpretation of the disputed clause. On the other hand, Pandit Nehru, as the Head of the interim Government made the following announcement over radio: "We are perfectly prepared to and have accepted the position of sitting in sections which will consider the formation of groups."

Bordoloi induced the APCC to write to Pandit Nehru for clarification on the two issues of mediation bv the Federal Court and sitting in sections.

The letter was sent on September 16 and a reassuring reply came to Bordoloi on Sepember 27. Nehru firmly said, "In no event are we going to agree to a Province like Assam being forced against its will to do anything."

Wavell was keen to bring the League to the interim Government and the Constituent Assembly. He persuaded the British Government to make a statement on December 6, 1946, giving its unilateral verdict on the grouping clause. It declared that the Provinces must sit in sections and decide issues by a simple majority vote in the event of an absence of agreement. If the Constituent Assembly should desire that this fundamental point be referred to the Federal Court, it should be done at an early date. Jinnah was given an additional assurance that if the verdict of the Federal Court went against the League's position, the British Government would have a fresh look at the whole issue.

Bordoloi was apprehensive, and he, along with the other Constituent Assembly members from Assam urged the Congress Working Committee through a memorandum submitted to the Congress President on December 9, 1946 (i) not to agree to the interpretation which has been put to sections 19 (5) and (6), (ii) to alter the decision to abide by the arbitration of the Federal Court on the disputed clause, (iii) to resist the imposition of condition by the British Government upon the Constituent Assembly. The latter should declare itself as a sovereign body and proceed to frame the Constitution by sticking to its own viewpoint in all matters including those relating to sections and grouping.

The APCC also sent protest notes.

Bordoloi did not rest there. He sent two of his emissaries, Mahendra Mohan Choudhury and Bijoy Chandra Bhagawati, to meet Gandhiji in East Bengal and to seek his intervention in the matter. Accordingly they met Gandhiji at Srirampur on December 21. Gandhiji read Bordoloi's letter, and made a very forceful statement in support of the Assam stand. The following extract from the statement will make the bold stand of the unique revolutionary very clear:

"I have told Bordoloi that if there is no clear guidance from the Congress Working Committee, Assam should not go into sections. It should lodge its protest and retire from the Constituent Assembly. It will be a kind of satyagraha against the Congress for the good of the Congress."

"Rightly or wrongly, the Congress has come to the decision that it will stand by the judgment of the Federal Court. The dice are heavily loaded. The decision of the Federal Court will go against the Congress interpretation of 'grouping' as far as I can make out, for the simple reason that the Cabinet has got legal advice which upholds their decision."

"The Federal Court is the creation of the British. It is a packed Court. But to be consistent, the Congress must abide by its decision whatever it may be. If Assam keeps quiet, it is finished. No one can force Assam to do what it does not want to. It is autonomous to a large extent today."

"It must become fully independent and autonomous. Whether you have that courage, grit and gumption, I do not know. You alone can say that. But if you can make that declaration, it will be a fine thing. As soon as time comes for Constituent Assembly to go into section you will say, 'Gentlemen, Assam retires'. For the independence of India it is the only condition. Each unit must be able to decide and to act for itself. I am hoping that in this, Assam will lead the way. I have the same advice for the Sikhs. But your position is much happier. You are a whole Province. They are a community within a Province. But I feel every individual has the right to act for himself, just as I have."

"If Assam retires, it does not block, but leads the way to India's independence. If we think independence is going to descend on our heads from England or somewhere, we are greatly mistaken. It will not be independence. We will be crushed to atoms. We are fluctuating between independence and helpless dependence. The Cabinet Mission plan lies in between."

"...If Assam takes care of itself, the rest of India will be able to look after itself. What have you to do with the Constitution of the Union Government ? You should form your own Constitution. That is enough. You have the basis of the Constitution of 1935. It is based on Provincial autonomy. The hill people are with you. Many Muslims are also with you. The remainder can be too, if you act on the square..."

"...If you don't act correctly now, Assam will be finished. Tell Bordoloi, I don't feel the least uneasiness. My mind is made up. Assam must not lose its soul. It must uphold itself against the whole world. Else, I will say that Assam has only manikins and no men. It is an impertinent suggestion that Bengal should dominate Assam in any way....Tell people even if Gandhi tries to dissuade us, we won't listen."[1]

[1]Political History of Assam, Vol. III, pp. 486-7; Appendix-1 (Sources–APCC papers, 1946, APCC office, Guwahati).

When Bordoloi handed over the note to the Working Committee, on December 21, it had to take a fresh look at the decision on the arbitration of the Federal Court on a matter vitally affecting Provincial Autonomy. Bordoloi attended the momentous session of the APCC at Gauhati on December 26 which reiterated the Province's right to frame its own Constitution. It asked for freedom to act accordingly. After the decision, Bordoloi accompanied by Sidhinath Sarma, met Gandhiji at Srirampur and again sought his advice. Gandhiji supported Bordoloi.

The AICC met on January 5, 1947 to discuss the December 6, statement of the British Government. Assam had a few delegates in it. While the resolution moved by Pandit Nehru went a good deal in assuaging Assam's fears, the final draft recorded a general acceptance of the British statement ; it also mildly referred to the arbitration of the Federal Court on the grouping clause. As a team, the Assam members found the resolution somewhat short of their expectations. Gandhiji however said categorically that, "the resolution passed by the AICC gives enough if not clear guidance to Assam, for it will not compel Assam to act against the declared wish of the people through the Legislative Assembly.[1] Bordoloi issued a statement on January 8, 1947 saying that though Assam was prepared to sit in the section in the Constituent Assembly, she would stick to the July mandate of the Assam Legislative Assembly. He expressed genuine fears that the Muslim League might try to impose its majority view on the minority of Assam members, and was apprehensive about it. This shows that he was not willing to compromise Assam's stand and kept his options open. The APCC approved his stand by passing a resolution on February 6, 1947

On February 20, Atlee announced the British Government decision to transfer power by a date not later than June, 1948. The Viceroy was changed. Lord Mountbatten replaced Lord Wavell. He persuaded the Congress and the League leaders to accept the division of India. So far as Assam was concerned, the new plan left it untouched, except for the Sylhet district whose future was to be settled through a referendum. The Cabinet Mission Plan was abandoned and with it the problem whether Assam and Bengal would be grouped together also vanished. Mountbatten accepted the fact that Assam would be a part of the Indian Union.

---

[1] Political History of Assam, Vol. III, p. 386, the quote is from Gandhiji's letter to Maulana Tyebulla, the President of APCC.

The anti-grouping movement under the leadership of Bordoloi won its point though indirectly. The referendum on Sylhet took place on July 6 and 7. On July 14, the results were declared with 2,39,619 votes going for Pakistan, and 1,84,041 votes maintaining status quo. The bulk of the Sylhet district went to East Pakistan, but the Radcliffe Boundary Commission later ruled that the four Hindu-majority thanas (Patharkandi, Ratabari, Badarpur and half of Karimganj) should be included in India.

The Mountbatten plan divided India, but advanced the date of independence by about ten and a half months. The Muslim League got the whole of East Bengal and a large chunk of the Sylhet district. Yet it was not satisfied. It laid claim for Cachar, the Khasi-Jayantia Hills, and Goalpara. Bordoloi soon came to know that the League had an eye on Shillong, one of the prettiest hill stations of the world. When he met Mountbatten, the latter casually asked him about the location of Shillong. This increased his apprehension that the Radcliffe Commission might concede the League's demand. He arranged another interview with Lord Mountbatten with the full knowledge of Gandhi, Nehru and Patel. At a party in the Imperial Hotel, Delhi, Bordoloi found Mountbatten alone and before he could broach the subject the latter told him, "On the day I met you, I could not explain to you certain things which were yet confidential. But I can speak to you now. Sir...was offered the Governorship of East Bengal. He had three small children and his wife (he mentioned their age). He could not keep them in Dacca in this heat. He was, therefore, wanting to know from me if there was any cooler place of higher altitude in East Bengal where he could keep his wife and children. He had just left my room when you came in and who could give better information about East Bengal and Sylhet than you ? I, therefore, wanted to know from you all about the place. And you probably thought that I was thinking of ceding these areas to East Bengal. And then you spoke to Gandhiji."

Suddenly he gave a big pinch on Bordoloi's arm and added, "As you know now, nothing could be further from my thoughts. I shall write to Gandhiji. But go and tell him all that I have told you."

In an earlier interview also, Mountbatten had tried to assuage the fears of Bordoloi regarding further ceding of Assamese territory to East Bengal. He had told him that the terms of the Boundary Commission were so obvious that it could not include the two districts in East Pakistan, even if it wished to.

The Sylhet referendum caused deep psychological worry to Bordoloi. "In this province, the aftermath of Sylhet's transfer and attendant evils of transfer of poor clerks rendered the political situation bitter," wrote Bordoloi in a note in moments of his deep agony. "And now I have received a few letters threatening my murder by unknown hands. I am feeling perplexed as to what would be the best way to fight these evils. Should I remain in the Government or go out of it? I wrote a long letter to Bapuji."

Bapu's reply came after some time. He said that Bordoloi's feeling was correct, but he would not hazard an advice. That would be blind leading the blind. His last words were, "Set apart some time every morning and pray."

Prior to this exchange of communication, Bordoloi had a meeting with Gandhiji sometime at the end of July or beginning of August, 1947. Bordoloi, as usual, came to share his anxieties about further ceding of Assam's land to East Pakistan. Before he could finish, Gandhiji suddenly said, "I have heard all about your attitude regarding the separating of Sylhet. Why did you agree to the referendum ?"

"I was not a party to it, "replied Bordoloi.

"Can anything happen in a Province without its Prime Minister becoming a party to it ?"

Bordoloi then told him all that he knew. "Both I and Mountbatten attended a lunch party. There he told me that he presumed I was indifferent about Sylhet going to Pakistan. I told him that while it was true that a large number of people in Assam Valley wanted Sylhet to be separated and at one time, even the Hindus of Sylhet wanted the same, the Congressmen of both the places wanted to live together as they fought together for ten long years, under my leadership for weal or for woe. Mountbatten also met the leader of Sylhet, Basanta Kumar Das (who was the Home Minister of my Cabinet) at a garden party the same evening. He agreed to the referendum. The Working Committee agreed to it. How can I fight the Working Committee ?"

"Did I not tell you that you should be prepared to fight any wrong ? Why did you not do so ? Seven years ago, you adopted Satyagraha. Do you consider that to be a mistake ? Was it not wrong to follow the Working Committee in this ?" Gandhiji was in a mood of deep spiritual agony in those days. "Who wants me now?" he said. Bordoloi knew that independence not only brought with it communal riots, hatred and partition of the country, but moral degradation also.

Assam, during 1946 and the early part of 1947, saw not only the unique anti-grouping movement, but also another kind of movement launched by the Muslim League. The Muslim League in Assam tried various means to mobilise Muslim opinion for Pakistan. One was the campaign for settlement of all encroachers from East Bengal on Assamese lands without any consideration for the legitimate interests of the Province. Another was political exploitation of religious sentiments of the Muslims. The third was evident in the method adopted by the Saadullah Government for enumeration in the 1941 census operations. The classification was made on the basis of community rather than on the basis of religion. The intention was to take the tribal population away from the Hindu fold and enumerate them as 'Tribals', and thereby reduce the number of Hindus in the Province. Bordoloi was opposed to this type of politics and he did oppose it publicly and firmly.

In 1946, the League intensified its campaign for Pakistan in Assam. But in the Provincial elections, it failed to win a majority. It was a great setback. The League Direct Action Day on August 16 was observed in Assam but it made no impact on the people. The Assamese Muslims were lukewarm towards any extremist action and to the idea of grouping of Pakistan. On February 19, 1946 the Muslim League directed its campaign against the eviction policy of the Congress Government. Even Jinnah warned the Bordoloi Government that a "situation would be created which would not be conducive to the well-being of the people of Assam." The resistance to evictions in the professional grazing reserves grew violent and in a number of places, the police had to resort to firings.

Bordoloi, however, stood firm and in this, he was supported by all secular and law abiding citizens. Even Mahatma Gandhi felt that the Muslim League campaign directed from East Bengal for legitimisation of large scale encroachment on professional grazing reserves was wrong in principle and violated the spirit of law. The campaign, however, continued unabated till April, 1947, when the Indian public opinion was fully aroused against it. The League planned to change the campaign into a regular warfare. But Bordoloi dealt with the situation firmly, and as a result, the 'invasion plan' mooted by extremists like Maulana Bhasani (Abdul Hamid Khan) came to nothing. The moderate led by Saadullah disapproved the militant guerrilla activities. Bordoloi's firm handling of the situation, indifference of the Assamese Muslims to extremist action, financial worries and Maulana Bhasani's growing unpopularity ultimately led to the collapse of the movement. The Assam Provincial Muslim League abandoned it formally on June 11, 1947. The movement had an inherent weakness, both in its leadership and volunteers from East Bengal. The Muslim League in Assam also suffered from internal dissensions. It was formally dissolved on June 30, 1948.[1]

According to Pyarelal, the Muslim League had two motives in sending *Khilji Dastas* (in imitation of Bakhtiar Khilji's invasion of Bengal in the 13th century) to Assam to take illegal possession of lands in the province and to refuse to be evicted therefrom. One was to relieve the pressure of overpopulation in East Bengal and the other, which was the main, was to alter the communal ratio of the population of Assam." The Bordoloi Government had to treat it as an administrative issue and evict the encroachers. The decision to prevent encroachment on Government lands had been taken earlier by the Assam Government long before as a result of an agreement with Saadullah, the leader of the Muslim League in Assam Assembly. Gandhiji supported Bordoloi's action saying that "illegal trespassers, merely because they happened to be Muslims or Bengalis, could not claim exception from the operation of the common law."[2] Important Muslim leaders of Assam including Sir Saadullah, were against this movement, which was violent and rapidly communal.

On 15 August, 1947 India became independent. The great struggle for retaining Assam's right to Provincial Autonomy and to decide its own future ended. Under Bordoloi's leadership, Assam gave a good account of herself. In Bordoloi's political career, this period was the most glorious and significant.

During his period of Premiership, Bordoloi was in regular touch with the Central Home Minister Sardar Patel. In his letter dated March 3, 1947 Bordoloi referred to the encroachment on grazing reserves by the Muslim Leaguers in order to settle the Muslims on those lands, and said: "Most of the troubles will arise out of the Government's policy of maintaining the inviolability of the grazing reserves which was agreed to by all parties including the Muslim League and also by the Government's attempt to

---

[1]Mahatma Gandhi–Last Phase : p.204; Pyarelal writes: "In Assam, there were 34.42 Lakhs of Muslims as against 67.50 lakhs of non-Muslims. But the latter included 24.84 lakhs of tribals. The Muslim League's plan was well known. It was to separate the tribals from the Hindus, give them separate electorates and promise of autonomy and convert Assam into a Muslim majority province by organising a mass immigration of Muslims from some of the densely overpopulated border districts of Bengal". This is a correct representation of the Muslim League's point of view.

[2]Pyarelal : Mahatma Gandhi - The Last Phase., Vol. I, p.160.

distribute available wastelands to all including Hindus, Muslim, tribals and immigrants themselves." Sardar Patel, in his reply to Bordoloi on April 11,1947, firmly pledged his support to Bordoloi eviction policy and said: "You will have my full support in your stand on legal rights. Not an inch of land should be surrendered to the illegal immigrants and you must stand solidly and firmly on the policy you are implementing." He was also ready to give military aid in case "civil forces were unable to cope with the situation."[1]

Bordoloi wrote another letter to Patel on April 18,1948 from Calcutta after attending the Inter-Dominion Conference held there. Pakistan at that time carried on a propaganda for inclusion of Khasi states and other hill areas on its border into its territory. Pakistan leaders also did not want to take responsibility of Pakistan immigrants in India who had illegally entered Assam Bordoloi wrote, "I am opposed to any matter concerning my Province being discussed in the Inter-Dominion Conference without the consent of my Government; I could not undertake the responsibility of committing my Government to a matter in which a major policy of the Government was involved."[2] This was Bordoloi's reaction to Pakistan's plea at the Inter-Dominion Conference for raising the above mentioned issues. He challenged Pakistan's right to speak on behalf of minorities in India. It appears that he was also annoyed at the stand taken by the Indian representative at the conference. He consistently maintained that Assam was opposed to the settlement of law-breaking elements and encroachers from Pakistan in Indian territory.

At that time Bordoloi was in bad health and he wanted to retire, "My heart is possibly damaged beyond repair," he wrote to Patel. He was compelled to reduce his working hours from 16 hours to 8 hours.

Sardar Patel promised to review the minutes of the Inter-Dominion Conference and wrote in his letter dated April 22,1948 in an affectionate tone, "I am very sorry to hear about your health. Assam needs you and we all want you to be at the helm of affairs there. At the same time your health requires careful attention. I would therefore suggest, you need not resign but delegate your functions to other ministers, keeping in your hands the direction of policy and other essential matters. I would advise you to so regulate this as to leave you with work for five or six hours so that you

---

[1]Sardar Patel's Letters (Mostly Unknown), Part II, p.29.

[2]S.P.S. correspondence, Vol. 6, p.97.

can have rest even while you are working." Sir Akbar Hydari, the Governor of Assam, in his letter to Sardar Patel dated April 6, 1948, endorsed the suggestion.

The sudden abolition of the post of Dominion Agent in Manipur by the Central Home Ministry on the advice of the Assam Governor, Sir Akbar Hydari, seemed to have displeased Bordoloi, who felt that they should have been consulted before such a step was taken. The Assam Provincial Congress Committee represented the matter to Sardar Patel and in his letter dated May 27, 1948, Sidhinath Sarma, the Secretary, characterised it as the 'most unpopular act.' The APCC evidently felt that the right of the Assam Ministry to 'advice the Governor' was vital for constitutional democracy. Bordoloi, whose health was shattered was willing to resign. But Sardar Patel felt that 'the question of Dominion Agent in Manipur had nothing to do with the Provincial Government.' He said that the Assam Ministry could have no grievance on this score and it could not be treated as a matter of confidence. He took upon himself entire responsibility of abolishing the post.

Bordoloi was persuaded not to insist on his resignation and ultimately he yielded. In his letter to Patel on June 22, 1948 he noted, "I could inform you that nothing would please me more than to serve India and Assam at this critical period but God alone will decide how long I could continue to do so." In his reply dated June, 1948, Sardar Patel wrote to Bordoloi that the decision which he had reached was in the interest of the Province and he would never regret his decision.

Bordoloi never repented his decision. But he knew his end was drawing near.

My Father

By Brig. D. Bordoloi, VSM (Retd.)

I was a kid then, may be ten or eleven years. Though nearly half a century has passed since then, I can still vividly remember the incident, as though it happened only yesterday. My father Late Lokopriya Gopinath Bordoloi never said a harsh word to any of us–my brothers and sisters. As a matter of fact, father and I hardly saw each other. because he was too busy with his own activities and I, with mine.

It was the day of Saraswati Puja the Late Jibeswar Goswami (Gopal) and I, student of MCME school, Uzanbazar, Guwahati had decided that after 'Puspanjali' and the feast at the school both of us would go over to his house at Brahmaputra Nadir par. His father was the Late Kumudeswar Goswami. Every year they used to celebrate the Saraswati Puja with great pomp and grandeur. The first thing that morning I did was to take mother's permission to attend the Puja and eat the evening meals at Gopal's house. We were terribly afraid of our father. To stand before him and personally take permission was beyond us children's dream. Our media was Ma who took the rap more often than not for giving me permission to visit this place or that and to play foot-ball which my father never liked me to play. That morning he gave me permission and asked me to come back before it was dark.

Anyhow, after the completion of the Puja and feast at our school, along with Gopal I went to his house. We played with the other children and made occasional trip to the Puja Mandap. By the time we finished our meals it was already dark and I wanted to leave for my house which was then located at Silpukhuri. I had to cross the Harijan colony (the site of the present St. Marys' High School, Chenikuthi) and was always afraid to do in the dark as the people there used to indulge in drinking and playing mischief on the road. At that time there was no city bus, no rickshaw or any other means of conveyance. There were only four or five cars including one taxi (Santosh Daat Silpukhuri) in the whole of Guwahati. I requested Gopal to accompany me but he would not hear of it and insisted that I stay back and spend the night with him. I vehemently protested as we had a strict rule at home, that we must be back home by dark . Gopal took me to his father and told him about my decision to leave. His father simply told me, "I will tell Maju (Father'a pet name) about it. I had to obey but spent a sleepless night on the verandah of the first floor of the house. Next morning before Gopal was awoke, I left.

It was just dawn when I arrived at the gate. I faced mother pacing the verandah. She appeared upset and it looked as though she too had spent a sleepless night. I sleepishly I opened the wooden gate and entered the compound. She looked at me tearfully and led me to father's 'Vakil Khanna', to the right of the main building. She showed me a small tin box and handed me a five rupee note. I was afraid to even ask her what that was for. Weeping, she told me that father was very annoyed with me for spending the night in somebody's house without prior permission. Therefore he had told Ma to tell me that as far as I was concerned, father did not care whether I was his son or not because, I had broken the discipline of the house. I did not deserve to live at home anymore. Ma further said that my clothes were put into the tin box and the sum of five rupee would take me to any place I wished to go. Whenever I was in need of money I could write to Ma and get it. At this, I broke into sobs. Blinded by tears, herself, mother went inside. Still weeping, I sat on one of the chairs and fell asleep. I do not know how long I slept but I woke up with a start, hearing father's voice. I jumped out of the chair and found myself staring into father's eyes. There was not the slightest trace of anger in them, instead there beamed compassion and love. He gently told me, "I did not expect this from you. Don't you ever do such a thing. Without discipline you cannot expect to become a good boy and later a good man".These words are still ringing in my ears. He called my mother and said that this had been a lesson to Bapa and he would never repeat the mistake. A smile crept in mother's eyes as she took the tin box from my hand and said, "Come inside."

Bordoloi, An Educationist First

By Lily Mazinder Baruah

"There can be no doubt that the bulk of the revenue for running this institution (University) shall have to be found from the toiling masses of the villages. The educated men instead of keeping in touch and improving the village, have left it to indulge in the comforts of the town. The whole outlook of the so called educated men has been one of self-indulgence and self-aggrandizement with neglect of and often times at the cost of the interest of the villages. This is of course an indictment against the modern higher education but it does not mean that we should perpetuate a recognised evil or at any rate should not take into serious consideration when we are out on a venture of higher education. To me, it is quite possible to bring in a new outlook into our society–an outlook of service and duty to our fellowmen, with a properly constituted educational centre, sacrificing leadership is as much necessary for the services of the masses as it is necessary to feed and clothe them. It is very necessary that our educated young men should be men with full knowledge of the need and necessities of our masses and of the means to satisfy them. They should be the fountainhead of the basic culture of communal unity and should represent a common meeting ground where all communal differences have found their settlement. They should be able to breathe freedom and exhibit character in all that they would feel, think and will. We can expect such young men to lead us and guide us and any institution that would train them should receive our support".

This is what my father, Late Gopinath Bordoloi, wrote about the Gauhati University.

A Gandhian by nature, father knew higher education to be integral to the development of a State. At the same time, he was not unaware to its repercussions on the society. Higher education would create a chasm between the village and the city. Therefore, the aim of education he envisaged in Assam was not of merely attaining individual degree but that equipped with their degree the young blood would enter society and serve the people.

This was but one of many dreams father had dreamt of Assam.

Education was one of his chief concerns and to me, my father was primarily an educationist. In fact, after his graduation from the Calcutta University he sought to be a Lecturer of History in Cotton College. It is learnt from some sources that his aim in life was to be a College Professor.

However, this wish remained unfulfilled. Some way or the other father came in contact with Deshabhakta Tarun Ram Phookan and gradually became his out and out disciple. Father became the Headmaster of Sonaram High School as per the wishes of his Guru, the Deshabhakta. Sonaram High School, as was then situated somewhere near the Jubilee Garden (present Water Works compound in Panbazar).

It may be that because he had personally suffered both physical and mental pains while pursuing his further studies outside Assam, he felt from the care of his heart, the necessity of a University in Assam. The wealthy students could easily manage to go outside Assam for higher learning but the meritorious boys of middle class families were deprived of further studies due to lack of an institution. Not to speak of Post Graduate courses, under-Graduate courses too were far from their reach. This was a heartache to my father. Himself and a few noted social reformers like the Late Dr. Harikrishan Das, Lokabandhu Bhubaneswar Barooah, Late Durgeswar Sarma, Late Gaurikanta Talukdar, Late Keshab Kanta Barooah and others put their head together to introduce a venture college for the poor students of the Gawahati. That is how the B. Barooah College came into existence, with my father as the first honorary Principal.

Regarding the University, one would well understand when one tries to go deep into the writings of my father written in the Prison in 1941 or the Editorial reports of 'Awahan' during that period. It happens that even if one has a clear perspective and aim of doing something one may not be able to fulfil it during one's life span. But my father was fortunate; God gave him the opportunity to implement his ideas. He steered clear the obstacles to achieve his goals. Gandhiji said 'When a man works for an ideal he becomes irresistible.' My father would go out in the scorching sun, collecting funds for the University. Never did he bother about his food.

A University was built. Late Radhakrishnan, the President of India, inaugurated it on an auspicious day in the old University Building on the banks of the Dighalipukhuri. But the University my father had visualised is definitely not the one of today. Because at the very outset, I would like to quote him–"The fundamental question is whether (i) A University is at all wanted and if so (ii) whether it should be as autonomous as possible. This reply was put forward by him. I am tempted to quote–"If it is an autonomous one, it will depend on the nature of the Government that would guide a particular society. A totalitarian State whether pseudo-democratic or otherwise would like to control every activity inside a State, whether goods, chattel or human being, must be according to pattern sought for by a few leaders of the society and any deviation would be severely put down by providing for State interference in all details. Freedom of thought, the highest gift of God to a human being is bound to go, and human nature with all its varieties and potentialities is degraded into a machine of a particular type for a particular purpose." To my father, the University in Assam had to be one where education was as free as possible, where there would be least possible State interference. I cannot resist the temptation of quoting him again."In the sphere of higher education, State interference should descend to a minimum. In other words, education,whether secondary or university, should be left in the hands of experts, who by virtue of their knowledge and experience, would be able to take an absorbing interest in it, detached from the gross party politics of the day. This body of experts must therefore have not only sufficient power to execute their will force, free from interference by anybody, except probably such as may be necessary in every extreme case."

It may be recalled that once when my father after becoming the Chief Minister, wished to discuss some problems with the Vice-Chancellor, the latter turned down the request. Father accepted the episode with a grace which no Chief Minister or any Cabinet Minister of present day politics can equal. He perhaps recalled that in his article, "A case for a University in Assam," he had himself put forward the propulsion that from politics, the Universities should face least possible interference. He was not a man of precepts alone but believed in practising them. I had heard Mrs. Bonilly Khongman of Shillong, an ex-MP, saying that "Mr. Bordoloi knew how to give due recognition to people of calibre, however subordinate they were."

Father was very dear to the hills tribal people; they mourned at his demise saying– 'we have lost our father, now that he has gone.' This affection was reciprocated by him. He wrote a descriptive article on them. And during his imprisonment, he regularly held meetings in which the problems of the plains and Hill tribal people were specifically discussed. How he felt for these people needs no explanation.

The rebel leader Late A.Z. Phizo in his Obituary message wrote– 'With only a few others, Bordoloi saw years ago admidst the gathering storm, a patch of blue sky. In that great vision of his and his unremitting contribution towards its realization will be found, truly depicted the impress of the character which neither death nor time can rob away. In life Bordoloi was a friend of the Nagas–a friendship he held so dear. Nagas have been made poorer today that he has gone."

Father's idea was to stay in close association with all the hill people who would remain as a league of power to protect the north eastern region from any enemy. With the plains tribal people, his policy was similar to that of the Ahom Kings to remain in harmony with them. After assuming power as the Chief Minister, father had celebrated a week long programme with the hills and plains tribal people. He was one of the framers of the Sixth Schedule. However, father was very much against communual representation in matter of Education. He said, thus, "I do not see in any reason, why it is necessary to reserve any quota of members from any community in any academic body or any body which will be concerned with academic administration. In order that I may not be misunderstood, I want to make it clear, I should not have the slightest objection to have all the fellows from the Muslim community or from the Scheduled Caste communities, provided the cause of higher education is properly furthered. Personally, I feel that in the Government of a University no distinction of caste, creed, colour race should be maintained and attempt should always be made to secure the best men to serve and advise this body."

According to my father, introduction of communal representation in the University would lead to political affairs. His exact words are: "If I object to the introduction of the principle of communal representation in the University, it is only for the reason that we may transfer the atmosphere of assembly politics in the sacred abode of learning and that we might be responsible for injecting into our youth the virus of communal poison."

After reading the significant thoughts that come to my father's mind, I can only say "Blessed is his soul that he is no more to see the Universities of Assam today."

Memories Only

By Lily Mazinder Baruah

I was not even in my teens when my father died. It was that short span of my life I spent with father. Not only that, but also fragmented; the frequent spells of political imprisonment often took him away from me.

Going through the letters from jail, it appeared to me that father sought to lead a life free from worldly affairs. And yet I remember him to be an ideal father. Where we children were concerned, nothing was too trivial to deserve his attention. He, himself, outlined our daily routine for us, and if there was anything he wanted from us it was discipline. Living in a joint family, with barely enough to make ends meet, my brothers had to do all the household duties. Yet they never forgot to sing prayers in the gosaighar (puja room) nor did they forget to spin yarn for their own clothing.

Father had always wanted us to be self-reliant and independent. Though he regretted that he could not provide us with a cook, he encouraged my sisters to learn how to cook. He would often tell us how important it was for a girl to know to cook, sew and knit even while pursuing her studies. I was very fond of accompanying my father wherever he went. Perhaps it was because I was the youngest and petted a lot, it was anguish after father died. Memories still haunt me: Shillong, the church bell, the cool breeze of the tall pines, the wind whistling in the meadows, the cuckoo's songs all these are still painful. The memory of the evening bugle at the Governor's House takes me back to my golden childhood days, days full of laughter and gaiety.

There are quite a few events that left indelible impressions in my mind. Father never liked me to dress fashionably. It so happened that once when I made a fuss about my dress he was harsh to me. That night he wrote in his diary "I had scolded Lily for making such a fuss about dressing. What does she know, how long will I remain as a Chief Minister, what will happen to them ? How will we survive ? Nobody in the family is bothered about that."

What we find in father is a bounty of human values. He had a belief that peace lies only in the ultimate merger with the great soul, God.

Father's concern and love for the neglected people was boundless. The people residing in the far north east of India lived forgotten. According to the British rulers' policies' the Government of India Act, these people of the hill areas were deprived of every facility that a citizen should get. NEFA, Naga Hills, Lushai Hills were categorized as Excluded Areas. Khasi, Jaintia, Mikir and Garo Hills were the Partially Excluded Areas. Although there were five representatives in the Legislative Assembly in a house of four hundred and eight members, they were not given powers.

While in the Jorhat Jail, in 1941 father wrote an elaborate article "Our Hills Brethren of Assam". Not only did he write the article he also discussed their problems, through ways and means to bring these people to light with a number of co-prisoners.

After he came to power in independent India, father's first move was to invite these people of the Excluded and Partially Excluded Areas to the capital of the State. The plains tribal people too were invited and a heart to heart get-together took place. The Chiefs of tribes were felicitated. Father, being an educationist thought the best reward to give these people was to educate them. And he did as a Chief Minister. He also took the portfolio of Minister for Education and travelled extensively to the NEFA, Naga Hills, Lushai Hills and chalked out various schemes for the development of these people.

All that father did for these people has not been forgotten. Even today the people in NEFA (now Arunachal Pradesh) sing "O Raja pabane, Gandhi Roja pabane O Raja pabane Bordoloi Roja pabane".

Vanlawma from Aijawl, a close associate of my father said the other day, I quote him "I hereby dare to mention that his endeavours to include Assam and its adjoining sister states in the Indian Union made Bordoloi one of the greatest architects and builders of the present India. Without his efforts the North Eastern part of India might have become a part of Pakistan." He added, that people in the Lushai Hills sing folk songs on father.

During my visit to one of the underground camps in Chedema, the leader welcomed me. They spelled out "Bordoloi laga chowali acho peace time to ahibi dei. Bordoloi to amar laga manu achili" (Bordoloi's daughter, come in the days of peace, Bordoloi was our man).

It was pure love and love only that father dealt with the tribals. Rather than resorting to the military powers, father believed love to be the protecting force to Assam. Love is the strongest weapon in the world. As a Gandhian, father believed in this.

Thoughts of my father sometimes fill me with elation, even pride, he was such a unique personality, a man of varied talents. He was a singer, an artist, a writer, a dramatist, a critic too.

Father was a lover of music, one of the jhuma songs of the tea-gardens father sang was "choto choto puthi machi, ki diya randhibo go, Biha rati bohu morilo ke boli kandino go". Another of his oft sung songs in the Nagaoian style "Ke ko katari bao, magi saoul emuthi pao, biroho kokaye bhath muthi randhi che topate topate khou."

Father's contribution to Assam was the prohibition of opium, establishment of a University in Assam, Medical College, Ayurvedic College, venture school and college. The venture college and school was introduced in order to foil the notorious Cunningham circular of 1929. Father believed in serving India by serving Assam. It was because he took pride in being an Indian that he wrote in his diary "Jana Gana Mana" may be recommended as a national anthem provided the name of Assam be included in it.

Had father not opposed the Cabinet Mission's plan regarding the grouping of Assam with Bengal to form a Muslim majority area as demanded by Jinnah, Assam would have lost its identity. Father was never tired of pleading with the Centre for Assam's tea, timber, and other natural resources. He always insisted on a greater autonomy for States.

Father was a man of firm conviction. It is because he never deviated from his beliefs, his ideas that he is respected as a National leader. I pay my tributes to this great soul who has enriched the soul of Assam, India.

Gopinath–a true Gandhian

By Prof. Chandrkant Mehta

Gopinath though a politician, was a true Gandhian; and his contribution to the propagation, and practice of Gandhian ideals is noteworthy.

Gopinath Bordoloi, after completing his studies first joined Assam Association, an institution wedded to achievement of Swaraj. Later on he was enchanted with the ideals, and especially the constructive programme of Gandhiji, and so he joined Congress. In 1920 he went to Ahmedabad to attend the annual session of Indian National Congress and met Gandhiji. His very first meeting with Gandhiji, totally converted him to Gandhism and he returned to Assam, with a firm determination to make Assam Gandhi minded. When he met Gandhiji, the Father of the Nation saw in him a spark to work for the downtrodden and so advised him, as to how to carry on the message of Swaraj, through the implementation of constructive programme. Gopinathji promised him to plunge headlong in the constructive programme.

Having promised Gandhiji to fully implement constructive programme when he returned to Assam from Ahmedabad, he was arrested and sentenced to one year imprisonment. On his release from jail he began to work for propagation of Khadi. In order to carry the message of Khadi to the length and breadth of Assam he moved on foot from village to village and founded many Khadi centres, through which he organised production and sale of Khadi. The response of the people was beyond his imagination.

He also undertook the work of propagating Hindi. He was elected Chairman of Assam Rastrabhasha Samiti. Gopinathji had already learnt enough Hindi to teach the language. His first pupil was his wife Surbala, who not only learnt Hindi but passed the examination with distinction. With the help of Rastrabhasa Samiti workers, he got school teachers of Assam to learn Hindi and then with the help of Hindi trainee teachers, he made the young generation conversant with Hindi. So Kaka Kalelkar, who was the person in charge of propagation of Hindi, when he came to Assam, was highly impressed by the commendable work done by Gopinathji where every village school had one teacher who was engaged in teaching of Hindi.

When Gandhiji turned to the problem of untouchability work, Harijan uplift work became a passion for him, and he started All Assam Harijan Sevak Sangh and though, orthodox so-called high caste Hindus put impediments, he was able to win younger generation to his side. He arranged community dinners in which Harijans and high caste Hindus participated. He led volunteers to Harijan Bastis and cleaned their streets and houses and he raised the status of Harijans.

He took upon himself the work of eradicating the evil of drinking by educating people and making them conscious of the evils of alcohol. He arranged picketing of wine shops and prepared ladies to picket. He paid special attention to the programme of eradicating illiteracy and recruited volunteers for showing the work.

He, during his Chief Ministership enacted several laws for the betterment of the tribal people and while taking measures to reform them he saw to it that their culture was well preserved.

During Cabinet Mission negotiations he was very much upset at the group clause of the proposal of the mission and had differences with the Congress high command regarding the same. He went again and again to Wardha to consult Gandhiji asking for his guidance. Gandhiji advised him to leave Congress, if Congress accepted group clause in toto. Whenever he was not able to take a decision and was in two minds he consulted Gandhiji and took his guidance.

Thus Gopinathji was true Gandhian and righteously followed him, whether there was call for satyagraha or engaging oneself in constructive work.

The fact that, in spite of Gandhiji's disapproval, Gopinathji wrote Gandhiji's biography in which he described Gandhiji as prophet, shows his devotion to Gandhiji. He also translated Anashaktiyog–Gandhiji's interpretation of Geeta–shows that he was a Gandhian to the core.

Assam as Visualized by Gopinath Bordoloi

By Lily Mazinder Baruah

The foreign national issue in the North-Eastern Region, particularly in Assam, is hanging on since the ten long past months. The people of Assam have suffered much but the problem is still far from solution. The memory of Gopinath Bordoloi often comes to my mind at this crucial time and I wonder how Bordoloi faced with a similar situation, would have reacted had he been alive today.

At the outset it is worthwhile to point out that Bordoloi's basic idea about welfare state centred round the villages, and this belief was further strengthened by Gandhian ideals of village reconstruction. Like Gandhiji, Bordoloi believed that the real strength of India lies in her villages. And by building a classless society and making villages self-sufficient the country could resist British imperialism far more efficiently. This is what Mahatma Gandhi advised Bordoloi and his colleagues, "The programme of constructive work is more than law and parliamentary work. Its compilation means complete swaraj won by truth and non-violence. What is true of you is true of every Congressman be he or she great or not. This is my message. Try to learn from the men here how it works and how ennobling it is."

Gandhiji wrote to Gopinath Bordoloi on 20th November' 44, "Concentrate on producing a solid scheme for villages and the names and qualifications of those who would work it. If you can do that, there might be no difficulty about funds even if you extend your allotment."

Gopinath Bordoloi, when elected as a member in the Assam Legislative Assembly for the second time, after assuming his office as the leader of the house, pointed out the grave defects of the Government of India in reference to services. I am tempted to quote his words:

"The two grave defects of the Government of India in reference to services :

(1) Cost of administration in services including pension charges (62% P.C. equivalent of ten annas 6 pies in the rupees) of this most the money, for whatever reasons it might be, must be paid, unless a radical change in the administration involving the substitution of the present constitution Act by a (mere equitable) Act. No civilized country spends that percentage.

(2) But in spite of this expenditure, the poorer classes of public servants have hardly a living wage. This is due to the fact that we are compelled to pay the higher services in thousands, where we might have paid in hundreds, even of provincial services. We are not privileged to reduce pay of the external service at certain times. In no civilized country this is true. The London Constables get 120 to 150 p.m. while the inspector get 300-350 p.m.

"The result is to create an aristocracy of services. They naturally come to look down upon village life as completely unsuitable to the status they enjoy and are inclined to look down upon the village officials equivalent to menials. The village life which is the heart of the country languishes, and a new and artificial town develops for the ruination and exploitation of the village."

"My sympathies are entirely with you because you live in the village and work in the village. I do sincerely believe that the present scale of pay of Mandals and Kanangoes is inadequate. But I feel the inequality is bound to continue till we can bring in a new order, find new state in the society."

I feel even being a Government servant, you can be helpful in bringing into existence that condition.

He further said that the cabinet in which such act was prevalent must be dissolved as soon as possible and the ministers should at once resign from their seats and come to work with the mass people.

Gopinath Bordoloi, while in prison worked hard with his fellow prisoners visualizing a modern Assam in independent India. The problems of both internal as well as external were worked out in details. The political, social, economic and cultural aspects were discussed, planned and finally chalked out.

After release, and attaining independence he did try to materialise his plans one by one under the guidance of Mahatma Gandhi.

The boundary question of Assam also deeply engaged Bordoloi's attention. He was not happy with boundary arrangement as prevailed in Assam just after independence. However, the merger of Sylhet with East Pakistan did not bother him the least. Because he felt that a part of the Province having a different linguistic and cultural background would rather be a hindrance in the way of emotional integration. But it was not the same story with Cachar and Goalpara, according to Bordoloi. Both these areas have been parts of Assam since time immemorial. And so were Rangpur, Jalpaiguri and Cooch Behar. In fact, Bordoloi took up the matter with Sardar Patel but unfortunately died before he could have done something about it. A vocal section of Cachar people wanted the area merge with East Pakistan but it was largely due to Bordoloi's efforts that

Cachar remained in Assam. Because he firmly believed that to push Cachar to East Pakistan could have been a great injustice to the indigenous people of Cachar who were, though mute, more closely related to the rest of the Province.

This apart, Bordoloi was very clear about relationship of the hillman and the plainsman. His love for the hillman is well known, and so they also treated him as one of them. But he knew that unless we treat them as our equal partners in the road to progress, they would look at us with suspicion. To do this it was essential to bring about emotional integration with the plainsmen and to let them progress according to their own genius. As Chairman of the Drafting Committee of the Sixth Schedule, Bordoloi said: "The most important fact that presents itself before this Committee was whether for the purpose of integration the method of force, the methods of use of the Assam Rifles, and military forces, should be used or a method should be used in which the co-operation of these people could be obtained for purpose of governing these areas... The point therefore that presented itself to us was whether we should raise in them a spirit of enmity or hatred by application of force or whether we should bring them up under the broad principle of Government by goodwill and love." And he preferred the latter.

It is interesting to note that the last official tour, Bordoloi undertook just a fortnight before his death was to the Lushai Hills. From Aizawl he wrote to his wife: "I arrived at Aizawl, yesterday after somewhat arduous journey. But the warm welcome I received from the local people has removed all the weariness." And equally significant was the tribute paid by A.Z. Phizo after his death: "With only a few others, Bordoloi saw, years ago, amidst a gathering storm, a patch of blue sky. In that great vision of his and his unremitting contribution towards its realization will be found truly depicted the impress of his character which neither death nor time can roll away. In life, Bordoloi was a friend of Nagas whose friendship they held dear. Nagas have been made poorer today that he has gone." Here are two men whose political aims and vision were poles apart but where awareness of age long ties between the hillmen and the plainsmen was identical.

He worked into the minute detail of setting up of a board of specialists to study the mode of living of the tribals, to investigate their real needs and, above all, their psychology.

In the same way regarding the internal problems Gopinath Bordoloi thought deeply of the minorities–Muslims, Tribals–plains and Hills, services in elective bodies etc.

In relation to All India Services in railways, posts and telegraphs Bordoloi felt that reservation should be provided for the people of the Province in all appointments in accordance with the number required for service in the Province in proportion to the population of provinces to the country.

Gopinath Bordoloi's conception of a socialistic state in India was based on two essentials–democratic and communistic or national socialistic state. But it was interesting to note that all throughout his life his basic principle was non-violence and love. According to Bordoloi, "a non-violent socialistic state can come only when individuals have learnt to live for others–consciously and conscientiously." While discussing socialistic state of Assam in independent India in the year 1941 he said, "I desire to mention, however, that the growth of communal feeling is due to a large extent of growth of the western idea of individualism and personal gain. But while in a free western country, people give much to the state or are meant to live in the state, in India our duty to society (the state) is altogether lost sight of, and we think of nothing but personal selfish gain. The so-called English educated Hindus had the loaves and fishes of the petty officers in the post. The minorities now strive after the same loaves and fishes. So called autonomy is increasing this craving, in view of supposed increased opportunities given under it. It is this politics for power, wealth and sordid gains which is killing the peaceful life of the country. While, therefore, I agree with most of the conclusion of Fakhruddin, I am in difficulty of the opinion that unless this sordid psychology could be removed from the mind of all the communities, the ill of communalism is not likely to go. The most effective way of fighting this psychology is by the constructive work among the masses, which will also include a system of education, which will remove altogether the idea of gain."

Bordoloi strongly felt that Assam had been unjustly deprived of her share in tea and oil. When he headed the Congress Coalition ministry in the late thirties, one of his first act was the inclusion of tea under the Agricultural Income Tax, despite opposition from the powerful European planters' lobby and earn thereby Rs. 40 lakh a year for the state exchequer. Similarly, as Premier of the first Congress Ministry in Assam, Bordoloi advocated for the inclusion of petroleum as a state subject. Though Pandit Nehru was sympathetic to the proposal, it fell through in the face of the opposition from interested quarters. Writing about this Smt. Hem Barua says: "Had his (Bordoloi's) plan been implemented, the petroleum and chemical portfolios would have remained with the state instead of with the centre. And then the question of granting autonomy to the state would never have arisen."

Lokopriya Gopinath Bordoloi - A Devotee of Mahatma Gandhi

By Abdul Matlib Majumdar

Today is the 29th death anniversary of Lokopriya Gopinath Bordoloi. When my father died nearly three decades back I was a mere child, and was too young to know the great role he had played in the political, economic and social life of Assam. To me, he was just a lovable father sharing my little joys and sorrows, despite his tight schedule of work as the Chief Minister of a problem state just before and during the early years of our newly won independence. I vividly remember how often my father would tell us about Mahatma Gandhi and about the latter's philosophy of truth and non-violence. All this went over my head.

But it was years later when I had been old enough to be able to go through his personal diaries and bunches of letters yellowed with age that I realized how devotedly my father had followed Gandhiji and how dearly he had loved Assam. He would consult every minute detail with Gandhiji before doing anything which concerned political, economic or social life of Assam. Here is an instance :

During those critical years preceding our independence the British hatched a plan known as Coupland's Scheme to separate some hill districts of Assam and amalgamate these areas with the hilly tracts bordering north east of the state so as to constitute a Frontier Province outside India. When Lokopriya Bordoloi saw through the game he sent the following telegram to Gandhiji:

"Bureaucratic scheme secretly hatched for separation of Assam frontier hills with northern Burma and possibly also Khasi and Garo hills now Partially Excluded Areas seem to be rushed through. Last month Viceroy met some hills people at Balipara and Sadiya specially sent to him in support of British domination of the hills. Governor is touring interior of the Excluded Areas apparently canvassing support of the scheme which it is feared include also amalgamation of Assam in Bengal thus giving virtual effect to Coupland's Scheme. The district officers in Excluded Areas all British are similarly preaching anti-Assamese propaganda. Whole proposal simply shocking to people of Assam also to the people of the hills.

Their leaders have openly expressed against this sinister move and people of Assam would under no circumstances agree to go to Bengal in order that a Province with linguistic and cultural basis in terms of the

Congress manifesto may be formed. Pray do the needful to prevent this grave mischief to Assam and India."

Similar was the case with Goalpara and Cachar. After Sylhet had opted for the erstwhile East Pakistan, a Boundary Commission was set up to determine the borders between Assam and the Eastern wing of Pakistan. At this stage a conspiracy was set afoot to include Goalpara, Cachar and some other areas of Assam in Pakistan. Bordoloi went to Delhi to explain Assam's case to the Indian leaders. The air in Delhi was thick with all sorts of rumours and Bordoloi's fears and suspicion grew more when he had found that some Khasi leaders were meeting Pakistani leaders. On the top of it, when he met Lord Mountbatten at the suggestion of Pandit Nehru, the Governor-General pointed to a map and asked him if Shillong and some areas of Khasi and Jaintia hills were in Pakistan. Although Bordoloi clarified this to Lord Mountbatten, he could not get rid of his suspicion and fear. So he went to see Mahatma Gandhi, and the meeting which later took place was vividly described by Bordoloi It was some time towards the end of July or beginning of August,1947, and Gandhiji was sitting in his usual seat with only Srimati Amrit Kaur in the room. I narrated to him my fears and troubles. But before I quite finished, he said: "I have heard all about your attitude regarding separation of Sylhet. Why did you agree to the referendum ?" I told him that I was no party to it. But immediately came that retort, "Can anything happen in a Province without its Prime Minister becoming a party to it ?" I then told him all I knew: how Lord Mountbatten at a lunch to which I was invited, said that he presumed I was indifferent about Sylhet going to Pakistan. I told him, however, that while it was true that a large number of the people in Assam Valley wanted Sylhet to be separated and at one time even the Hindus of Sylhet wanted the same, the Congressmen of both the places wanted to live together as they fought a common fight together for ten long years under my leadership for weal or for woe. I told him also how Lord Mountbatten met the leader of Sylhet, the then Home Minister of our Cabinet (Sri Basanta Kumar Das), the same evening at a garden party and how latter agreed to the referendum and how the Working Committee of Congress endorsed it. I then put to him, "How can I fight the Working Committee ?" Then he said rather firmly, "Did I not tell you that you should be prepared to fight any wrong ? Why did you not do so ? Seven years ago you did a mistake in adopting Satyagraha in trying to follow the Working Committee."

Then referring to the subject under discussion he said,"I can do little for you. You had better go to the Sardar." I said, "I shall surely go to him, but Bapu, you must do something." He was then as if thinking aloud–

"Once you agree to an evil, you do not know where it will lead you." I was sitting there full eight to ten minutes mute, while he was talking to himself and partially to Srimati Kaur. I read in his face a bitterness and a despair which, during the course of twenty-five years' experience, I had never seen before. He spoke in low tone," I am never a man given to suspicion, much less act on suspicions. But looking at things around me, I feel suspicious of even the best actions of the Britisher." Then he became silent. I again repeated, "Bapu, will you not do anything for me ?" He did not reply but told me again, "Go to the Sardar." I obeyed him and went to the Sardar the next morning. I narrated my doubts and fears in the same was as I did to Bapuji; but Sardarji said that if I had felt so strongly, why did I not speak to him earlier. I came back with the impression that he considered I was childish in my fears.

But Bordoloi was not childish in his fears. The real story behind the Shillong episode came to light with an element of comedy when Lord Mountbatten disclosed it to Bordoloi at a party hosted by Sardar Patel a few days later. The Governor General said, "On the day I met you, I could not explain to you certain things, which were yet confidential, but I can speak to you now. You see, Sir...was offered the Governorship of East Bengal. He had three small children and his wife (he mentioned their age). He could not keep them in Dacca in this heat. He was, therefore, wanting to know from me if there was any cooler place of higher altitude in East Bengal where he could keep his wife and children. He had just left my room when you came in; and who could give better information about East Bengal and Sylhet than you? I therefore, wanted to know from you all about these places. And you possibly thought that I was thinking of ceding these areas to East Bengal, and then you spoke to Gandhiji"–with that he gave a big pinch to my arm.

Only a true Gandhian devotee can confess his follies and weaknesses so sincerely as Bordoloi did. But his fears and suspicions were, after all, not unfounded in so far as Shillong was concerned . But he was a man of too large a heart not to believe what Lord Mountbatten had explained to him by way of a joke.

Lokopriya Bordoloi strictly adhered to Mahatmaji's advice to Congress members in the Legislative Assemblies. I feel like quoting a few lines from the circular issued in 1945 to the members of the Congress party in the Legislative Assembly : "As regards the attendance of members under restrictions,I repeat Mahatmaji's advice to the effect that members should not generally apply for permission but if exigency so demands, they may do so in consultation with their Leader..."

Mahatmaji's advice to the duties of legislators was such "Members of the Assembly outside jail should attend the Assembly in order to register their views on important matters such as Land/Settlement, Food, Evacuation etc. Internee M.L.As should not apply for permission to attend the Assembly but if the gravity of the situation so demands, they may do so. In cases like these, exigency is the governing factor and that is to be decided by the party or its leader."

It may probably be due to Bordoloi's sincere devotion to Gandhiji that he could steer clear his leadership in a very smooth way. In spite of so many oppositions, he could succeed in overcoming almost all the political crises that stood in his way.

Bordoloi very neatly handled the problem of the Tribal Sangha in 1945. He could prevent the plains tribals from going away to merge with the Muslim League. He managed the whole thing so skilfully that it did not hurt the sentiments of the tribal people. Bhimbar Deuri, a Minister in the Bordoloi Cabinet, wrote to Bordoloi: "It appears that you have been carefully weighing the effect of my appointment on the tribal people of the plains particularly the Kacharis who form their majority...with our joining the Congress the mental and spiritual weariness from which I suffered from 1946 up to the time of our joining the Congress has disappeared. None on the earth is happier than I am at the Tribal Sangha's joining the Congress.

In most of his letters, Gandhiji used to write to his dear disciple Bordoloi in this way,"There should never be the slightest departure from truth and non-violence. There should be perfect fearlessness." He followed the Mahatmaji's advice both in letter and spirit. His friends, admirers, colleagues could well understand these impressions on him. Abdul Matlib Majumder, one of his Cabinet colleagues, commented that Lokopriya was a man of principle and honesty. He used to oppose in the Assembly saying, "I will lose all the seats but still I will be honest."

Mira Ben said in a letter to Bordoloi sometime in 1948 "It made me feel more strongly than ever what I have often felt before- namely, what a tremendous task you, who are Gandhiji's friends and followers have taken upon your shoulders in trying to carry his way of life into the political world...and assure you of my deep sympathy and for what it is worth of my unswerving support in your heroic attempts to give life and reality to Bapu's ideals in this Province."

The last meeting Bordoloi had with Gandhiji at Birla House a couple of days before the latter was killed may not be important from historical point of view. But the meeting as described by Bordoloi as poignant with feelings and it shows how great a devotee of Gandhiji he was : "It was 2 o'clock when I arrived at Birla House and directly went to the yard where Gandhiji was lying on the cot in the December sun of New Delhi. Maulana Abul Kalam Azad Sahib was discussing with him the condition under which Gandhiji would be prepared to break his fast. I went and caught hold of his feet for a few seconds and kept standing near his legs for about 10 minutes while the conversation was going on. He only smiled at me. I had full opportunity of studying his face and the pose in which he lay on the cot. He was speaking in low but distinct tones with usual emphasis. He had the Burma hat given to him by Thakin Nu on his head, and his whole face was aglow with a radiance that I had not seen in him for several months. He was protected from the western sun by Dr. Sushila Nair and some other ladies. But nobody could miss the beaming happiness that was radiating from his face, apparently arising out of divine duty done. Every moment of the talk, however, made me anxious about his condition. It was passing the seventh day of his fast, and I decided not to speak anything, although I came with determination to ask him to break the fast.

Immediately after the Maulana had finished he beckoned me to his side, with a smile which will linger in my memory all the rest of my life. I took one step towards him, and told him that I had nothing to say and, with a namaskar left his side to the place where the Maulana was talking with Dr. Nair and others. I did not listen to the conversation, but all the time I was contemplating on Bapu's fast and the duty that the same imposed on us. Little could I imagine then that this was the last time that I would have the chance of meeting him. Today I feel an agony in my heart when I feel that I did not go near him even when he beckoned me, although I did so from the tenderest of feelings in me."

The death of Mahatma Gandhi came to Bordoloi as a stunning blow as it did to his countrymen. But its description is no less poignant than Pandit Nehru's famous "Light is out." I now felt it must be real and felt so stunned that I became mute for the time being. I did not really know what to do, where to go; and again came the conviction that it cannot be all true. I then sought a call with Dr. Bidhan Chandra Roy, and in 5 minutes, I got him to be only told that the light of India and the world had gone out from us forever. To me, he had always been a force influencing or trying to influence every thought and action of my life. I know that I could not even expect to live up to what he wished of us, but the very fact that he was looking at us even from distance, used to inspire us. During the last six years I felt that he infused in me a strength which only a spiritual leader could bless his follower with. His advice was seldom in the nature of do this, and do that, "but always to inspire me with courage to fight out anything that I consider evil or wrong."

This obituary indeed written with tears of a man who had been a true devotee of Mahatma Gandhi and his lofty ideals.

Lokopriya Bordoloi dreamt Mahatmaji on the third August '50 beckoning him and saying that "lots of things are to be done. You come soon." And strangely enough, he passed away two days after the dream.

CHAPTER VI

Obituaries

Editorial on the death of Gopinath Bordoloi published in the Assam Tribune, 7th August 1950

Late Sj. G.N.Bordoloi

At a time when she was least prepared for it Assam has sustained a heavy loss by the death of her Chief Minister, Sj.Gopinath Bordoloi. The sudden and unexpected death has been a veritable bolt from the blue. Who among the many that saw Sj. Bordoloi return hale and hearty on Friday night from the theatrical performance in the Bhaskar Natya Mandir at Uzanbazar could expect that within a few hours the great man's heart would cease to beat? Though Sj. Bordoloi had been suffering from ill health for a long time none could dream that he would be cut off from our midst just on the threshold of his sixtieth year. Sj. Bordoloi overworked himself and refused to be weaned from his duties always inspired with a sense of integrity and justice. Sj. Bordoloi devoted his time and energy exclusively to the cause of the country. So he has died in harness and Assam is definitely poorer by his death today.

Sj. Bordoloi's life is crowded with events as he had lived and worked in one of the most eventful periods in the history of the country. Only a brief reference here is possible. With the late Deshabhakta Tarun Ram Phookan and Karmabir Nabin Chandra Bordoloi he was one of the earliest followers of Mahatma Gandhi in Assam. He suffered incarceration several times. After the Congress had decided to enter the Legislature in 1937 Sj. Bordoloi became leader of the Assam Congress Assembly Party. In 1938 when Netaji Subhas Bose, the then President of the Congress, came to Assam Sj. Bordoloi, under his instruction, formed the Congress-coalition Ministry which resigned after the outbreak of war in 1939. In 1942 Sj. Bordoloi was present at the Bombay session of the AICC which under Mahatma Gandhi's advice adopted the "Quit India" resolution. As soon as he returned within the borders of Assam he was arrested at Dhubri and like all other Congress leaders of the day was thrown into prison for an indefinite period. In Jorhat jail he developed eye trouble and was thus released after about two years, though a little earlier than other Congress leaders in incarceration, both inside and outside the Province. He did not rest idle to enjoy a period of convalescence, but devoted himself heart and soul to the cause of a separate university for Assam. In the elections of 1945-46 Congress candidates were returned at the head of polls and could thus form the single majority party inside the Legislature. In February, 1946, Sj. Bordoloi formed the Congress Cabinet in Assam with himself as Chief Minister and that position he retained up to the time of his death. Because of Sj. Bordoloi's influence Congress Ministers of Assam have worked on the whole as a happy family and such dissensions inside the Cabinet as have happened in some of the sister states remain yet unknown in Assam. Sj. Bordoloi has worked under five Governors since 1946 and he has been regarded as the ablest man for the premiership of the Assam Government. Shri Sri Prakasa, the former Governor of Assam revealed in a speech on the eve of his departure from this Province in May last that Sj. Bordoloi wanted to tender resignation more than once but it was the Governor who had insisted upon Sj. Bordoloi's retaining his post.

Of late Sj. Bordoloi was much interested in the tribal and hill areas of Assam. He realized it fully well that without cordial relations between the hills and plains of Assam, this frontier state could not be turned into a bulwark of strength for the Indian Union in the present context of the subversive activities that are being carried on inside and outside the borders of Assam. As a matter of fact, Sj. Bordoloi had called a Press Conference yesterday forenoon at the Circuit House herewith special reference to the subject of tribal areas. But before the public could benefit from his recent experiences as acquired in the tribal and hill areas, death laid its icy hand upon him. In Sj. Bordoloi's death Assam has lost more than a political leader of great eminence. He was a man of many sided action, and from his early life he took a great deal of interest in music and sports. His keen attachment to sports, even when burdened with official duties was quite apparent to all, when in 1938, during his term of premiership, he played at a cricket match in Shillong. This is perhaps something unique in the whole history of Premiership in India and elsewhere. Besides, Sj. Bordoloi was a man of letters and he wrote a few books in Assamese. Sj. Bordoloi has died but he has left behind a name which his grateful and countrymen will not forget. We offer our homage to his memory and our heartfelt condolences to the members of the bereaved family.

"By his (Bordoloi's) death a void has been created in public in Assam and India which it will be very difficult to fill... Shri Bordoloi had borne the burden of administering a most difficult province in very trying times. He was greatly loved and respected not only in Assam but outside the province as a great fighter in the cause of freedom and good and considerate administrator...

Dr. Rajendra Prasad

"...for all of us and for Assam particularly this (Bordoloi's death) is a very great loss of a brave fighter for freedom and one who in high position as Chief Minister of Assam faced courageously the many problems of that state".

Pandit Jawaharlal Nehru

".. it is difficult to think of the state without Gopinath Bordoloi. He had identified himself so completely with the interest of his state, and for years the political life had so much intermingled with his great personality that we had come to think of the two entities being always synonymous.

I know it for fact that his health had not been too well for the last two years ... He mentioned to me his innermost desire to resign his office but when I told him that his services were the paramount need of his province, he cheerfully obeyed the call of duty and this he did right up to the end..He has died in harness, full of glory and achievements. The unity of Assam was his great ambition. It was a great source of gratification that the Constitution recognised that unity and I am sure that he was happy that he could achieve it within his lifetime.

The state has yet to consolidate this unity and cement its bonds. It has yet to infuse into the different elements, which constitutes its policy, a spirit of oneness and loyalty to its common ideals. None was more fitted to achieve this difficult task than Gopinath Bordoloi. But alas, fate has removed him at a time when the state needed him most. I can only hope that his successor, and his colleagues will follow the path on which he trod, and inspired by his example will devote themselves to his unfinished tasks with unity and faith. His death is equally a loss to India. A devoted Congressman, he throughout participated in the freedom battle without regard for self and with complete determination to sacrifice for the country's cause. Those who knew him loved him and wherever he went he carried with him the hallmark of a loyal and disciplined soldier ever willing to render every service to the motherland. As a colleague in the working committee his advice was always helpful. We all mourn his death as that of a loyal and devoted colleague and of a selfish and zealous public worker whose ruling passion was service above self..."

Sardar Vallabh Bhai Patel

"... I counted him (Bordoloi) amongst some of my best friends. Undoubtedly he was one of the noblest sons of India. He had placed before himself a very high ideal of private and public life. I came in close contact with him for the last twelve years and more and I never found him descending from that high ideal on a single occasion. I had many occasions of talking to Bapu about him and knew that Bapu had a very high opinion about his character and statesmanship... Bapu more than once advised Gopinath to give up all public work for a time to recoup his health: 'your health and life are national assets...you should not be negligent of these.' This was Bapu's message to him through me... But public life in Assam would ill-spare him in the most trying time of Hindu-Muslim tension, as also during the bitter days of Bengali-Assamia controversy. I found him not only impartial and just, but always thinking of the best interest of national solidarity.

The Gauhati University was a thing nearest to his heart, and he often thought of resigning from the premiership of Assam so that he could give his undivided attention to the University. His death is a great loss not only to Assam, but to the whole of India. He was one of those noble souls that had imbibed the spirit of Bapu".

Kaka Kalelkar

"Four lakh Gorkhas of Darjeeling Hills share your grief at sad demise of our beloved Bordoloijee".

All India Gorkha League–Darjeeling

"People of Mishmi hills both tribals and non-tribals overwhelmed with grief at untimely demise of Shri Gopinath Bordoloi honourable Chief Minister. Convey their message of deepest sorrow and sincerest condolences. We pray in silence for peace to soul of deceased".

Sadiya

"Kindly communicate the following message to the bereaved family of late Chief Minister Hon'ble Sri Gopinath Bordoloi. The Public and Officers of the Garo Hills (Tura) assembled in a public meeting held at 4.30 p.m. at the Tura Town Hall on 6/8/50 under the presidency of Co. Friend, Inspector General of Assam Rifles express their deep sorrow at the sudden and untimely demise of Hon'ble Shri Gopinath Bordoloi late Chief Minister of Assam and express their heartfelt sympathy to the bereaved family".

Garo Hills

Jamiatulema Hind deeply mourns loss of one of greatest sons of Assam, Gopinath Bordoloi.

Lifyurahman–New Delhi

"Kindly accept my heartfelt condolence–in your sad bereavement, in your husband the whole nation has lost a trusted friend and leader".

Chief Minister–Orissa

To Hon'ble Medhi

"Poignantly grieved hearing Bordoloi's demise. Assam loses its great leader, deep sympathies to Assam. Please convey sincerest condolences to bereaved family".

Basanta Kumar Das
Dacca– Pakistan

Governor of Assam

"I am deeply grieved to learn of the death of my friend Sree Gopinath Bordoloi, Chief Minister of Assam. Please convey my sincere condolence to his bereaved family".

Maharaja, Manipur
Howrah Camp

"Heartfelt sympathy untimely demise friend Bordoloi".

Abul Kasham
Assam Assembly Now refugee
Ulipur Pakistan

"Extremely shocked hearing premature death of your husband. May God bless departed soul and give you consolation".

Ali Haidar Khan
Pakistan

The Governor of Assam

"Deeply grieved at tragic death of Chief Minister. Convey sincere condolence to bereaved family".

Doctor Maikee,
Minister of Pakistan

"Extremely shocked to hear of your husband's sudden demise. Entire Assam plunged in grief for loss of undisputed leader. He departed while engaged in piloting state in midst of thousand intricate problems notwithstanding failing health. His devotion to duty to fight against imperialism and lifelong sacrifice and suffering for country will ever shine and live in his admiring countryman's heart. Please accept most cordial condolence from one who had privilege to know your noble spouse intimately in varying circumstances while in jail as also when he was in pinnacle of glory".

Satindradev - Silchar

"Shocked at sudden demise of hon'ble Bordoloi, Chief Minister of Assam. For refugees in Cachar offer deepest condolence. May his soul rest in peace".

Premdra Gohain
Joint Secy., Central Refugee Board
Cachar

"People of the Mikir Hills express their profound sorrow at the sudden demise of their beloved leader the honourable Chief Minister Sreejut Bordoloi and offer their deepest condolence to the bereaved family".

Kharsing Terang

The Mikir Hill People Association while setting upon certain deliberation affection the people inhabiting the Mikir hill learn to their greatest grief about the sudden and untimely demise of hon'ble Gopinath Bordoloi, Premier of Assam.

President
Mikir Hills People Association

"Extremely shocked sudden demise Hon'ble Chief Minister. Irreparable loss to Assam".

Hema Chakravarty
President, District Congress, Silchar

"Meeting Udharband Public expresses deepest sorrow at Premier's premature death conveying condolence to bereaved family".

Udharband Public, Cachar, Assam

"Please accept on behalf of myself and the Indian Tea Association, Surma valley branch our sincere sympathy in your great bereavement. We feel your deep loss of your husband as the Leader and Premier of Assam can never be replaced".

Morley,
Chairman, Indian Tea Association
Member Legislative Assembly

"Extremely shocked at sudden demise of Chief Minister at a time when country needed him most".

Upenda Sankar Dutta
Ex-President Cachar DCC

"Public of N.C. Hills assembled in a meeting under Presidency of SDO at Haflong on seventh August and expressed their deepest sympathy and resolved to convey their heartfelt condolence to the bereaved family on the sudden demise of late hon'ble Chief Minister".

President, SDO
Haflong

"Deeply grieved sudden demise of revered leader Shree Gopinath Bordoloi Chief Minister Assam".

Suresh Deb
Surama Upatyaka Union, Karimganj

"Sincerest condolence, sudden demise of your distinguished husband country shares your loss".

Capt. Subodh Dutt
Hailakandi

"Our condolence at your terrible loss".

President Kaburganj
Panghat, Rural Panchayat

"Cachar Muslims deeply grieved at sudden premature demise of most beloved Chief Minister, Champion of peace and cause of minority offer sincerest condolence".

Makabir Ali Majumdar
Muzzafar Ali Laskar
Rashid Ali Laskar
Rahamatualla Majumdar

Hon'ble Sri G.N.Bordaloi's sudden and untimely death is a bolt from the blue on Assam. The cruel and sad news shocked all people irrespective of party allegiance. Loss is irrepairable and the void caused by his death is never to be recouped. Late Bordoloi was the post and pillar of the state. His amiable character was a solace to the country. He was the only man who was taken into confidence by all people of hills and plains. He was the bridge between the centre and the state. The newly born Sreemanta Shanker mission could see the light of the world through his sincere and untiring efforts.

He wanted to make it a national social service organization. He actually believed that we could establish friendship with hill people who suffer from abject poverty and ignorance only through humanitarian services. We would gratefully remember him best. *He was a true follower of Mahatma Gandhi and a true Congressman.* May his departed soul rest in peace.

Haladahar Bhuyan
Secretary, Assam Congress
Parliamentary Party

"Heartfelt consolation demise your illustrious husband".

Kaviraj Hareshchandra Bhattacharya
Secy., Cachar Ayurveda Seva
Silchar

A Portion of His Diary
1950

Saturday 21st January	Left Gauhati by air on way to Delhi.
Sunday 22nd January	Arrival in Delhi at 1 a.m. night.
Monday 23rd January	Met Ayyangan over communication and the ordinance.
Tuesday 24th January	Left Delhi by night Air Mail most tiring journey.
Wednesday 25th January	Morning Dum Dum 10.40-Kahikuchi 4 p.m.–Shillong - felt giddy and...
Thursday 26th January	Republic Day observed with myself only standing near the flag, H.E. doing all the ceremony.
Saturday 28th January	Was out for Gauhati for a propaganda tour among tribals to complete what I started in Dec. last. On a venture all the people of the state.
Sunday 29 January	Korkapara (Boko area) - social education rally and a good and simple exhibition. Come back to Gauhati. A big crowd of 3000 people gathered. Read address and presents from Korkapara Biniadi Vidyalaya and the people of the Mouja.
Monday 30 January	Left for Barpeta arrived there at 12. After lunch went to attend a meeting at Bhella where I explained the significance : attendance 4000.

Unveiled Bapuji's portrait at Barpeta after half an hour's speech - attendance 4000. Mahila samitee meeting.

Tuesday
31 January

Speech at Pathsala after leaving Barpeta in the morning. Went gala where a mixed crowd of tribals and others of about 4,500 accumulated. Spoke to them on the necessity of living ourselves as one family. Received 3 or 4 addresses. Halted at night at Pathsala.

Wednesday
1st February

Proceeded to Masalpur and arrived at 10.30. The meeting started at about 3 p.m. It was also the anniversary day of the compulsory education day and at least 500 boys and girls of different schools came, received several addresses.

Explained the value of real education and the necessity of working as one family the tribals and non-tribals all together. Total attendance would be 4,500.

Halted at Nalbari at night.

Thursday
2nd February

Went to Sarthebari : felt as if the road built was over a depth as less as 12 ft. from the normal level. The land appeared fertile though infested with water hyacinth. The people complained: but did not seem to be doing anything themselves.

A big 'naam' took place and with the presence of myself the crowd grew as big as 10 thousand. None of the leaders like Akhoy Babu, Mahendra Choudhury spoke. I had to do this for more than 45 minutes. I was presented with addresses and some presents. I felt the thrill of 'naam' and felt very happy.

Spoke to the local Congress committee who were more prone to discuss Govt. than to help the people.

Halted at Nalbari, which reached at 6.30. Could not attend the District Working Committee meeting.

Friday 3rd February	Attended the District Congress Committee between 8 and 9.30. Left for Gagra where a Co-operative society was functioning; went to late Harinder's Gossaighar etc. Old art completely lost. But many people appeared devotional. The object of the meeting apparently who to get some grant for the High School. Attendance in the meeting was poor - not even a thousand attending. Arrived at Nalbari at 3.30 and addressed a big meeting of about 3,000 people where the Constitution was explained. Left for the meeting and halted at Kamalour Bungalow for the night.
Saturday 4th February	Left for Goreswar, lunched and addressed a tribal gathering of about 5000. On Goreswar people (Tribal) education. The heart of those innocent people appeared quite sound. I am only sorry that their progress in education has not been as rapid. Received affectionate addresses. Arrived at Guwahati by the last ferry and arrived Shillong at 9 p.m.
Sunday 5th February	Heavy file work.
Monday 6th February	Cabinet meeting and a heavy day.
Thursday 7th February	Could not finish all the files, but nothing of importance was left. Left Guwahati at night.
Wednesday 8th February	Met Kala Saheb in the morning and was with him till 9.30 a.m. He is proceeding to Sadya at 2 p.m. I inspected my house.

(1) University development meeting at 3 p.m. which went on till 4.30 although it was to have been finished by 4 p.m.

(2) 4.30 - Committee of the Relief plan with the D.C. Requisition offer etc. till 5.30 p.m.

Thursday
9th February

Tezpur by air with Bhaiti. Addressed the Library Conference at Basseria at 2 the functions having started at 1.30.

There was an attendance of less than 1,000 people. As usual address was given.

The L.B. Chairman presented to me an address in the midst of a crowd of 3,000 men. Did not find Marwaris present.

Explaining Constitution to general public.

I explained the new Constitution, the implementations of the provision and our duty in that connection - the necessity of social feelings.

Discussed at night

(1) the grant of the Missamari Hungar to the College etc.

(2) Harijan colony (?)

Friday
10th February

Inspected the Missamari Colony after having seen the Collage site. I enjoyed the dance by the Santals etc.

Missamari
darrang College

This co-operative work has only started; I missed; it would take a long time to make it a complete success – of course in all details. The people are much too dull to be fully co-operative. Came back to Gamuguri to see the High school. But had to speak a few words to the gathering crowd of 300 men and women. Then came and inspected the basic education building –a big cluster of good houses. Addressed a meeting of 500 people. Lunched and immediately started for Bihali, where I addressed a meeting of 400 men– receiving addresses everywhere. Then came to Barangabari, where I was late by 1 hour; some 500 people were there, and by the time I reached Kalabari Aided H.E. School. It was 6.30 when the crowd had all left. Received, however, an address, went back to Gohpur Bangalow, ate and slept.

Saturday

11th February

Left Gohpur and arrived at North Lakhimpur at 9.30a.m. having halted on the way.

North Lakhimpur

Subansiri

Received addresses. Addressed a meeting of the Scheduled Caste people of about 400 men. After lunch came to Pathalipam where an address was presented, M.E.Schools of Kadam and Pathalipam. A crowd of 2,000 men listened to my address.

Went and saw the ravages of Chalohoa 3 mls. from there and came back and halted at Durrlong, Mukh.

Sunday

12th February

Subansiri with all its ferocious beauty

Was charmed to see the river in the morning after a very prolonged sleep at night. In the morning went to Subansiri 3 miles up the river, which although flowing, over boulders was nearly half a mile here, 3 miles up only 100. yds. or less. The water there was four feet deep at several places, the same river which was not more than 4 ft. deep here.

Earthquake Irony of Fate

The nature, it seemed to me, was in the process of formation. Rocks were being formed. At one place (Ram Mrigaya) a single rock seemed to as high as 1,000 ft. high. The path the Daflas got down was shown to us by the Miris who took us on their boat, S.D.O. Phookan was telling me about Hydro Electric possibilities. I was only thinking of the Earthquake, which brought down an avalanche of earth and timber which lay strewn on the bank of the river. The whole land appeared to me so strangely wild that is weird and uncanny. Returned to Bungalow at 12.45 having started at 9 in the morning.

At 3.30 went to see the site of the New Subansiri Bund. In the meantime several deputations all for the settlement of land came. It seemed to me that in the land of lands, there was no land - Subansiri being responsible for this. Got down in the Miri Village–the women folk came and gave some present of Mugu but I refused. I hope they have excused me.

Dictate letter to H.E.Panditji regarding general election while meditating, how the ravages of the floods could be mitigated, ate and slept another long night.

Monday
13th February

Got up at 5 and was waiting for dawn. At 8.45 went to see the fishing operation of the Miris. They caught a dozen of them, small ones, having surrounded the fishing area with a net. It was an interesting operation, it was a game day. In the morning a cock, a duck, and a big deer were killed. The fishermen gave me a present of two fish.

Came back at ten and met the Asstt.Recruiting officer and the Executive Engineer, Embankment and Drawing and discussed Subansiri Bund for an hour.

Khirod Gogoi P.A.

Corrected the Dictation prepared by Gogoi.

Wednesday
1st March

Arrived Goalpara at 5.
Met Hindu and Muslim leaders including M.L.A.s and Ex-M.L.A.s and one Mofiruddin (alias Maji Mahajani).

Goalpara
Immigration Act

The latter bitterly criticised the utterance of Sj. Bhubaneswer Goswami. But I pacified and told them that the only way to maintain peace was to trust each other. I told them that while Immigrant Expulsion Act would be enforced it would be a Government action, and individuals and communities would not be justified in taking the law in their own hands. The law would be enforced severely and without any.....From the talk it appeared that all Hindus and Muslim were extremely panicky.

Thursday
2 March

Left Goalpara at 11.30 and came to Bangaigaon straightway with the D.C. and S.P. of Dhubri and S.D.O. Goalpara after fixing up a programme of seeing as many places of up as possible.

Visiting Riot-town places in the District of Goalpara

(1) at Bongaigaon - about 1,500 stranded people D.C. called some of the Matbars (village head) there at my instance and asked them to stay back for which all arrangements for safety would be made. Out of 5, none agreed to stay back and only said, "Hazoor, make immediate arrangements for leaving the place". When we got on a trolly for P.

(2) Basugaon, all looked pitiously on me and saluted.

I felt as if a dart was in my heart. On the way we found houses and villages burnt on both sides said to be belonging to immigrants. Met a party of Boros with bows and arrows on the way. On being accorded they said that they were afraid of the immigrants.

(3) From Basugaon we went to Vidyapur, the place of Raja of Sidli where also some Muslim houses were said to be burnt. Raja and Rani were panicky.

(4) Then we went to Champak where we talked to a number of people not found to be panicky - the military having taken their post there.

(5) We then came to Bilaspara, where I addressed a large meeting at about 7 p.m. It was then said by Mr. Umruddin that houses near Lakhipuja were on fire. We proceeded to Lakhipuja and found there that a large number of Muslims were leaving their houses taking only some property in bundles. We asked them to go back and said that military were there and would shoot anybody they met committing mischief. Fire became visible on the other bank of Gourang, the S.P. could not trace the miscreants although a party or two went towards the side of the fire. Arrived Dhubri at 9 p.m. and after a hurried dinner at D.C.'s place, slept and dreamt hideous dreams.

Friday
3 March

Visiting riot-from places of Goalpara

Wanted to start early after meeting a group of representatives of people but could do so only at 9.30 up to which we remained in the hope communique printed. We passed through the road towards the east; again the D.C., I.G.P., S.P.etc accompanying and saw Congress flags in some places belonging to Hindu hung up in the houses. They told us that Bazar people wanted them to do so. At one bazar about 20 miles from Ganipur they said that some people whom they did not know asked them to put them up for their safety; they would not tell the names. Went first to Fakiragram; we saw some houses burnt near the station. They could not say who did it. Then I talked with L.S. and S.D.C. who said that the Muslims... Basugaon were completely panicky and were arranging for evacuation. We came back to Lakkhigang and again found people mourning. Before going to Fakiragram, we found on the way hundreds of people with women and children leaving their houses in an interminable stream. We sent back to their villages only a few of them all afraid of going back. From Gaurang river and round about one could see a most heart rendering scene.

Old villagers about 40 to 50 in all were burnt, with the grannaries still burning, cattle and poultry straying and the whole area up to 1 1/2 of Kokrajahar Thana in ruin and desolation. At Kokrajahar ate our food - rather scrumptious ladies not Bengalees who refused to us food. Addressed a big meeting of tribals (7000 to 8000) and explained that no crime would be tolerated and the government would bring all offenders and looters to book. Then came to Dachim Salmara, where we addressed a meeting of about 8000 men asking Hindus and Muslims to work together against the arson and looting etc. Met some people from Abhayapuri side coming towards Chapan side quite panicky. They told us that there was fire and Muslims were attacking; sent back the Police with.

To inform military and myself went alone to Iagighopa Ghat having met Muslims on the way.

Saturday 4 March	Last night before I went to bed sick, some people of Goalpara came. Khagen Babu, the President, Goalpara Congress Committee had been with us all these 2 days constantly and had seen everything for himself. I sent words to Muslim representative that things were worse than I imagined. I wanted to send the S.D.C. even last evening to Abhyapuri ; but he accompanied us to Dhupdhara, his jurisdiction and saw the Inspection Bungalow which the R.C.P.I. was said have burnt last night.
Back in Shillong	Arrived Guwahati at 11.45. At 1 we left for Shillong. A large number of files awaited me.
Sunday 5 March	Draft for a communique was given to me; I had hardly any time to examine it and left it with a slight note for change.
Monday 6 March	In the last two days files were cleared. Karimganji affair did not develop any further although I heard that panic continued in the most severe form. At 7 I left for Guwahati and left Guwahati at 2.30 p.m. by air to attend Panditji's call to meet him at Calcutta..
Calcutta meeting with Panditji on riot.	After the evening dinner he talked to me. He said, you shall have to pay compensation for losses to the people. I said Government had not yet been able to take any action under the undesirable Immigrant Expulsion Act and that a state of lawlesness had suddenly developed and that I had run about in these areas. He said we should stop the law from operation at present. Srimant M.Sarabhai told me that Gowalka's hand was there. J.E. Katju talked about the situation in the country and said it must be treated as an all India question. I told that the question of settlement of refugees come only after law and order. I went back at 10 p.m. to sleep at Murleedhar's place which was fixed by Mazumdar for sleep.

Tuesday
7 March

Next morning I read the communique. I found that the points that I mentioned were not incorporated. They were that the crimes exhibited were only repercussions of Pakistan's action on the Hindus.

At 12.45 again there was to be a lunch and we waited from them till 1.45. Panditji and I came out of conference; I did not know to what effect. After lunch we went to the secret chamber where 4 Chief Ministers, Saxena, Dr. Shyama Prasad Mukherjee were present. More or less the memorandum prepared by a Committee of relief etc. was rediscussed. Panditji went away after some time. I said that policy of makeshift would not do.

In the conference, I refused to take anybody from the Goalpara side so long as the lawlessness continued and left even the Karimganj side to be done by the Government of India. I said we were embarrassed with so many difficulties shortage everyway that we would not be able to have anything done. Saxena agreed to go to Karimganj, himself came back at 3.30 and drove about and went to Hiwatsingka's place for dinner and at 9.30 came back and slept.

Wednesday
8 March

Arrived Kahikuchi at 10-35. Opened police Conference at 11.15 and spoke the policemen.

Left for Shillong at 1 and arrived at 4 to do the files that came and worked till 8.30 p.m.

In the meantime the reports from Sarbhog was alarming and decided to come to Sarbhog with Sri Mohendra Chowdhury after Cabinet meeting. H.E. was pleased to send some Assam Rifles to Sarbhog.

Thursday
9 March

Cabinet meeting was started at 9.30. Somehow I could not come that day on account of other urgent work and decided to start next night after arranging for a plane. Sri Mohendra Chowdhury was already prepared to be sent next morning.

Friday

10 March and 11 March

Left for Gauhati by special timing in the evening. Next morning I was told that on account of bad weather the plane would not arrive at 8.a.m. but would be late. I arrived Kahikuchi at 10 and at 10.35 the plane took off and landed us at 11 at Sarbhog. Met Mohendra, Akhoy Babu, the A.D.M., A.S.P. Bora and all drove to Sarbhog Police Station. Then a number of people mostly Hindus wanted that I should address the people, I did so. The situation excepting on the Roha side where there was firing, seemed well under control on that day and I was happy that the trouble would no more spread. I came to Roha within 3 mls. of which the firing took place and although within 3 mls. there were no immigrants I found the people so panicky that I was surprised. At Barpeta I was met by Ronf and Ataur Rohaman and also by the other leaders at a meeting. I thought that they would express sympathy at the suffering of the distressed people; but everybody except the Congressmen spoke only on the method of evacuation ... whether peacefully or otherwise.

On riot Sarbhog and Barpeta

I heard that Muslims of Abhayapuri had also came to attack and killed 3 Hindus and to quell the disturbance, Military had to open fire on the 6th. The same Muslims came to Barpeta side and similarly killed 4 Hindus near Roha. They were resisted by good works of the S.D.O. on the 6th but on the 7th Police opened fire and killed some Muslims. The result was a complete evacuation of this locality by Muslims and they all moved towards Baghbar side to which Muslims from all North Goalpara area also moved. It was reported to me by the Mauzadar that about 25,000 Muslims had gathered there. A report said they looted some Langa Hat and looted the house of ... I talked to the S.D.O. to see to the orderly evacuation of the people who wanted to go ; but to assure all people that people who wanted to stay should be sent back and to assure them full protection.

Sunday
12 March

Left for Gauhati at 7.30 with Mohendra Choudhury and thought that this was last of a bad dream. But by the time we reached Shillong at 2 p.m. news came of similar depredation at Khairabari of eviction of Muslims setting fire to their houses.

In the meantime I had to be ready for tomorrow's session of the Assembly.

Monday
13 March

Assembly is sitting ; but mind was all along disturbed with these occurrences. The Governor's address was delivered by him ... a long speech as usual; but apart from the enunciation of our policy full of sentiment. The Thanks Motion was moved by our Chief whip, Sj. P. Sarma and seconded by Mrs. Bonelly Khongman. The Budget speech was read by Mr. Medhi ... a good speech also. In the party meeting it was decided that I would reply to the amendment of the opposition.

Met H.E. with H.M. 7 and the C.S. to discuss the situation, the appointment of P.S.C. and left him at 5.30. A most stringent set of directions to the police was to be issued to the S.P.s and the D.C. Arrangement for better evacuation of those who would leave Assam was also made. Plan for rehabilitation was thought out by me for (1) temporary cultivation of land. (2) Disposal of property including seizure of paddy by Procurement Deptt.

Tuesday
14 March

In morning the amendment. Dr. E.H. Choudhury spoke about the shortage of sugar of fine cloth. But Saadulla tried to find everything good in Pakistan ... and all bad in India. This C whip, Sri Moti Bora etc. attacked severely and asked Saadulla to go to Pakistan.

Mr.... gave credit to Government for all that they did to Saadulla's incidental attack that the lot of the common man (meaning Muslims) was not safe in Assam, I gave a rather lengthy reply, stating Pakistan was responsible for this state of things.

We had a party meeting again this afternoon.

Wednesday
15 March : At 9.30 we had a Cabinet meeting to discuss attitude to the resolution and other matters.

At 3 p.m. we sat to decide Saadulla's request to shorten the Assembly. I was myself very anxious to leave the House to the disturbed areas see things for myself, arrange for cultivation of fallow lands, to the relief of displaced persons. It was accordingly decided that sittings should continue to finish all business that it would prorogue on the 28th March. In the meantime the necessity of passing of two legislature, Enhancement and Disciplinary Power Bill for giving wider powers to the Commandants of Police Battalion and Amendment of the Assam Public ...became necessary. H.E. who under direction of H.P.M. India was touring the affected area had to be wired to.

After finishing all the files I got ready to go to Barpeta, from which place more widespread damages by fire etc. came to me.

Thursday
16 March

Barpeta again on riot

Started for Barpeta at 7.30 and arrived at Ranja at 11.45. Met a number of representative people, talked to them and secured the Co-operation of the Peace Committee for

(1) Seizure of the paddy through Procurement Inspector.

(2) Seeing to the custody of the unclaimed cattle & property with the co-operation of the people. Both Hindus and Muslims seemed to work together, but examining deeper, found that mistrust was yet there. Went up to Khundikar at 4 p.m. and found the houses burnt and a number of immigrants crying. The lane belonged to a landlord of North Gauhati. After taking tea went to Juroni and from there to Rangya Station waiting room which looked so unclean and dirty.

Boarded the Saloon, which was so kindly provided by Mr. Arora, C.A. Rly. and arrived at Barpeta Road, where I slept for the night, after having met D.C., S.P. and S.D.O. Akhoy Babu, Mohendra, Madhusudan and other Congress workers. Slept for the night.

Friday
17 March

At 8 o'clock had a conference of D.C., S.P., S.D.O. and others. Heard that even last evening fires were there South of Sarupeta Station. But at 9.30 up to which conference lasted Mohendra told that he had heard about the firing programme to continue even today.

The following was settled that S.P. put a sort of ... for further programme of the miscreants (2)S.D.O. should obtain authenticated information about the situation in Tarabari and Bagbor side. The Mauzadar of the neighbouring Mauza of Bagbor told that 30,000 Muslims had accumulated there (3) Issue a bulletin explaining Government policy.

At 1.30 after we had finished our food, the a/c of Barpeta Police Station came and told some villages of his Thana were burnt by ... but did not seem at all anxious. On my asking why he came there he said that he had come to take orders from S.P. I said the S.P. had gone to the area concerned and he should proceed to the spot also. An hour after I got anxious to hear that several villages were still burning. With Mohendra Choudhury one or two Congressmen rushed to the area. On the way we found a/c and one Ajoy Mukherjee on a truck at Bhabanipur talking to people. They did not pursue going 3 or 4 mls. We found that almost all the Muslim villages were burnt and that the S.P. had arrested 17 Hindu people from different places. Came back; at night news came that Ajoy Mukherjee was arrested.

It seemed to me that a/c was equally to blame for failure to prevent the riot. The D.C. who followed us to the fire.....areas came to the same conclusion.

Saturday
18 March

No more fires were there. We assured the people that Police would help them : some in that region seemed steady in spite of the fires. But the large mass of people of Barpeta Road. etc. had all come to the big field on the other side of the Station. About 5,000 people gathered of whom 900 left yesterday. Today another 12 to 13 hundred left by train. Some of the Matbar were swindling the unfortunate displaced Muslims by realising Rs. 700 per ticket whereas it is only R. 1-12 as. From reports heard 40,000 with tickets had already left by train. To this surely can be added those without ticket. I was sure that atleast 60,000 had left by that end apart from those by steamers etc.

Addressed a meeting at Howli at 3 p.m. A crowd of 5,000 people gathered. Heard many Muslims were near about the Muslim locality. Head master and some Muslims were doing all that is possible to maintain peace. I told D.C. that it possible they found accumulated were without food and shelter they might be helped.

About three miles from the Station there was fire. Mohendra Choudhury, Akhoy Babu and the Police went there and found a Muslim singing and setting fire to houses one by one.

Instructed the S.P. and the D.C. to follow some defined policy in arresting the spread of the crimes, to keep an eye on the property and cattle of the persons where houses were burnt and to take the strongest measures. Again reiterated that all land must be brought under cultivation and no land could be waste.

Sunday
19 March

At about 7.30 D.C. Dhubri was there in the Station. I called him to the breakfast table and learnt the situation and asked him about rehabilitation of the displaced Muslims, as also the reception of the Hindu refugees. He said the morale of the Muslims was not strong enough to move to areas beyond the Rly line;

a few of them had been rehabilitated. As regards Hindu refugees the difficulty is being created by the so called Refugee association who were inviting people to come although for law and order position the Dist. authorities have not been able to give requisite attention.

Decided to go to see the mass of people accumulated on the banks of Gauranga as wished by H.E. which place we arrived at 10.30 and left by 11. The people got scattered and about 2 to 3 thousand men and women in most distressed condition were found lying with water and wind-driven sands of Gauranga River. Rice was being given to them only.... D.C. telling me that D.D.P. not co-operating with him. I told them to go back. Some agreed; I was told they would represent a batch of 2,000 D.C. arranged to go to Bejni as formerly fixed up to settle some of the displaced persons.

Came back to Gogighopa, leaving a big crowd on the River Ate our meals and at 4 started for Gauhati where we did not stop and drove straight to Shillong.

Loose Leaf Diary of Lokopriya Bordoloi

11.11.48

I forgot to bring my diary and I have not made use of the same for more than 2 months. But the glory of what I see today is making me repent that I should not have given up the habit of recording my impressions. The same spirit of repentance overtook me when I had my tour in the tribal areas of Charduar, Margherita, Sadiya and Passighat. These, besides grandeur and beauty of nature, were the impressions of my meeting the various tribes– the Nagas of Tirap Frontier Borders, the Abors and Mishimis of Sadiya and Abors Gallong and Padongs of Passighat area. About the beauties of nature, I seem to catch back the charm by what I see today. Yet the scenarios, that I saw in the frontiers of Assam in October last were not such as I had seen here for the first time. Two years and four months ago, I had visited all those areas. I forgot myself in the work of the Advisory Sub-Committee; but yet in those moments, when I could feel round me, I got lost in the wonder of God's creation in tnose areas, the nature and men.

Today, however, these scenes being new, I feel completely overwhelmed. From the earliest childhood I heard about the beauty and the holiness of Haridwar, the inaccessibility of Risikesh and Lashmanjhola. A halo of sanctity pertained to the very names of those places. The feeling of retirement from the turmoil of politics has been ever agitating me and I thought, a little withdrawal from human company might possibly tone up my mind and let me realise how I should conduct myself in future. Whatever might have been the underlying thought they passed away as soon as the car passed through a variety of scenery–the first 7 miles of open waste, then miles and miles of sugarcane cultivation, then a township - Modinagar, then a crowded town–Meerut and the Dwara Mills area. Muzzafar Nagar, altogether different atmosphere began to surround us from Roorkee. Our road lay through the bank of the Ganges, which, we found were bounded in various places by huge dams. The channels of other streams falling into the Ganges were similarly diverted or its channel filled with water for irrigation. The S.D.O. of Haridwar told me it was a great and interesting work and I am proposing, if possible to examine the whole system and a porportion of the work at Haridwar.

This bunding has probably taken away much of the natural beauty of Mother Ganges, yet the place is not less delightful. The temples and big buildings abut on the river as also on the hills, on which also have been created several temples. The uncontrolled channel is just to the east of the controlled channel; but I have yet to examine it more critically tomorrow.

After lunch brought ready from Sj. Rohini Chowdhuri's place, and a little rest, we started for Rishikesh and Lashmanjhola at 3 p.m. and here that we were struck with the abundance of the natural beauty of the surroundings. We went to Lashmanjhola first but spent more than 1/2 an hour in wrongly going to Badan Kashan Road. At about 4.45 we were at Lashmanjhola. I felt the impulse of rushing the heights, where we were. I came down about 1/4 of a mile; but immediately felt the impossibility of going down and therefore, waited there to see Mukti and Nadia Babu go near the Bridge and fetch Ganges water for us.

When they came back we got into the car, which was brought to where I was standing. On the other area were built a splendid mansion so it looked the view of which fell full on us from a height of 1000 ft. A boat was ferrying a number of pilgrims almost every 20 minutes from the other side to western side. I myself noticed some pilgrims - among whom the number of the aged seemed to have a fair proportion. Many appeared full of devotion; but there were sightseers like myself even among them.

We then drove to Rishikesh. It was getting dark and I could see the beautiful waters and touched it only glimmer of the evening. The scenery struck me as superb. Waters of the Holy Ganges rushing through the millions of rounded pebbles and stones with a forest on the other side of it. The ghat was beautifully made to go up to the waters and people flocked there in the evening. What struck me was the devotion of the ladies, large number of whom sat in choristers facing the river. Many are seen in contemplation–particularly those who were sitting singly. To my mind, came immediately the difference of outlook of a Westerner with an Indian–the former utilizing these scenarios of nature as places of pleasure–while the Indian using them for devotional purposes.

Arrived Haridwar at 7 p.m., had kichri and slept disturbed by cough all the night.

Statement by Sri Gopinath Bordoloi as the Leader of the Opposition Party in Assam Legislative Assembly on Mass Literacy Campaign

Mass Literacy Campaign (Friday Sept. 20, 1940)

Congress Party in Assam Legislature Not to Co-operate

The Congress party in the Assam Legislature is not co-operating with the mass literacy campaign. The reasons for this decision are explained in the following statement issued by Sjt. Gopinath Bordoloi, ex-Premier and leader of the party.

Although not officially informed I have been told that the Government of Assam will inaugurate the second year of the mass literacy campaign which was initiated and started by the Congress Coalition Ministry. A number of enquiries has been made as to what attitude I should take in the matter. Having initiated the scheme myself and taking considerable pains to prepare the same in the consultation of the Heads of the Department, it seems it is a great pity to me that I shall not be able to render co-operation which I so much desired. It is true that, the same scheme prepared by us has more or less been maintained; but it seems also that there has been departure from the original both in regard to principles involved as well as in the personnel chosen by the Government in conducting the campaign. So I have been compelled for the present to decide to withhold our co- operation.

The Reason

My reasons are as follows : The Sub-Divisional Committees have been ..... of the powers that we propose to give them. Under the revised scheme prepared by the present Government the selection of centres have been left for the D.I's and SI's of schools, the said Committees are merely to help the DI's. Although the Deptt. Notifications No. 1142, 331 dated 4-9-40 say that one of the function of the Sub-Divisional Committees is organisation of local centres, it is clear from the provision made by the paras 9-13 of the revised scheme of the mass literacy campaign that this function will be more or less advisory than having the power of execution. I feel that it is mainly through the local boards, the Local MLAs and some influential representatives from the public, that the Government should have composed the Committees in order that adequate co-operation should have been received from the local centres where the works should be carried. I thought that under a Constitution as desired by us, it would not only safeguard the power of the Department under the scheme but it would have ensured better co-operation from the public.

Party Politics

The personnel in Central Sub-Divisional Committees have been based on considerations of party politics. It is not known why names like Dr. U. J. Sword of the American Baptist Mission should have been omitted from the Central Committee to make for persons whose only qualification is affiliation to the Government Party. Similarly in the Sub-Division Committees the persons whose only qualification is allegiance to the present Government Party have been included apparently to include persons otherwise fit and desirable. If the Committees are to represent political parties, as has been done by the Government, the Congress Coalition party as the opposition should have been allowed representation in the proportion of its strength. But the Government nominated only one member in the Central Committee and an insignificant number in the Sub-Divisional Committees. It should have been only fair that as the initiator of the scheme the Congressmen should have been given due opportunities in working the scheme, more than any other partymen. It seems, therefore, clear, that the Government do not want any co-operation from the Congressmen and want simply to carry on according to their party consideration.

Line of Action

In this connection I would state that no meeting of the Central as well as the Sub-Divisional Committee has been held for deciding the line of action prior to the inauguration of the scheme. It may be noted that no student or public organisation have been invited to co-operate in the campaign.

In passing I desire also to point out that the proposed increase of pay of teachers under the revised schemes is an eye-wash. The last Government proposed for every three persons made literate a remuneration of Re. 1 to the teachers while the present propose the same remuneration for five students regularly attending a centre.

Yet I want to make it clear, that our co-operation will be fully at the disposal of the Government, if the defects I have pointed out are rectified. At present the Government have left us no option but to act in a manner we have decided to do.

From G.A.Small,I.E.S. (Retd.)
Shillong, Assam.
To
The Chairman,
British Parliamentary Delegation,
C/o The Secretary,
Information and Broadcasting Department,
New Delhi.

Dated Shillong,
the 11th January,
1946.

Sir,

In the hope that some members of your Delegation may be able to visit Shillong, the Capital of Assam, I am writing this letter to try to give you some idea of the problems facing the people of this province, and of their fears regarding the future.

I claim to be able to write some authority, as I was for thirteen years Inspector of Schools, serving in both the Assam Valley Circle and the Surma Valley and Hill Districts and subsequently having been Director of Public Instruction, Assam from 1928 to 1941, when I retired as a protest against the nepotism of the Assam Government.

At the time of my retirement I was Honorary Secretary of the Joint War Committee, and Honorary Treasurer of the Assam War Fund and in May 1942 I became Assistant Red Cross Commissioner for Assam, and organized the War Depot at Gauhati. I resigned from this work in June 1942 on account of double hernia. I have been provincial commissioner of Boy Scouts, Assam since 1924 holding the Silver Wolf, and the Scout ranks of Deputy Camp Chief and Akela Leader ; and I am Honorary Secretary of the Shillong Citizens' Association, and the only European member of the Gauhati University Trust Board.

1. It is common knowledge that the Government of India, and possibly the British Government, have in mind to form a Frontier Province outside India by combining the Northern part of Burma with the Hill Districts of Assam and the Hill Tracts outside the Assam Borders.

2. The Hill Districts of Assam are the Lushai Hills, the Naga Hills, the Khasi and Jaintia Hills, the Garo Hills and the Mikir Hills.

The Transfrontier Hill Tracts are the foothill of the Himalayas, inhabited by uncivilized tribes such as the Abors, Khamtis, Misimis,

Akas, Daflas, Singphos and the border of the Naga Hills inhabited by wild Nagas and Kukis.

3. In my opinion it would be grossly unfair to the Assam tribal people to bring them under the same type of Government as the transfrontier tribes.

It would also be grossly unfair to the Assamese people to separate the Hills of Assam from the plains to Assam.

4. The province of Assam consists of the Hills Districts mentioned above and the two river valleys, the Brahmaputra Valley and the Surma Valley.

In the Brahmaputra Valley, commonly called the Assam valley, the people are Assamese, a race completely different from the Bengalis; although the colloquial dialect in northern Bengal is similar to Assamese.

Culturally the Assamese have little in common with the Bengalis, as Assamese written histories date back as far as the 14th century, while written Bengali is of only the last century. The Assamese kingdom once spread as far as Bihar and the United Provinces; and the colloquial dialect as far as Gonda and Baraich is similar to Assamese. In religion the Assamese follow the Mahapurushia form of Hinduism, which has no followers in Bengal.

In the Surma Valley, which takes its name from the Surma River, there are two Districts, Sylhet and Cachar. Sylhet is purely Bengali; it was part of Bengal till the partition of Bengal and it is a permanently settled district, whereas the Assam Valley and most of Cachar are temporally settled areas. Sylhet is almost entirely Muhammadan, while till recently the Assam Valley, and to a slightly less extent Cachar were almost entirely Hindu; although in the last few years, through the efforts of the Saadulla Government to encourage the immigration of Muhammadans from Bengal, the Hindu majority has been decreasing.

5. The people of the Hill Districts adjoining the Assam Valley have always been in close touch with the Assamese for purposes of trade, although they have had no cultural link. In the Naga Hills the lingua franca is Assamese, and it is used as the court language. Assamese is also spoken by the Mikirs and the Khasi and Jaintia Hills. These Hill Tribes have always been in close contact with the Assamese and Assamese and Ahom kings married the daughters of Hill Chiefs.

6. The Hill tracts outside the borders of Assam along the foothills of the Himalayas are inhabited by the Abors, Mishmis, Khamtis, Datlas, Akas, Singphos, and those on the East by Nagas and Kukis.

These people are backward, uncivilized and practically savage, hardly removed from the head-hunting stage, and obviously requiring a completely different type of Government from the people of Assam Hill Districts.

7. The proposal to separate the Hill Districts of Assam from the rest of Province, and to include them with the Transfrontier Areas of Assam and the Northern Hill areas of Burma in a new British Province or Protectorate, if carried into effect, will have the following effects:

(a) The remainder of Assam, i.e. the Assam valley, Sylhet and Cachar, will not be large enough to form a separate Province; and the obvious intention is that these districts will be attached to Bengal. This will not affect Sylhet very much, as it was always a Bengal District, and the people are purely Bengali; although the position of Sylhet as the least important district of Bengal will be very different from its position as the largest District in Assam ; but it will affect the people of Cachar, who have close connections with Assam and some of whom are Assamese; and it will vitally affect the people of the Assam Valley, whose linguistic and culturally identity must inevitably be swallowed up by Bengal.

(b) The Hill Tribes of Assam, instead of continuing the advance in education and culture that they have been making recently, will come under the Non-Regulation type of Government, which its advocates call 'paternal' but which really aims at keeping the people in ignorance so that they will not give any trouble, and cannot protect themselves by law.

(c) A number of British Civil Servants, who will soon be deprived of their soft jobs in the Assam or other Secretariats will find new and even softer jobs in the new protectorate, where there will be no High Court to insist on Justice or interfere with the autocratic rule of the I.C.S.

(d) Education will be entrusted, as it always was in the past to Missionaries, whose whole object is not to educate but to produce registered converts.

(e) The Hindu majority in Assam will be absorbed in the great Muslim majority of Bengal.

8. All these statements require support by facts and figures, and I am prepared to give them to your Delegation if any of your members visit Shillong, where you will be able to hear the other side and compare the evidence. The following points, however, may be considered as supporting the case against the partition of Assam.

ASSAM VALLEY

(1) Language: Sir Edward Gait made it quite clear that Assamese is a much older language than modern Bengali, which is in fact an invention of English Missionaries, modelled on Sanskrit, with a complex grammar entirely different from the language spoken by the ordinary people of Bengal. When the British first occupied Assam they brought with them, Bengali clerks, who regarded Assamese as a vulgar dialect of Bengali. Bengali was made the Court language; and it was not till the end of the 19th century that Assamese was recognized as a separate language. If Assam becomes part of Bengal, Assamese as a separate language is doomed.

(2) Education: I can only speak of conditions at the time of my retirement in 1941; but at that time the system of education in Assam was very much sounder than that in Bengal. Inspection was careful and systematic. Experimental methods were constantly being tried and originally among teachers was encouraged. If Examination results alone are to be considered the Assam results in the Calcutta University Matriculation Examination were 25% higher than those of Bengal; but we aimed far more at a high standard of vernacular education, and our Middle-Vernacular schools were the best in India. In Bengal purely vernacular school education in the higher stages does not exist. After the primary stage there is only the Anglo-Vernacular school, with its urge to the University.

If Assam comes under Bengal, education in the mother-tongue in Assam will cease after the primary stage; and all teaching will aim at the University and the production of "Babus".

Efforts are now being made to establish in Gauhatian an Assamese University, in which the medium of instruction will be Assamese; but there will be no hope of such a University under a Bengal Government, and the possibilities of real work in anthropology, archaeology, entomology etc., for which Assam offers unrivaled chances, will be lost.

(3) Government: When in competition with the enormous needs of Bengal, the needs of Assam will be completely neglected. The Bengal secretariat will know nothing about Assam and will care less. Assamese officials will be superseded by Bengalis, and the few representatives of Assam in the Bengal Legislature will be ignored. This is not merely conjecture, it is what actually happened when Bengal was partitioned, and Assam was joined with Eastern Bengal in the province of Eastern Bengal and Assam. The present prospect for Assam is even worse than it was then, as the remnants of Assam will be attached to the whole province of Bengal.

(4) Post-war Reconstruction : All intelligent plans for post-war reconstruction in Assam depend mainly on Hydro-Electric development, for which the province offers enormous possibilities. The sources of power lie in the Hills; and if they are separated from the plains districts there will be no such development by the Government of the latter, nor will the Hills Government welcome any such development. Bengal will be too busy with her own schemes to worry about the remnants of Assam; and development of the Assam valley, Cachar and Sylhet will be out of the question.

THE HILLS

It would be hard to conceive of any proposal more unfair, more retrograde, more selfish, or more short-sighted than the proposal to form a British Frontier province or Protectorate including both the Assam Hill people and the Trans-Frontier tribes.

In the first place, if India and Burma are to be given-self-government in the near future, how can a purely British protectorate exist on their Northern Frontier?

Secondly, in the Burma Hills the lingua-franca is Burmese, while in the trans-frontier hills bordering Assam the lingua-franca is Assamese. The two languages are of completely different types, Burmese being tonal, while Assamese is a direct descendent of Prakrit,

Thirdly, to force into one semi-military province, as is the obvious intention, the Hill people of Assam proper and the half savage or altogether savage of the border hills will be grossly unfair to the former, who are progressing far faster, educationally, culturally and industrially than the people of the plains districts.

The Lushais are a rapidly developing race, which sends hundreds of boys to High school and Colleges, and sent hundreds of men to the fighting forces and Medical Services during the war. Several Lushais obtained King's commissions. The Lushai women are also rapidly becoming educated, and their hand-loom weaving is unsurpassable.

The Khasis are a matriarchal people whose women have the highest percentage of literacy in India. They are wealthy and progressive, good carpenters; stone masons and machines, and grow the best potatoes crop in India. Persuading Government to open Government Primary school in the Garo, Naga and Khasi Hills, but the effort has been half-hearted and opposed by the District officers.

The opening of schools in the Hills has also been opposed by the non-Christians, because there are no non-Christian teachers, and the entry of Christianity into a village means the end of all tribal custom.

Tribal dances are forbidden, and the drinking of the homemade rice bear means excommunication.

Even now Government has not opened a single Training school for teachers in any of the Hills.

In spite of all this the Assam Hill people are striving hard for advance and if given a chance will equal any of the peoples of the plains; but if the proposed scheme goes through their future is without hope.

It is certain that if the Assam Hill people are forced into a Tribal Frontier Protectorate education will be put back ruthlessly, as being likely to cause trouble. To show the attitude of the present Government towards education in backward areas I may mention that some weeks ago I was asked whether I would work out a plan for the future education of the Transfrontier tribes. I agreed to do this, and made out a programme of work according to which I proposed to spend about one month visiting the frontier areas and discussing the local needs with the local officers. As remuneration I asked for the same rate of pay as I was drawing before retirement. The Governor withdrew the offer on the ground that it was not worth spending so much on the scheme. The total sum including travelling allowances would have been about Rs. 3,000.

Obviously the Governor does not think the future education of some ten Hill tribes of any real importance, if he is unwilling to spend this sum on a scheme fully worked out by the only expert on the subject in Assam.

GENERAL

Although some of the Assam Hill people are not very highly advanced, culturally or educationally, there is a vast gap between them and the Trans-Frontier people. To bring them all under the same type of Government would be a gross injustice to the former.

The Garos live at the extreme west of Assam, on a range of Hills that jut out into the plains of Bengal; and they can only be approached from the West. These people are more backward than the Khasis; but not because they are not anxious for advancement. The only reason is that the Government of Assam has kept them backward.

Those Nagas who live under British rule belong to several tribes which are defiantly backward, because the Assam Government has treated them like semi-prehistoric animals in a museum, to be dressed up and shown off to visitors in tribal costume, but otherwise to be repressed.

The Mikirs are a small tribe living in hills in the middle of the Assam Valley plain. So far as they speak any language but Mikir they speak Assamese, and the school books are written in Assamese character.

They have no future apart from the Assamese people. None of these tribal people have nothing in common with the North-East Frontier tribes. All of this have men and women at the Universities and if they had been given a fair chance they would have been at least on level terms with the people of the plains.

That this is true is clear from the manner in which Government has dealt with the education of the Hill people from the time of the occupation of Assam. In each case Government has handed over the whole responsibility to a Missionary body, and has washed its hands of any responsibility in educational matters.

The Missionary body in the case of the Naga, Mikir and Garo Hills was the American Baptist Mission, a Mission whose members knew nothing about education, but only wanted to send home sufficient returns of converts to guarantee their salaries. I can amplify this if necessary.

The Missionary Body in the Khasi and North Lushai Hills was the Wolsh Calvinstic Mission. Its interest in education was confined to making its converts sufficiently literate to be able to read the Bible and the Hymn Book. It has been in the Khasi Hills for over 100 years, but has not yet produced a dictionary or a single respectable text book for primary schools.

Comparatively recently the London Mission has been working in the south Lushai Hills. Some of its members are first class educationists and they are making education popular and intelligent.

After I became Director of Public Instruction I succeeded in a few words. It is high time for the ordinary law of India to rule in all the Hills of Assam. That at present the High Court has no jurisdiction in criminal matters in Shillong, the Capital of the province, is a disgrace to the British Government. Capital punishment is inflicted in these Hills by Executive Officers not by Judicial officers.

If all the Hills are lumped together in a Frontier province, educated, half-educated and completely savage all treated alike, the Province may be easy to govern for the present; but it will have in it the seeds of rebellion; for the different types and standards of education and culture cannot mix.

If the Assam Hills people were all brought under the ordinary law of India, as they should have been many years ago, as part of the Province of Assam, which would include the Assam Valley and possibly Cachar, while Sylhet might be permitted to return to Bengal, the province of Assam would be an easy province to manage under the ordinary Government of India, and there would be no need for special treatment of its Hill Tribes.

If India is to be responsible for her own Government and her own defence in future, why should there be any attempt by the present Government to break up Assam of its two parts, and to keep one part under foreign Government. Even if it were desirable from a military point of view to form a kind of frontier buffer state on the East of Assam, the inclusion in it of the Assam Hills seems futile, as there are no direct means of communication between any of them.

If such a state is essential it should consist of the Trans- frontier tribes only, and its Headquarters might be at Sadiya.

I enclose an outline map showing the Hill areas.

I am sending a copy of this letter to Sjt. Gopinath Bordoloi, the former Prime Minister of Assam, whom, I understand, has been asked to meet you.

I repeat my hope that some at least of your Deputation will be able to come to Shillong.

Your obedient servant
(G.A.Small)

This letter is written by G.A. Small, IES (Retd) Shillong, a Scotsman who was in-change of education of Assam for a period of thirty years. He was a great friend of Late Bordoloi, together they fought for the cause of unity and integrity of Assam of the forties (Assam then included present State of Arunachal) against the sinister of the British Government made at the time of transfer of powers to create a Transfrontier British state by separating the Hills people of Assam from their brethren of the plains. Mr. Small's letter in the form of a memorandum submitted to a British delegation who came to Shillong in 1946, helped in foiling this move.

MY CHILDHOOD MEMORIES

DR. INDIRA GOSWAMI
(Mamani Raison Goswami)

I still remember those days in Shillong when I was studying in Pine Mount School. My father was at that time the Director of Public Instruction in undivided Assam. We stayed in a huge bungalow allotted by the Government. Our house was called "Crinolin" because it faced the Crinolin falls. It was a breath-taking scene. The compound was full with various types of plum and peach trees, and wild roses, and pine trees.

Our bungalow and the one where the Chief Minister of Assam, Gopinath Bordoloi, lived with his family, were of the same type near each other. Bordoloi's bungalow had a thatched roof like all the government bungalows of those days. It was a very spacious structure built in the middle of a sprawling compound.

My father used to speak to us about Gopinath Bordoloi with great pride, especially about his Gandhian philosophy. People used to say that probably Assam would have been a part of Pakistan if Bordoloi's towering leadership had not guided the destiny of Assam through the difficult days of partition. But at that time I was too small to understand all this political talk. However, it was in those days the common topic of conversation between the elders.

Afterwards we came to know about the dreams of Bordoloi and how much he strived to fulfil those dreams. Among his many valuable achievements can be counted the establishment of Gauhati University, the eradication of opium addiction which was eating up the population of Assam; and then his work for the upliftment of the Harijans and the down-trodden people in general, and his genuine love and sympathy for the tribals and his work among them. All this he did, not with any political ambition but with the pure motivation of his heart. Even the astute politician like Phizo of Nagaland repented on the death of Gopinath Bordoloi stating that Naga people had lost a dear friend and leader.

At present, with all the turmoil in Assam and the deteriorating relationship between the plains people and the tribal people, a brilliant and wise leader like Bordoloi would have brought hope and solace for Assamese people.

My childhood memories are still green. We used to visit the residences of the Governor Jairamdas Daulatram, Gopinath Bordoloi and sometimes Bishnuram Medhi who later became the Chief Minister of Assam and the Governor of Tamil Nadu and even Mahindra Mohan Choudhury who also later became the Chief Minister of Assam, and then the Governor of Punjab. When I was doing my Ph.D. in the Oriental Institute of Philosophy, Vrindaban, Mahendra Mohan Chaudhury, while as a Governor of Punjab, came to visit our temple. He reminded me about my childhood days in Shillong, how he enjoyed the hospitality of my parents.

Governor Jairamdass Daulatram was a very popular figure at that time. He often used to throw big parties at his official residence on the bank of Ward Lake. These parties were lavish affair where many eminent men and women, celebraties and others were invited. My father and my mother were always invited to these parties. Sometimes the Governor also invited the students of Pine Mount School. I also visited his palatial home several times. His daughter, who was much older than us, would show us around the grounds of the Governor's house. They had a beautiful, well-laid-out garden where lovely roses, dahlias and other seasonal flowers, of variety of colours, grew in abundance. It was a delightful place to roam about and play, with brooks and shady paths. I remember in particular the willow trees with drooping branches and red flowers.

As far as my memory goes, this type of parties were never held at the Chief Minister, Bordoloi's house because with him, simplicity was the main motto of his life and his way of working. I remember vaguely that I had seen a loom in Gopinath's house. I learned later that he used to spin threads and weave the cloth himself for his dresses, on this loom.

Working on loom and weaving is even now a household art in many Assamese homes. It is a well known fact that Sualkuchi on the Southern bank of Brahmaputra, is a place of weavers and famous for their fine workmanship. During the British rule, the weavers of Sualkuchi paid the land revenue tax by bartering their fine silken "muga" and "pat" cloth. The wife of Vishnuram Medhi was very famous for her art of weaving. Her adopted daughter Manju also studied at the same time in Pine Mount School. She was an extremely beautiful little girl at that time.

I was too young at that time to come into much contact with Bordoloi. I used to see him coming and going while I played with other children in the compound of his bungalow. Sometimes he would stop for and enquire about my father. It was such a long time back and I hardly remember anything in greater detail. I remember that we children collected pine cones from the ground of Bordoloi's bungalow and made golliwog dalls out of them.

One impression which has remained with me about Bordoloi is that he and his family lived a plain and simple life even though at that time he was in the highest position of a Chief Minister. He believed in plain living and high thinking. This was one of his great qualities. Another thing which struck me was his genuine concern for people and their welfare.

Bordoloi was also a very good singer himself and he used to sing the devotional songs. Afterward I came to know that he was very fond of devotional hymns composed by the two saint composers, Sankardeva and Madhava Deva. The Vaisnavism taught by Saint Sankardeva is based on Bhagavat, with Krishna as the supreme diety. It has a profound belief in monotheism akin to monotheism of Sankara Charya.

Gopinath Bordoloi was a rare leader of exceptional calibre who was in tune with Assam's heart beats, who understood its problems, and its hopes and aspirations. He knew and understood all sections of Assamese society from the very poor to the more affluent, from the plains region to the hill tribes, from the farmers in the fields to the labourers in tea gardens, from villages to towns and cities. He was a leader who inspired confidence and extracted love and affection from the people. The Assamese people felt safe and secure under the umbrella of his leadership.

After the death of Gopinath Bordoloi, I remember distinctly seeing Lily, his daughter, standing on the school verandah, totally grief-stricken and heart-broken. I could not say anything. We just stood there silently sharing the feeling of loss. Though Lily was senior to me, we were very intimate friends throughout till today.

I shall never forget the one great lesson I learnt from the Bordoloi family, — simple way of living, worthy deeds and high thinking. A scholar A.W. Hare has rightly said, "The greatest truths are the simplest; and so are the greatest men." This is certainly true about Gopinath Bordoloi.